I Have Given Them Your Word

Sunday Homilies for

Cycles A, B, C

edited by Douglas Fisher

Paulist Press

New York ◇ Mahwah

Library of Congress Cataloging-in-Publication Data

I have given them your word.

    1. Church year sermons. 2. Catholic Church—Sermons.
3. Sermons, American. I. Fisher, Douglas.
BX1756.A212 1988   252'.6   88-2489
ISBN 0-8091-2961-2

Published by Paulist Press
997 Macarthur Boulevard
Mahwah, New Jersey 07430

Printed and bound in the
United States of America

CONTENTS

Introduction

Service, Resources for Pastoral Ministry is a quarterly publication of Paulist Press. It was begun under the guidance of Robert Heyer, nurtured to prominence by Jean Marie Hiesberger and is now edited by Douglas Fisher. An important and oft-praised dimension of this publication is the homily section which offers homily possibilities for each Sunday of the year. *I Have Given Them Your Word* is a collection of some of the best homilies from *Service* in the 1980s, composed in such a manner that there is one homily for each Sunday in the three year cycle.

The homilies collected here are as different as the people who wrote them. Many use stories from tradition, history, literature, the arts and everyday life to capture the imagination and bring out the power of the Scripture in our world. Some take the popular Jungian approach to the biblical images. Others offer a prayerful and challenging meditation. No matter what the approach, each homilist whose words are contained herein has attempted to fulfill the vocation of a preacher: to make extraordinary things ordinary and ordinary things extraordinary.

St. Augustine once said that preaching is "Mystery talking to mystery about mystery." Perhaps these homily suggestions will be of help as the mysteries of preacher, listener and God come together in a union of Spirit ignited by the Word.

CYCLE A

1st Sunday of Advent

Cycle A

Is 2:1–5
Rom 13:11–14
Mt 24:37–44

A common experience of people in this season could be an entree into opening out Jesus' message in Matthew's Gospel, "keep a watchful eye." It is at this time of year when we "keep an ear tuned" to the wants and needs of our loved ones. What should I get my wife for Christmas? Didn't she mention that her overcoat is not warm enough? I remember she really admired pearl earrings she saw in a catalog. She has a new job—maybe she needs a picture for her office? It is a time for being aware—a time for looking beneath the surface.

This experience is analogous to what Jesus challenges us with in today's Gospel. Pay attention to and reflect on your world. God's grace rarely is so obvious that we can't miss it. Or perhaps it is so obvious we miss it. This story could elaborate on the point:

There was a little fish who swam up to his mother one day and said, "Mom, what is this water that I hear so much about?" Laughing, she responded, "You silly little fish. Why, it's around you and within you and gives you life. Just swim to the top of the pond and lie there for a while; then you will find out what water is."

Another time there was a little fawn who walked up to her mother and said, "Mommy, what is this air that I hear so much about?" Smiling, she answered, "You silly little deer. Why, air is within you and around you. Air gives you life. If you want to know what air is, stick your head in the stream and you'll find out."

Finally, there was a certain young man who was beginning his spiritual journey. After having difficulty knowing where to turn, he asked a holy woman, "What is this God I hear so much about?"

Invite your congregation to look around this week for the God who is hiding in plain sight.

The awareness Jesus calls for has other dimensions as well. The "watchful eye" means more than awareness of grace in the present. The eye has the capacity for vision. What is your vision of life? How broad a field does my vision take in? Do I have "tunnel vision," or can I see something of what God sees—the vast array of human possibilities? A "vision story" comes from the popular television show, "Family Ties." In one program, Alex, the 18-year-old with tremendous business ambitions, is working in a small corner grocery store. He is good friends with the kind-hearted manager and enjoys the diversity of the work. But it is just a grocery store and leaves no opportunity for "climbing the corporate ladder." To the great dismay of the manager, Alex leaves and goes to work at a huge department store. There his only job is to stock "cat-toys" and he is referred to as "number 28." But he can see his future in front of him—manager of cat toys, then manager of all pet supplies, manager of housewares, all the way to president of the chain of stores. His goal is in sight— but the road is lonely, impersonal, and very narrow. Alex takes some time to look around and reflect. What does he really want? What does he really want to be? Alex, aware of his feelings, having checked out his "vision" with his heart, decides to go back to the grocery store.

Now let's take the awareness of Advent to another level—that of social justice. How aware are we of the oppressed in our world? Anyone with "a watchful eye" must be aware of a "haves and have nots" world. There are many things a preacher can get into here. One suggestion is to challenge the congregation to an awareness of solidarity with all people—oppressed *and* oppressors. What separates us from the poor, what separates us from our ideological enemies is obvious. It takes a "watchful eye" to look deeper, to find what unites. Martin Luther King did this very well. He looked for common ground with his enemies—a place, no matter how small, where they could stand and say, "At least we are together on this much. Now we can begin." King saw common threads because he looked so intently. Perhaps we too can look for a unity of heart with the oppressed and with oppressors and move our world to new actions of liberation.

This is a season to look for gifts. Perhaps in the looking we will discover a gift for ourselves—the gift of a God waiting to be born in us.

Douglas Fisher

2nd Sunday of Advent

Cycle A

Is 11:1–10
Rom 15:4–9
Mt 3:1–12

In personal and communal life, there are times when all that seems left is a "stump." Yet those of experience and wisdom know life can come from stumps.

Isaiah knows God is not finished yet with Israel. Though things are in a political mess under Ahaz, God had promised earlier to Nathan that the kingship of David (son of Jesse) would endure. Isaiah perceives a "shoot" emerging from the political/spiritual "stump" of Jesse.

All nations yearn for the "ideal leader." Israelites were no less expectant of an "ideal king" to emerge to lead them. They wanted a utopian situation wherein peace and justice reigned.

The Jews wanted a leader so great that his light would attract foreigners (Gentiles). According to the early Church, this "ideal king-messiah" occurred in Jesus. But it was not in the way the people of Israel expected it! He was not a powerful political leader. His "kingdom" ideas were not land-bound or army-protected.

Andrae Crouch sings: "Jesus is the answer for the world today, above him there's no other, Jesus is the way." Believers see Jesus' leadership as real. Kingship occurs in their hearts, and inspires them to spread that kingdom in love and justice.

Sometimes we would all like a leader who would sprout up and wave a magic wand to solve all problems. We must reflect on our expectations. If they are not balanced or tolerant, we can kill growth, limit opportunities, and miss significant persons. Self-righteous expectations can blind us.

Our expectations about leadership must be perceptive and understanding. Conservatism is needed "to preserve that which has always been, is, and will be true." Liberalism is needed to give to those truths and to the non-essentials of the faith the modernization of appearance and expression called for. Jesus' own leadership expressed both. He fulfilled the Law and gave new teachings.

Both Isaiah and Jesus were "dreamers." Both saw how things should be, and worked to make them realities. Both hoped for "harmonies" among peoples, marked by love and justice.

The dream to be fulfilled is a kingdom of harmony. If we seek to make it real, it becomes possible. Jesus calls all to this "kingdom living." John the Baptist prepared the way for Jesus: "reform your lives." They are to be "re-formed" in Jesus' way. We are not only to laud his words/deeds, but to make them real in our lives. We must decide and respond.

Some who came to Jesus were not ready for an internal "heart change." Their claim to faith was external allegiance to Abraham. Jesus called for an inner change with a "faith-lineage" grounded in truth. The fruit in one's life indicates true descendancy.

John foresaw a greater baptism, not only of water (an external sign) but also of an inner "enablement" through the Holy Spirit. Christ would enable us to do that which needed to be done. The force of the Spirit would bring inner conviction, plus "kingship" power: making us able to live justly. Kingdom living is to be marked by the qualities of wisdom, understanding, counsel, strength, knowledge, fear of the Lord. These are the kingship-gifts of the Holy Spirit.

Such was the life of the apostles. So too, this was their teaching, which we are to be devoted to. Harmony will emerge with our effort.

Let us learn to respect differences. Let us love and tolerate differing ideologies, faiths, and lifestyles. Let us seek truth in all matters.

Jeffrey Archambeault

3rd Sunday of Advent

Cycle A

Is 35:1–6, 10
Jas 5:7–10
Mt 11:2–11

Matthew, the man who records for us Jesus' comments on John the Baptizer, seems utterly convinced (as we may find it hard to be) that we are greater than John, at least in the sense that we participate in a blessing that John saw only dimly. For Matthew, John did not really understand what he spoke of. The reality loosed in the world by Jesus' life and death far surpassed what John had imagined. It even surpassed his visions of judgment. John's warnings of fire to come are subordinated to Jesus' teaching that God is closer to us here and now than we are to ourselves, and the closeness bespeaks love, not hatred. The deepest symbol of God's nature for Jesus is not judgment but healing, not fire but friendship, not punishment in the pit but resurrection unto life. Surely the Christian Scriptures do not lack warnings about the consequences of sin, but their most pervasive interest is in the joy and peace that comes from a clear conscience and an uncomplicated and unconditioned faith in God.

Take the reading from James as an example. After a sharp warning that the wealthy have misplaced their trust, James urges, in the simplest terms imaginable, that Christians be patient with the trouble of life, that they stop grumbling and complaining. Wait, he says, for the coming of the Lord, as the farmer waits patiently for the coming of the spring rains and for the quiet growth of his crop. In an impatient world, be patient. Watch for the growth of the kingdom. Hardship and suffering notwithstanding, our eyes are to be fixed on the "judge who stands at the gate," and from that vision we are to draw our patience.

And James believes that it is possible for us to live "steady in the heart," as he puts it, just as Matthew believes that we are better off than John who first pointed Jesus out and who preached the fiery cleansing. How can that be? What divides us from John, what makes patience possible for us?

As always, the Church answers the question by pointing in two directions, to the future and to the past. We have hope because we have a vision of the future, a vision we share with our Jewish brothers and sisters and which is expressed so magnificently by Isaiah the prophet: What is a desert now will not long be so; it will be a garden of delight and joy. Life will be transformed. "Say to those whose hearts are frightened: Be strong, fear not! . . . He comes to save you." The future is God's and we can rush toward it patiently. What divides us from John and makes us more blessed than he is the death of Jesus which shows us clearly how to live with the intractable evil of the world, and the resurrection of Jesus which shows us how close to us God already is. We are blessed because the God of the future is already here. God is present to us in forgiveness and love even now.

We celebrate and revive our hope and trust in God's future on these Advent Sundays. We remember as well the time when God came among us bringing forgiveness and love in the man Jesus of Nazareth. And, as long as we are gathered here in the church of God, God's forgiveness and love are touching us deeply again in the man Jesus of Nazareth. This is the reason for our ability to suffer patiently: The God who has given us a vision has also given us a man to share it with.

Helen A. Lutz

5

4th Sunday of Advent

Cycle A

Is 7:10–14
Rom 1:1–7
Mt 1:18–24

Today's gospel reading provides us with a wonderful portrait of Joseph. There is very little about Joseph in the Scriptures, but this one passage of six verses tells us he was a person of many dimensions. In looking at the Joseph of Matthew 1:18–24 perhaps we can discover some dimensions of ourselves and our own capacity to "father," to nurture the Christ who wants to be born within us.

Three aspects of Joseph I will discuss here are Joseph as: (1) quiet "dismisser" of injustice; (2) dreamer; (3) receiver of life.

When Joseph realizes Mary is "with child" before they have lived together, he decides to divorce her quietly. Here is Mary, a woman he loves so much he wants to marry her, and he is willing to divorce her quietly. He does not commit himself to her, nor does he scream and shout at her for supposedly having relations with someone else. When faced with conflict, Joseph reacts without passion. He just quietly lets things go.

Is there a "quiet dismisser" within us? Are there events which, although obviously unjust, we just ignore? Think about your relationships. I know there are times when my wife expresses a complaint or a need and, because it will inconvenience me, I just quietly ignore her. I don't commit myself to helping her, I don't fight it out with her, I just ignore her. Are there ever times when you do that? Look at your place of work. Do things ever happen which are unjust but you "look the other way" because you don't want to get involved? Go to the global level. Psychological blocking is commonplace in relation to the nuclear arms issue. We would rather not think about it because it is uncomfortable. Meanwhile, missiles are stockpiled at an ever accelerating rate and we allow other people to plan the destruction of the world.

Within Joseph, there was a "quiet dismisser." Does one live within you? In what relationships, in what areas of your life?

Joseph, of course, is more than that. Joseph has the capacity to dream, to see things differently—in a very radical way. Imagine envisioning that your wife has conceived a child by the Holy Spirit and that child is going to save people from sin! Joseph, obviously, did not stay simply with what he saw.

What is your dream? Where is it that you look and imagine things differently? Where is it that you say "things do not have to be what they appear"? The preacher could help the congregation to get in touch with their dreams. We have all had the experience of asking someone, "How are things going?" and the person responds, "Oh, the same old routine." How lifeless! All of us have the experience too of asking that question and getting a flood of dreams, hopes, goals coming through. Which person would we rather be? Joseph was a dreamer. Are we in touch with our dreams?

A third dimension to Joseph is "the receiver of life." Joseph follows his dreams and receives Mary into his home as his wife. He takes in life and treats it with acceptance and warmth. Am I in touch with the hospitable, caring dimension of myself? A story to help in imagining this comes from a woman with an autistic son. The boy would spend hours moving in a disoriented way and making strange sounds. His mother tried to teach him motor skills and normal responses but she also tried something different. For an hour a day she did what he did—she moved as he moved and repeated his sounds. This very unusual method worked. The child felt accepted. He no longer felt like a stranger in a strange land. In this way, the mother really did welcome the boy into his home with acceptance. Very gradually the child overcame his autism.

There is a dimension to me which is accepting, loving, and kind. Joseph was in touch with this dimension within himself. Am I?

It is to this person that the Father trusts his only Son. The man is complex—a quiet "dismisser" of injustice, a dreamer, a receiver of life. He is not perfect by any means. But he is God's choice to nurture his Son.

Within us Jesus awaits birth. He is within our very imperfect selves. But the Father, who has created us in his image and likeness, has entrusted us with the Spirit of his Son. It is up to us to nurture him as a father and bring Jesus to life within us.

Douglas Fisher

Christmas Day

Cycle A

Is 52:7–10
Heb 1:1–6
Jn 1:1–18 or 1:1–5, 9–14

Christmas seems to be one feast for which we have found symbols that really express the meaning of the event. The traditions—both family and church—of Christmastime richly retell the ancient story of the Incarnation in sensual realities which capture the incredible truths of today's readings in contemporary experience.

The Gospel, John's magnificent prologue, is replete with images reaching to capture who Jesus is for us. We taste both the awe—"He was in the world and the world was made through him"—and the poignancy—"yet the world did not know who he was"—of the coming of Jesus. Yet, for all the beauty and depth of John's prologue, we are left with the realization that it is still inadequate to describe the profound mystery of the God who became a human person. The Word, ironically, leaves us speechless. And so, we are drawn to the symbols of Christmas which, though wordless, speak to us of "the glory of an only son coming from the Father."

"The real light which gives light to every person was coming into the world." So much of the beauty of Christmas is in its light: colored bulbs on trees and mantels and around windows and outdoor evergreens; spotlights on manger scenes, candles on tables, and the glow of fires in hearths. We know from all the modes of Christmas lighting that light's significance goes far beyond its usefulness. Somewhere deep within us, the traditional lights of Christmastime remind us that "a great light has come upon the earth," a light which "shines on in darkness" to illumine, to warm, to beautify our earth and our lives.

"Whatever came to be in him, found life" John writes, and reflecting this expression are the living symbols of Christmas: trees and holly and mistletoe, the poinsettia plants and Christmas roses. The circles of wreaths and the ever-greenness of garlands echo the promise that Jesus' temporal life will bring us life eternal.

We send cards and packages by mail, as God sent his son by miracle. The good news of our love and friendship, written or wrapped, expresses again the message of God's love enfleshed and sent to us all.

"The Word became flesh and made his dwelling among us." This incomprehensible truth sends its roots more deeply into my being as I finger, like beads on a rosary, the ornaments which grace our Christmas tree. Each one speaks to me of the Word made flesh as I recall the people they signify.

Our traditionally first-hung ornament is a wooden heart which proclaims our first Christmas as husband and wife. I realize how the love in our marriage is an on-going sharing in the faithfulness of God's love for us. The drummer-boy ornament recalls our son's pre-school Christmas play role, and I wonder again at the marvel of sharing the Christmas story with our own child. Several of the ornaments are satin and sequin globes made for us by a blind friend. These proclaim to me the beauty of our human lives, whatever our handicaps or limitations. There are dough ornaments, some boldly outlined in fluorescent colors, which my son and I made when he was very young. I am aware of the delights of parenthood—the teaching and the learning—and the special bond which Jesus used to image his own bond with the God he called "Abba." I see among the branches the gift ornaments from former students, apples, schoolhouses, blackboards, which remind me of the faith shared with and enriched by those students. There are other gift ornaments, surprises found on the doorstep, from our parish Kris Kringle custom. These remind me of the extended family which our parish has been for me, and the new friendships which have gifted our lives and expanded our appreciation for the uniqueness of many different kinds of people. Delicately placed is an aging paper chain garland forged by friends and neighbors at our tree-trimming party several years ago. Its fragility speaks to me of our humanity, and its need to be frequently mended is a call to be reconcilers and peacemakers as Jesus was. There are ornaments which recall friends who are dead now, and these especially bring me to gratitude for the gift of Christmas and the promise of Easter. A new ornament, a beautiful china bird, is perched on a prominent branch. A gift from my new pastor, it glows from within and reminds me of the special joy of new beginnings.

Each ornament is unique and each light glows with its own hue, but together they make one picture. In meditating on our tree, I, like Ebenezer Scrooge, am visited by three Spirits; the Spirit of Christmas Past, which brings memories of how I have met the Christ; the Spirit of Christmas Present, which enriches today's celebration with eyes of faith; the Spirit of Christmas Yet to Come, when we will finally come to share in his divinity, who humbled himself to share in our humanity.

Carole M. Eipers

Feast of the Holy Family

Cycle A

Sir 3:2–6, 12–14
Col 3:12–21
Lk 2:22–40

Today, as we celebrate the feast of the Holy Family, we are invited to reflect on ourselves as "family." There are at least two sometimes unexamined presuppositions of which we might try to become aware. The first is that there is only one kind of family, i.e., the so-called nuclear family—wife, husband and children under the same roof. While in some sense this is the ideal to be aimed for, and Margaret Mead assures us from her very long perspective of the history of the human race that the nuclear family will not soon become extinct, in reality, we are surrounded by, and part of, many different kinds of "families." Sociologists list at least five other types: (1) the single parent family; (2) the mixed family—husband and wife both with children from a previous marriage; (3) the childless couple; (4) the divorced or widowed person alone; (5) single persons who see their family unit primarily in terms of close friends. Then there is the family of the local community, the state, the nation, the world. As we reflect on family relationships today, it is important to keep this broad perspective in view, and to be mindful of the struggles and joys attendant on each of these lifestyles.

The second sometimes unexamined presupposition is the way in which we might look to the Holy Family as model of family life. The truth is that we know next to nothing about the daily ups and downs of the Holy Family. So we must approach the scriptural texts with care, taking into consideration the milieu and the theological objectives of the author.

Yet another complication in dealing with family ties of the "blood relationship" variety is the immense diversity in our experience of family, and the extreme depth in our psyches to which these ties go. In any gathering of people, there will be as many experiences of family as there are individuals. We are all familiar with some of the more pronounced of these. On one end of the spectrum, there are those of us who have very positive, affirming relationships with parents and siblings. These graced families seem to cope well with difficulties, and maintain honest communication among family members. Some families may live in close proximity to one another and be very involved in each others' daily lives—for better or for worse. Others may live at some distance, a factor which creates yet another dynamic in family relationships—for better or for worse. Most of us probably give "mixed reviews" to family involvements—there are some good times and some bad ones. And then there is the other extreme—those of us whose family relationships seem engulfed by alienation, silence, bitterness and resentment.

What all this adds up to, is that we cannot glibly or facilely talk about family relationships. They are too important and too complex for us to be satisfied with pat or pious answers. Today might be a time to reflect on our family relationships in honesty and simplicity, in order to come to some insight about what is operative in us as we relate to family members of all kinds.

But the question remains: How can we talk about this in light of the Scripture, and in terms of our Christian commitments? One possible approach is to focus on the first part of the reading from Paul's letter to the Colossians (verses 12–17).

These verses have got to be among the most beautiful in the New Testament. The passage is like a jewel—describing the Christian life that one chooses to live at Baptism. Words such as "chosen ones," "holy," "beloved," reflect back to the community of Israel, and underline the development from the old to the new Israel. We are a people with roots, with connections, with a history that is still moving forward.

In general, these verses call us to become new people. We are challenged to take on a new personality, as it were, and in one sense, this new personality is that of Christ himself. One could spend months reflecting on all the dimensions and ramifications in one's life of each of the characteristics of this new life—mercy, kindness, humility, meekness and patience. And these are not to be experienced casually, but must be "heartfelt."

In the last analysis, I cannot get very far on my own. An integral dimension in this whole endeavor is to acknowledge that I need other people to pull it off, and ultimately, it is only possible in and through the power of Christ, which is always available to us as believers in the promptings and presence of the Holy Spirit who breathes within each of us, in our families, in our communities, in our world.

Elizabeth Dreyer

Epiphany

Cycle A

Is 60:1–6
Eph 3:2–3, 5–6
Mt 2:1–12

Matthew's story of the magi from the east is an account of a sacred journey, a search for salvation. As such, it is a paradigm of our own faith journeys and helps us to appreciate other paths to God.

We are searching for someone to enlighten and save us. Our journey has many ups and downs, numerous mysteries and loose ends. At times there are only glimmers of light on an otherwise dark horizon.

The journey of the magi was like this too. Raymond Brown, in *The Birth of the Messiah,* calls the magi "wholly admirable." Sincere searchers for truth who come from afar, they stand in stark contrast to the faithless King Herod and his Jerusalem court. The magi have learned all they can from openness to nature and, though led only vaguely by a star, they stay with their journey. They seek information from the Jews and their Scriptures, and continue to travel with hearts ready to pay homage. Finally, when their journey ends in the simple village of Bethlehem, the magi are not distressed to find Jesus among the poor and nameless rather than among kings and priests. They experience an intense joy, and put their gifts at his service.

Our journeys of faith are often like theirs. We wonder where God is to be found in our lives and in the world. We try to discover God's purpose and to follow it. We puzzle over how best to use our gifts in the service of Jesus. There are long periods when the direction is not clear. We ask others for their insights and seek out spiritual guides to show us the way. We also have our epiphanies. We recognize revelations of God in the events of our lives, in the beauty and power of nature, in the words of Scripture, in the eyes of a friend. Sometimes these are only faint signs, like a star against a night sky. But as T. S. Eliot reminds us in his poem, "The Dry Salvages": "The hint half guessed, the gift half understood, is Incarnation."

What stands out in the story of the magi is the quality of their journey. Their hearts are receptive, ready to respond when a revelation appears. They are faithful searchers, sensitive to the fragile signals of transcendence present in life. They do not place conditions on the revelations of God, but recognize God's grace however it comes. In his book of modern parables, *"I" Opener,* Herbert Brokering tells a parable that shows how such readiness enables us to hear the good news: "Once there was a church where they couldn't find the Bible one Sunday. The minister asked if anyone had good news from the Lord. No one admitted having any, so they all started leaving. One man said his wife had just had a baby this morning. The people decided that this wasn't a word from the Lord, and they went home. The man stayed for a whole hour. He was sure this was good news from the Lord" (p. 54). Our moments of epiphany or revelation do not always come in the way we expect.

Today's readings not only tell us about our own journeys; they challenge our attitude toward other searchers. All three readings repeat the same theme: all nations shall walk by God's light and share in the promise. The magi of Matthew's Gospel are Gentiles, and Paul reminds his hearers that Gentiles are co-heirs and members of the same body as Jews. We sometimes set boundaries to God's love and salvation. The sincerity and genuine faith and goodness of outsiders challenge those of us who see salvation as confined to the established churches.

Today's readings remind us that we cannot know with assurance how God acts in other people's lives. Salvation is open to all. Moreover, those we consider outsiders may see truths we have missed in our own sources of revelation, sending us back to them with a new receptivity to their truths of love and justice.

Kathleen R. Fischer
Thomas N. Hart

Baptism of the Lord

Cycle A

Isa 42:1–4, 6–7
Acts 10:34–38
Mt 3:13–17

I often ponder the countless walks I have taken along the shores of Lake Michigan, awed by that expanse of water and the life that it supports upon and beneath its surface. People are drawn to bodies of water, aware that they represent a power and meaning difficult to describe but demanding our attention, if not our respect. There are probably many reasons for the universal attraction to water, not the least of which is the fact that it is the source and sustainer of life. We come from its very bosom.

Today's Gospel places us at the center of the Judeo-Christian tradition about who we are in relationship to water. The consciousness of Israel and her Jewish descendants was that of a people brought forth miraculously from water. The Jews remembered and celebrated that God had brought the chosen people from the waters of the Sea of Reeds and made them into a beloved people and a mighty nation. Their stories, particularly their most fundamental Story of Exodus, focused on and dramatized the import of their being brought out of or over waters. It was—and is—basic to their very identity.

This moment, however, was not isolated from the larger picture in the Jewish mentality. These were a people rescued and chosen for a *purpose*. Israel was to *live* as a people brought up out of the waters. Her self-consciousness was to be that of a people raised up, brought out to be a *sign* and to live faithfully for the sake of others. Israel was called forth from the waters to be servant. Generations would resist this calling, but prophetic voices and religious rituals served as pointed reminders of this reality: "I, the Lord, have called you for the victory of justice . . . as a covenant of the people, a light for the nations . . ."

In today's Gospel, Jesus rises out of the waters of the Jordan in this same Servant tradition. Jesus' own self-consciousness is shaped as one called for a purpose. The "voice of the Lord," which speaks repeatedly from the beginning of time calling forth life and naming what is called forth as good, calls Jesus to a new and exemplary role. Jesus is to be Servant like none other. His life, like that of his religious ancestors, is to be that of one called out of the waters to bring reconciliation, justice, healing, sight, light. Unlike his ancestors, Jesus would embrace this role totally, testing it to its limits and revealing its cost.

And what does this mean for us? We, too, as baptized Christians, are a people come "directly out of the water," called to live in solidarity with all others, "washed" for a purpose. As with Israel and with Jesus, our being brought through or out of water has meaning only insofar as we are willing to embrace this identity and live it out.

If it takes a long time for the impact of this message to sink into our consciousness, we can take consolation in the fact that Israel, too, only gradually came to understand what this meant. She repeatedly recoiled from and resisted the task, needing to be called back again and again. Jesus' own awareness of what he was called to do seemed to unfold progressively. Its meaning brought him pain and fear against which he struggled to the very end.

But starting slowly, realizing late, or failing frequently should not deter or discourage us. We hear in these readings that Jesus is anointed and empowered to do what he must do. The same Spirit of God is given to us, too. Each of us can probably think of times in our lives when we have recognized God's empowering Spirit enabling us to serve in ways we did not think possible. The results of our servant actions—those same effects named of the servant in the Isaian song—can flow from our efforts *because* we are empowered. People can be led to see, can be released from the many things that imprison them, can be brought up out of darkness by a servant community called and empowered to act on their behalf.

From the beginning of time, the Voice of the Lord speaking over the waters has called new life into existence or given new meaning and direction to those who heard the voice. Our task is to heed the voice that has spoken our own individual names and called us out of the water, identifying each of us as members of a servant people. Our task is to live the identity that we have been given.

Joan R. DeMerchant

2nd Sunday in Ordinary Time

Cycle A

Is 49:3, 5–6
1 Cor 1:1–3
Jn 1:29–34

Both the prophet Isaiah and John the Baptist have something in common in today's Scriptures. They hear voices. Isaiah hears the Lord. John hears "the one who sent me to baptize with water." Now before we think of Isaiah and John as different from ourselves, it might be good to consider all the voices we hear within our own minds. Everytime I try to get away with doing something slipshod, I hear my father's voice saying "Anything worth doing is worth doing right." Playing pick-up basketball I can hear my first coach saying, "Look for the open man." When I am with someone who is troubled, I hear the words of comfort which have been spoken to me by friends and counselors. All of us have many voices within us all day. Do you ever hear a mocking voice? A cynical voice? A hopeful voice? A challenging voice? A sad voice? We could all take the time to trace those voices down to people and events in our lives.

It is important for the homilist to go beyond this meditation on voices and deal with two key terms used by John the Baptist. He speaks of "preparing" and "witnessing." Our inner voices can be a real key to what has prepared us and what we witness to now and in the future. Those voices do not determine us. We can choose to follow the voice which once told us, "You can't do that!" or we can choose to follow the voice which said, "You have enormous potential."

Here is a story which might illustrate my point. In the play *Mass Appeal*, a young deacon ascends the pulpit and gives the following homily (paraphrased):

People often ask me why I want to be a priest. It goes back to a time when I was very young. In those days I had goldfish. I was very proud of those goldfish. One night, while I was asleep, there was a malfunction in the heater. The temperature in the tank went sky-high. When I came down the next morning the fish had been boiled to death. I remember crying and wishing I could have had ears to hear them crying in the night. If

I could have heard them shouting in pain, then I could have run down and saved them. Why didn't God give me ears to hear fish cry? Then one day in church, I looked around at the faces there. People seemed to be in so much pain! They looked as if their lives were miserable but they weren't saying anything. I wished I could have ears to hear their pain and save them. I decided then to become a person who would develop ears to hear the cry of the people, and priesthood seemed to be a good way to do it.

It takes a lot of work to develop the kinds of ears which can hear another's pain. It also takes a lot of energy to hear the Lord's voice among the many voices in our minds. Once we hear the voice of hurt and suffering—in ourselves and in others—do we choose to witness to the Lord's voice of hope? We can choose to follow that voice or the other voices of despair, cynicism, failure. The choice is ours. Again, a play might serve as an illustration.

At the end of *Camelot*, King Arthur stands on the stage a sorrowful man. His beautiful wife Guinevere has loved his favorite knight of the Roundtable, Sir Lancelot. This has led to the downfall of his kingdom, as what was once a peaceful utopia has been split apart into warring factions. In the midst of the ruins, a young boy comes to Arthur and asks to join his Roundtable where "all are equal and where might serves right." The young boy tells Arthur the tales he has heard of the glorious Roundtable. Arthur believes those years were "the real years," an example of what the world can be. In the midst of failure, in the midst of mocking and destructive voices, he chooses to recognize this voice of hope from the past. He sends the boy forth to tell those stories to whoever will listen. This is the voice which Arthur chooses as the truth.

Ask your congregation to take some time this week to listen and distinguish the many voices within them. Perhaps they will hear the voice which John heard. Maybe someone will hear a voice which sounds like the Lord's voice—a voice which consoles, a voice which invites us to live fully, a voice which asks us to give witness with our own voice of hope.

Douglas Fisher

3rd Sunday in Ordinary Time

Cycle A

Is 9:1–4
1 Cor 1:10–13, 17
Mt 4:12–23

Humanistic psychologists such as Abraham Maslow and Carl Rogers tell us that essential to a healthy personality and good community life is a sense of mission, purpose or vocation. Each person and group needs to have a work that can be done with commitment. If this is absent, the individual or society experiences *anomie*, or a sense of meaninglessness. Our readings speak to us of mission and vocation and what happens when this is absent from our lives or that of the community. Israel has experienced the "dark night of the soul" with the destruction of the Northern Kingdom (Is 8:23). The people have experienced a traumatic setback and they are now in the grip of the powers of darkness: alienation, meaninglessness, displacement and a lack of direction. However, these powers do not have the last word. The prophet offers them the Lord's words of comfort and hope. Their sorrow and darkness will turn to joy. This darkness is not uncommon in our own day with the numerous peoples who have been displaced by the darkness of war. The "boat people" are a tragic example of the rootlessness that each of us experiences. We all share to a certain extent their homelessness and feeling of alienation. Large segments of our population, for example, the young, are searching for role models and values which will sustain them beyond the pleasures of the moment and the bread of this world, which fails to give lasting nourishment. The young long to be nourished in the Spirit. The widespread use of drugs and alcohol, along with the rising suicide rate for teenagers, give vivid witness to the need to belong and be at home with a sense of vocation or purpose in life. The elderly, at the other end of the age spectrum, often experience the bitter pain of rejection and a feeling of being obsolete in a society that worships the young and the new. The challenge of and need to proclaim the Lord's words of comfort, acceptance, and hope are as pressing today as in the days of Isaiah.

The Apostle Paul knew well the crisis of vocation or mission. Saul was a good Jew and very dedicated to the ways of the Torah. But he encountered the risen Lord, and for him the whole of reality was changed. As is often the case, we must be blind before we can see; we must lose before we can appreciate our gifts, and die in order to be reborn anew. After his initial conversion, Paul went to Athens to preach Jesus in the idiom of Greek philosophy. The result was a total disaster. Paul, writing to the Christians at Corinth, shares with them a deep insight born of bitter personal experience: Jesus cannot be conformed to the world; Jesus must be proclaimed in faith and one can only come to Jesus as Lord in that same faith. There are limits to human reason and power. The Cross is the wisdom and power of God, which alone can save and heal the brokenness of our human condition. We cannot preach Jesus according to our own agenda and make him into our image and likeness. We can only accept Jesus and the scandal of the Cross on his terms.

The experience of crisis and vocation reaches its climax in the gospel with the call of the disciples. In the midst of their everyday world, with its routine concerns and needs, Jesus challenges these fishermen to build upon that which they know best. Jesus' call is an invitation to "come and see" that alone which endures and gives life-relationship with Jesus in service of the Kingdom. Jesus does not reject or trivialize that which has structured these men's lives. Jesus enriches and adds depth to it.

It is not easy to say yes to Jesus and the Kingdom. Many go away sad. Jesus' call is a challenge to repent and experience a change of heart. What is called for is a new direction and focus, a new value system. The old values and beliefs no longer hold sway. All is made new. It is painful to give up the familiar, the certain, the expected and the taken-for-granted. It is painful to journey into the unknown with no explicit guarantees. One must truly walk by faith and live a life of hope in things not seen. So radical is the call that one may even have to give up family and friends. Two masters cannot be served. The house of one's being cannot be divided. Jesus and the Kingdom must be the ultimate concern of the person who says yes to the call of discipleship. The coming of the Kingdom in the person of Jesus ushers in a new age. The brokenness and alienation that we all experience through sin will not have the final word. The Kingdom is the active presence of the God who cares and heals. The dead are brought back to life; the lost are found; the unaccepted are greeted with the kiss of peace; true liberation is extended to the whole of creation in which Christ is all in all.

Rev. William F. Maestri

4th Sunday in Ordinary Time

Cycle A

Zep 2:3; 3:12–13
1 Cor 1:26–31
Mt 5:1–12

Today's Gospel tells us what kinds of people are happy. It is a topic of immediate interest to us, for we all long for happiness. Jesus calls blessed the poor in spirit, those who feel the suffering of the world and weep for it, the defenseless prophets, the peacemakers. If we were to write our own beatitudes, the list would probably sound very different from Jesus': Blessed are the rich, for they will possess luxurious homes and current fashions. Blessed are the beautiful, for they will be sought out by others and have many friends. Blessed are the powerful, for by their influence and strength they will control others. Blessed are those who win, for they will be judged shrewd and successful.

When we recognize whom we consider happy, we realize what an inversion of conventional values the beatitudes are. We tend to think life belongs to the strong, young, wealthy, powerful, and beautiful. Jesus reveals the norms of the new age he came to inaugurate. In so doing, he turns our value systems upside down. The only true source of happiness, he says, is a heart renewed by the Gospel in mercy, simplicity, and reconciliation.

In Richard Attenborough's film, *Gandhi,* there is a scene which conveys how challenging such a call to conversion can be, but also how it is the only way out of our present problems. A young Hindu from the slums, who has been both a victim and a perpetrator of violence in the struggle between Hindus and Moslems, comes to see Gandhi. To avenge the death of his own son at Moslem hands, the Hindu has killed a Moslem boy. "I am going to hell," he says. His tormented face tells us that he is already there. Gandhi lies on a cot, nearly dead from his fast to protest the Calcutta riots of 1947. He looks at the young Hindu and says, "I know a way out of hell. Find a child whose parents have been killed in the riots, adopt and love the child as your own. But let it be a Moslem orphan and raise the child as a Moslem." In other words, blessed are the peacemakers, those who refuse to perpetuate the cycle of violence, those who accept the most radical of Jesus' commands—love your enemy. Only such peacemakers will find a way out of the hell which hatred, quarrels, and war produce in the human heart and in our world. The spirit of revenge only keeps it all going.

The beatitudes, like the rest of the Sermon on the Mount, call us to a radical conversion. In Jesus' kingdom, we must seek to establish justice for the poor and take responsibility for making peace. Jesus tells us we will find joy by traveling light through this world as we espouse these deeper values. Such renewal need not be played out on the world stage in struggles against powerful governments. We can be poor in spirit by shifting our focus from acquiring things for ourselves to a recognition and concern for the needs of others. We can show mercy by letting go of our harsh judgments and the demanding standards we apply to others' behavior. We can be single-hearted and hunger and thirst for holiness by letting God's gift of salvation into our world of pain and darkness. We can learn to grieve with those who suffer, allowing such sorrow to move us to action on their behalf. As the gospel call to conversion slowly transforms our hearts, the new age will begin to dawn in our families, parishes, neighborhoods, and cities.

Paul reminds us in the letter to the Corinthians that if we go against the dominant values of our culture, we must be prepared to be considered fools. To follow Jesus in a society where aggression is the norm, money the measure of respect, and power the way to success, is to risk being condemned as naive. Like the prophet Zephaniah in the first reading, Paul advocates a deeper wisdom. Gandhi himself, in his espousal of nonviolence, chose such wisdom. He refused to harm or dehumanize his adversaries. Evil, he believed, must be fought without weapons or hatred. Such is the paradox at the heart of the Gospel: Weakness is strength, foolishness is wisdom, and death is the way to life.

Kathleen R. Fischer
Thomas N. Hart

5th Sunday in Ordinary Time

Cycle A

Is 58:7–10
1 Cor 2:1–5
Mt 5:13–16

It must have been a magical moment when—after thousands and thousands of years of life—human beings first conquered fire. Long before there was any history to record it, there was that moment when humans were no longer prisoners of darkness, when darkness could be dispelled at will, when light and warmth were at our service, when people could gather around the warmth of the fire against the cold of the long darkness of night.

And at the beginning of this month of February, in the state of Wisconsin where I live, the LIGHT still speaks powerfully to me and my modern contemporaries. In a month which is often filled with long nights and gray days, unbroken by any major holiday to give cause for celebration, I eagerly await the coming of the light we can't yet control—the sun with its brightness and warmth, the yellow days of summer which mean vacation, longer days, and a more carefree style of existence.

In general, light is awaited, is welcomed, is positive and encouraging—and today's readings have some of that flavor. But there is another reality here. For sometimes the light lets us see more than we would want. The light in the house doesn't just dispel the darkness; it can also illuminate the dusty corners, the accumulated junk, the ugly decoration, the decaying woodwork. And we can be faced with the task we might rather ignore.

Then there is the dark side of our own lives; not only the deep darkness of sin and evil, but also the shadow elements in our lives, those parts of us which speak of weakness, of incompleteness, of limitation, those parts which need healing and acceptance, yet which are also easier to ignore or avoid. Exposing these parts of ourselves to the light does not come easily—even if we're the only ones who will see.

Today's readings also speak of this other dimension of light—light as the revealer of that which is hidden, ugly, or evil. The promise of warmth and light, the "light breaking forth like the dawn," is tied to removing oppression, feeding the hungry, and satisfying the afflicted. If these things can be done, "Then light shall rise for you in the darkness."

We want the light, yet the work of removing the darkness is difficult, and we have a mixed record so far. In one lifetime technology has done amazing things. My father remembers well his first apartment which had electric lights—and this not in isolated or rural America but in the midst of our second biggest city. It was just twenty years later that the Rural Electrification Program brought electric lights to the rural areas. And less than twenty years later the world learned of another, even brighter light—the deadly light, brighter than any sun, which cast its brightness over the citizens of Hiroshima and Nagasaki. A light had come which brought the incredible darkness of death in the midst of incredible brightness.

Technology has moved quickly, but humanity has not moved as fast as the Scriptures would demand. The afflicted, the oppressed, the homeless are all too much with us. To use Teilhard de Chardin's image, we need again to discover fire—the light of love and goodness to dispel these darknesses which make us less human, less like a family of sisters and brothers, and therefore less like God's people.

People today need to see in a special way the light of human love and warmth to dispel the chill which would say that the task is too big, the need too great, the effort beyond our abilities. They will be convinced not so much by what we say that they should do, but more by what we, as Christians, actually do. "Your light must shine before all so that they may see goodness in your acts and give praise to your heavenly Father."

Stephen C. Gilmour

6th Sunday in Ordinary Time

Cycle A

Sir 15:15–20
1 Cor 2:6–10
Mt 5:17–37

"Eye has not seen, ear has not heard, nor has it so much as dawned on people what God has prepared for those who love him." Thanks, Paul, I needed that! Especially after that first reading! Sirach's words are surely from another age. It's been a long time since I've heard, "If you choose, you can keep the commandments." The word around today is that it's impossible. Sirach seems to imply that there is an objective morality after all—and worse, he places the responsibility squarely on my shoulders.

You know, Paul, I'd rather believe some of my contemporaries. They tell me to give up. Quit trying to love. Quit struggling for answers. "Everybody is out for themselves," they say. "You're a fool to even talk about common good and community." To believe what Sirach says makes one an anachronism in today's society, Paul. It's so much easier to join the crowd.

I guess there was a contemporary "wisdom" among your Corinthians too. You reminded them that real wisdom "is not a wisdom of this age." This discerning of God's wisdom from other "wisdom" can be difficult. You ought to know, Paul! After being knocked off your high horse, you had no doubt that conversion meant pain. You knew suffering intimately, yet you held on. I wonder if some well-intentioned Corinthians didn't try to make you rationalize some comforts for yourself, and perhaps to alter some parts of the Good News that didn't seem all that good to them.

If we try to make your words more palatable, it's no wonder we pick and choose among the words of Jesus too. If I were to edit the Bible according to today's society one of the first lines to go would be from today's Gospel: "Say 'Yes' when you mean 'Yes' and 'No' when you mean 'No.'" That's a hard line to follow. All the things Jesus says about the commandments may give us occasional trouble, but this integrity stuff is a day-in, day-out challenge. People who have integrity find it doesn't always pay off. They end up as failures in business or in relationships. They can be trusted and people who can be trusted can be used. They won't strike back, so, one can use them, feign an apology (for they are forgiving too), and then use them again if one needs to.

It's tough, Paul. I see it happen; I see people learn to play the game, to compromise their integrity to succeed or simply to belong. I see people learn to say "Yes" when they mean "Maybe" and to say "No" if it furthers their purpose. I see people who have the meaning of their "Yeses" and "Nos" so mixed up even they can't tell the difference anymore. Yes, in the 1984 Socially Acceptable Version of the Bible, that yes and no line would have to go.

Perhaps today's whole Gospel has to be struck. After all, here is Jesus trying to expand our notion of law and stretch our understanding of love, and we snap back asking, "How much can I get away with?" It is a game: listening to Jesus' words, then trying to rationalize our foolish expenditures and selfish motives. I've seen it, Paul; I'm sure the Corinthians had their own version.

Then, there's that bothersome line about leaving our gift at the altar and being reconciled. Let's get this straight, Paul. We've advanced beyond that. It's one thing to let someone crawl over and beg my forgiveness. I can be amazingly condescending in accepting an apology. (I keep a secret tally, though, allowing for far less forgiving than 70 × 7.) But this Gospel seems to imply that I am the "crawlee." How naive of Jesus to imagine that our lying and cheating would lack the subtlety that keeps it secret. What folks have against me they don't even suspect I have done, so clever and cunning have I become. What Jesus asks here is to go and admit my wrongdoing and to apologize as well. If we all had to undo the week's dirty dealings and to admit to our "Yeses" that were really "Nos" before we approached the altar, the church would be empty until at least Sunday night! What about all those well-planned liturgies? What about the collection? Where would Christianity be if we spent all our time being reconciled?

Forgive me for playing the devil's advocate on these issues, Paul. I really only intended to thank you for reminding me of the promise. "Eye has not seen or ear heard, nor has it so much as dawned on people what God has prepared for those who love him."

Forgive me for playing the Devil's advocate, Father.

Carole M. Eipers

7th Sunday in Ordinary Time

Cycle A

Lev 19:1–2, 17–18
1 Cor 3:16–23
Mt 5:38–48

Computers are everywhere, and even seem to have a life of their own, multiplying rapidly! And one of the first things the novice user quickly learns is that most computers, for all their sophistication, are really very unimaginative. They will accept information, questions, or directions only if given in exactly the right way. Make the slightest deviation and you are reminded, sometimes quite directly, that YOU have made the mistake, and that your program will not work.

The computer functions on the basis of an internal logic or law—it has been programmed to work only if this law is respected. In the midst of its memory chips and electronic circuitry there is a wonderful wizardry, capable of great things, but only if its internal laws are followed.

I'd never want to push the comparison too strongly between human being and computer, but humans too have an internal law, something built in to our makeup as persons, that must be followed if we are to be capable of the great things within our possibility. It's in this light that I like to think of the law of love found in the readings today: "You shall love your neighbor as yourself," "Love your enemies."

Rather than think of this law as an order, something imposed from the outside, something we wouldn't want to do unless we were commanded, I find it more helpful to think of this law of love as a principle, an explanation of how we function, an explanation of what's really at the heart of things. People are made for love, and if this internal law is not respected, they will become less than human or even die.

It might seem trite to say that people die without love, but it's true. Research has shown that newborn infants who must be supported with high medical technology and equipment begin to suffer from the lack of loving and human contact—being held, fondled, rocked. Research confirms that deep parental instinct which says that babies should be loved and fussed over. Occasionally we meet adults who try to survive without love—maybe they were burned in one relationship and resolved never to be caught again. Maybe they never had a chance to develop a deep and caring relationship and now are scared to try or not sure how. They become "cold fish," never venturing, never risking involvement beyond the surface—and they think they will survive this way.

My experience says that this is not the way it ought to be—this is not what life is all about, this is not what human beings are capable of. We are made for something greater; we are made for a love which draws us out of ourselves and renews us by keeping us in relationship to others who also love us.

Two things more need to be said, lest this sound too much like a kind of warm and fuzzy humanism. First of all, anytime we learn something about what it means to be deeply and most profoundly human, we are also learning something about God, for we are the work of that Creator. And anytime we learn something about God, we discover something about ourselves. It is this link between God and us, sealed in a special way in the incarnation of Jesus, that reveals the basis of the law of love. "Be holy, for I, the Lord, your God, am holy; you must be perfect as your heavenly Father is perfect." God and his people are both known for the love they give in abundance; both come alive and do great things out of this love.

Second, the Scripture is clear and honest about the fact that there is a certain amount of "stretch" involved. Even though the law of love is what will make us most fully human, and most fully God's people, its practice is not always easy. There are times when we consciously or unconsciously say "enough." And then we get reminded: "Love your enemies . . . for God's sun rises on the bad and the good . . . and if you only love those who love you, what merit is there in that?" To go the extra mile, to be even more generous than asked, these become the mark of the follower of God.

Stephen C. Gilmour

8th Sunday in Ordinary Time

Cycle A

Is 49:14–15
1 Cor 4:1–5
Mt 6:24–34

In Matthew's Gospel today we hear Jesus say "Do not worry about what you are to eat." This brings to mind a story a Filipino friend of mine told me once. He said, "Your typical American opens his kitchen cabinet and says, 'What will I feed the dog today? What will I feed the cat today?' In my country hungry people sit and think, 'What will I eat today? The dog or the cat?'"

That story illustrates what Jesus does in today's Gospel. He breaks open our tiny worlds of self-concern. We can all get caught up in our own problems, our own worries. But that can lead to an alienated, lonely world. Just think for a minute about what you worry about—are some of those things a worry to you alone? Jesus points to a wider world. He points to the kingdom—a world where our lives intersect with that of the Filipino, the Indian, the person next to us in the pew. Jesus invites us out of our self-centered worries to relationship, community, kingdom.

It is interesting that Jesus says, after telling us not to worry about tomorrow, that "each day has enough troubles of its own." Jesus is being very realistic here. If we expand what we think about, what we care about, what catches our attention and our passion, then there are bound to be new problems—"enough trouble" to keep us busy. A Peanuts cartoon provides a graphic illustration. The first scene is of Lucy and Linus watching TV. In each succeeding frame Lucy is demanding something from poor Linus—popcorn, a change in channel, and finally his beloved blanket. The blanket is ripped away from him, leaving Linus in a dazed heap. His response is "Brothers and sisters shouldn't be in the same family."

What does it mean to be in the same family? When our worlds intersect, problems arise—*and* we get in touch with who we are. When we allow another in, we allow in a God who calls us to forget self and narrowness and come alive—to live in touch with the heart and not just with food and drink and clothing.

One final story about the God who cajoles us into "setting our hearts on his kingdom and his righteousness." A priest friend of mine was recently on his way from his Long Island parish to celebrate a wedding at St. Patrick's Cathedral in Manhattan. He was driving along, going through the Midtown Tunnel, thinking about the wedding. He had never witnessed a wedding at a church as glamorous as St. Patrick's and he was wrapped up in imagining it. He was also a little worried because with New York traffic he knew he would get to the church with little time to spare. As he came out of the tunnel and waited at the first traffic light, a boy of about 12, poor and black, started to wash his windshield. The priest didn't like this intruder into his worries. He really didn't like him when the light turned green and the boy was still at work. And he disliked him even more as he fumbled in his pocket for change and couldn't find any—which meant he had to take a dollar from his wallet. The frustration was rising. He was going to be late for a very important wedding with very important people in a very important church. Why didn't this nobody kid leave him alone?

And then it hit him: "What is a Christian really all about? Is a Christian allowed his own sheltered world or does that poor kid mean something? Is there room in my heart for one more? Perhaps I live and love in a world bigger than the one I create."

Just when we are safe and secure and have our own worries lined up, God breaks in and asks us to "set our hearts on his kingdom first."

Douglas Fisher

9th Sunday in Ordinary Time

Cycle A

Dt 11:18, 26–28
Rom 3:21–25, 28
Mt 7:21–27

Jesus was and is a phenomenal teacher. He taught with "power and authority," not like the Scribes and Pharisees. And he taught with images: images which allow us to hook onto something real in our reflection on our lives. This week you have the opportunity to explore the images of rock and sand with your congregation. The goal is to meditate on where we build our houses—what we allow to count in our lives as foundational.

Think about sand for a minute. Envision a sandy beach with the sun setting over the ocean. It is attractive, isn't it? A little romantic? But what would happen if you built a house there? Jesus the architect warns it would have a great fall in a storm. But don't we all sometimes build our houses on the attractive sand and then watch them fall in crisis?

Ask yourself and your congregation what it means to build a house on rock. What are the foundations of life? I will suggest two here: gifts and friendship. You might be able to think of many more.

How are gifts a rock to build on? In the movie "Chariots of Fire," one of the English runners who will compete in the Olympics says: "God not only made me, but he made me fast. And when I run, I feel his pleasure." God not only made you, he made you with gifts. What are they? "God not only made me, but he made me . . . what?" Generous? A good listener? A good parent? A great dancer? A wonderful joke-teller? Compassionate? Trustworthy? When you activate that gift, you feel God's pleasure. He is delighted he made you. You are a joy to him. And when you know your gifts, when you know yourself, you have a house built on rock, a house built on thanksgiving. You can live with strength and conviction.

Another rock in life is friendship. Father Robert Lauder illustrates this well in a review of a play called "K2" (*America*/July 16, 1983). "K2" is about two men, Taylor and Harold, who are stranded on a ledge of a mountain, K2. What happens there is described by Lauder:

When it seems that Harold will not make it down the mountain, the crude, vulgar apparently self-centered Taylor confesses that the one important reality in his life is his friendship with Harold and that he wishes to stay and die with his friend. Pulling a switch on Jesus' statement, "A man can have no greater love than to lay down his life for his friend," Harold suggests that Taylor's love can best be shown by descending the mountain and bearing Harold's testament of love to Harold's wife and children. If Taylor descends K2 he will not be like Camus' Sisyphus mocking an absurd universe, but rather an apostle proclaiming a gospel of love.

Patrick Meyer's vision is not a Nietzschean nihilism but an optimistic glorification of human nature, a celebration not that God is love but that human love is as close as anyone can get to anything divine. Friendship is the only religion worth engaging in, and love of one another is as close as anyone ought to get to adoration.

A person can build a life on friendship. A Christian can see Jesus in these friendships. And a Christian believes he or she can experience a friendship with Jesus himself. That will be a house that will remain when hit by the rain, floods, and gales of life.

Each life has some sand and some rock in its foundations. Ask your congregation to remember this during the Eucharist. As the Eucharist is celebrated, perhaps all could look for the "rocks" and truly give thanks for personal gifts and for friendship. Being in touch with that, perhaps your congregation will leave the church a stronger, more confident people.

Douglas Fisher

13th Sunday in Ordinary Time

Cycle A

2 Kgs 4:8–11, 14–16
Rom 6:3–4, 8–11
Mt 10:37–42

Dolores was the oldest of eighteen children. When the last child came into the family circle, she was given the name "Anne Welcome." Though she was last, the family wanted her to know that she was wanted, warmly received and welcomed.

Human welcome is one of the gifts everyone hopes for. It says that others open themselves to us in hospitality. No Christian virtue is more desired than hospitality. The document, *Environment and Art in Catholic Worship,* states that the foundational virtue needed for quality worship is hospitality. Perhaps this is why Catholics now talk in church. It is to welcome fellow believers who have spent the week scattered in the tasks of human and Christian living. Perhaps this is why we think that ushers are more than collection takers. We want to create a spirit of hospitality and welcome to newcomers, catechumenal candidates, the elderly who may need assistance, and the handicapped who enter our circle of worship.

It may seem that it costs something to be hospitable. The woman of influence offers table sharing and a room of hospitality for Elisha. The Gospel continues this Jewish sense of hospitality by indicating that Christians are to welcome the holy person and are to offer a cup of cold water "to one of these lowly ones because he or she is a disciple."

Some people seem to have a natural sense of welcome and hospitality. But it costs something to forget oneself for the sake of another. We have to put ourselves out. Sometimes the cost seems minimal—a gesture of courtesy, a moment to pause and greet another, an arm to take as one enters a stairway into a church building. But the cost is deeper than meets the eye. Authentic hospitality means dropping the socially learned attitude of suspicion of others, especially those very different from our tastes or backgrounds. It also means allowing the other person room and space so that we do not become curious, a busybody or someone who smothers the other with kindness galore. The cost is presence without intrusion and an attitude that Christ is present in the guest.

Christian heritage prided itself on the virtue of hospitality. Rooms were set aside in church buildings for the sojourner. The church was to be an inn of hospitality. Monies were to be collected for those without any means of welfare: widows, orphans and the poor. Eucharistic bread carried by a traveler from one local church was mingled in with the bread at another Assembly in order to indicate hospitality and communion of one community with another. Ancient writings indicate that affluent Christians gave because others had need and they would receive the best gift in return, the prayer of the recipient for them.

While hospitality costs something of ourselves, there is a surprise in store for us. When we are welcoming and hospitable, we receive the word of the other. That word may be God's and it may be effective. Because of her hospitality, the woman receives a word from Elisha that she may not have heard without her hospitality. This word of God is effective and results in fruitfulness: she will be gifted with child. The guest offers a word of surprise; the guest becomes bearer of good news in the environment of hospitality.

Our modern world evidences bearers of God's good word to us in a spirit of hospitality. We who give become the recipients of a much more wonderful hospitality from God. One could think of Carol Houselander in England during World War II. She was so effective with emotionally ill persons that doctors sent her patients to receive her word of healing. Tom Dooley became bearer of good news by laying down his life as a doctor for those who were poor and of a different background from him. Oscar Romero and four American churchwomen became bearers of good news by laying down their lives for fellow Christians so that God's hospitality could displace the despair of war. There are examples of modern holy women and men who are bearers of good news, whose word is effective both verbally and in action. We have a responsibility to listen to these prophets of hospitality and we may want to seek out who these persons are in our own midst.

John J. O'Brien

14th Sunday in Ordinary Time

Cycle A

Zec 9:9–10
Rom 8:9, 11–13
Mt 11:25–30

While driving in a 35 mile-per-hour zone the other day, I suddenly found that my car was the "leader of the pack." The other vehicles had decelerated, leaving me quite alone—though I was only traveling at the posted 35 mph. The reason for this turn of events became apparent as I spied the radar-equipped patrol car on the side of the road. Once we had passed the radar's range, the other cars sped by, leaving me in the dust.

I laughed; then I began to think about yokes. There are drivers who are "yoked" externally: the sight of a patrol car, a radar line, a policeman, and they obey the speed limit. There are drivers who are "yoked" internally: radar or not, they drive safely and lawfully.

In today's Gospel Jesus says, "Take my yoke upon your shoulders . . . "—not a very appealing invitation at first glance. The yokes in Hebrew Scripture often denoted slavery and oppression. The first realization we must come to in order to understand what Jesus offers is that we are all yoked already; we are all motivated, driven by the values we hold.

There are life-yokes which are external. Some people are yoked by what others think. Their actions are controlled by others, whether those others are bosses, or colleagues, or the "Joneses." There are life-yokes which are internal. The yoke which Jesus speaks of is an internal yoke—one which functions whether there is a "cop behind the billboard" or not, whether anyone sees what we do or not.

Once we can admit that we are indeed yoked, we can examine whether our yoke is external or internal. If we are yoked internally, there are a variety of yokes to which we may find ourselves submitting. There are the "Seven Deadly Yokes": pride, covetousness, lust, anger, envy, gluttony, or sloth. One of these may be the primary motivating force in our life. They are deadly because to live with any of them as our goal is to seek isolation from others and ultimately death.

Jesus invites "Take my yoke." The implication is that this is not a yoke which he places on us, but rather, one which he shares with us. What was the yoke which Jesus wore? What was it that motivated him during his early life?

Jesus names his yoke for us: "My food is to do the work of the one who sent me"; "Not my will but yours be done." Certainly Jesus was not controlled by others. If he had been, his life would have been devoid of sinners, tax-collectors, prostitutes, and children. We see no trace of his being moved by the deadly yokes for selfish gain. The only yoke that Jesus wears and offers to share is his Father's will.

To accept the yoke Jesus wears makes sense only if we believe what Paul says in today's second reading: that we are debtors. Until we know that all is gift, we fight all yokes and end up settling for inferior motivation in our lives. Jesus, gentle and humble of heart, invites us to be gentle and humble too, to have faith that the Father's will for us is life-giving.

"Rejoice!", the prophet Zechariah says in the first reading. Your hero comes, not in a limousine, nor even on a white stallion, but on a donkey. This man who invites you to share his yoke does not promise a share in pomp nor possessions. He comes, not to conquer your enemies, but to free you from false yokes which promise more than they can deliver. He comes to share his own yoke—his Father's will—and if we plow with him, the furrows which we dig will one day be a foundation for our place in the Kingdom.

There is no radar to scan how we measure up; no officer of the law waiting around the bend to punish us if we are not faithful. There will only be the knowledge that we share the yoke of Jesus himself. What's good enough for him is good enough for me.

Carole M. Eipers

15th Sunday in Ordinary Time

Cycle A

Is 55:10–11
Rom 8:18–23
Mt 13:1–23

One of the strongest of human needs is the need to belong to and be a part of something larger than the individual ego. We all need to feel that we have roots that extend from the past, give meaning to the present, and promise hope for the future. Much of our searching is for a home: a place where we can feel secure and accepted. Even more than a place, a home is a state of being, a fundamental condition of being-in-the-world. One of the clearest symptoms of our modern discontent is the present state of *strangeness*. To be alienated is to be a stranger: a stranger to the world, others, the self, and ultimately God who is the Ground of all Being. The modern complaint of alienation is voiced by many across the strata of our society. The young feel the loss of community in a world which often seems indifferent to their searchings for a truth beyond the bread of this world. Many young people turn to cults which promise a strong sense of identity through community, sacrifice, and discipline. The elderly feel the alienation of a society which often pronounces them useless or a burden. Alienation can also be experienced in various crisis stages of life when our careers no longer seem promising or our children have moved out leaving us with a void that demands filling.

This feeling of alienation and homelessness is not unique to our own age. The Israelites knew well what it meant to be displaced. The most traumatic experience of their history, the Exile in 586 B.C., brought on a profound communal identity crisis. "Weren't we God's People? How could this happen to us? Was the Lord our God really all he was made up to be? Is our God faithful to his promises? What went wrong? After a period of deep reflection and suffering a biblical insight emerged: God is faithful and loving, but God respects human freedom and God's people can reject him and be left to their own designs. This can lead to the unfortunate consequences of destruction and homelessness. Only by dwelling in God's creative word, expressed in the covenant, can people reach their true destiny.

In our first reading, Isaiah offers hope to the people in a distant land that through God's grace they will experience release and freedom. The people will once again have a home through the generosity and faithfulness of God. To celebrate this homecoming, a new covenant will be established. It will be greater than the first—no longer exclusively for the Israelites, but extending to the Gentile world as well.

The new covenant comes to the Israelites in the depth of their alienation as a beacon of hope which exceeds the power of mere human ability and expectation. This theme is developed by St. Paul in his letter to the Romans. All those who are guided by the Spirit are children of God and heirs as well. Salvation and full life with God is promised to all who endure the baptism of suffering in the present with a hope of future glory to be revealed. In the midst of suffering we can endure with fidelity and longing because, through the power of God, suffering will be transformed into newness of life. Such longing and growth through suffering is not limited to humankind but extends to all of the created world. All of creation waits in eager longing for the second coming of the Risen One.

The theme of alienation and homelessness has special meaning for us as citizens of the twentieth century. These past eight decades could rightfully be termed the "Decades of the Homeless." In this global village we are more aware of that which divides us than of our common humanity and relatedness to the Father, through Jesus, in the Spirit. Violence becomes the easy and rationalized answer to all our problems. The great wars and so-called lesser conflicts of this century have given renewed viability to the Gospel's call for finding the hidden presence of Christ in the least of our brethren. These least are easy to reject and pass by for often they act and speak in a manner different from our own. They are strangers and evoke all kinds of feelings of suspicion and distrust in us. However, the more distant and strange they seem, the more present is the Crucified and Risen One.

Today, new waves of immigrants are landing on our shores, testing our commitment to the Gospel. We too were once aliens and strangers in this new world. We too benefitted from the charity and love of others. We are now being challenged to remember our past and offer hope to those who come searching for freedom and a more human form of existence. As Christians we can never be indifferent to our brothers and sisters who set up tents in our midst. Each Christian community is the present testing ground for the courage to accept our brothers and sisters as we would accept Christ himself.

William F. Maestri

16th Sunday in Ordinary Time

Cycle A

Wis 12:13, 16–19
Rom 8:26–27
Mt 13:24–43

In the old cowboy movies (still occasionally shown on television), there were certain unmistakable clues as to who was who. The good guys were invariably in white hats; the bad guys in black hats.

Jesus, the good rabbinic storyteller, portrays a more ambiguous scene. The wheat and the weeds are mixed up so closely together that to root out one will destroy the other. And so the owner must wait, must be patient, must live with the mix until the end. The seemingly efficient slaves, who think they can immediately distinguish the weeds from the wheat, must learn a lesson of toleration.

It is the rabbi Jesus who is wise, and not the movie makers. Good and evil are not so neatly separated, in ourselves or in the world. There are weedy patches within the best of us, and perhaps rich wheat among the worst of us! And luckily enough, the Master/God is willing to live with this, willing to be patient and tolerant until the end, willing to be merciful and allow repentance.

Mercy and power are strangely like the weeds and wheat; like the efficient field hands, we presume that they cannot exist side by side. Mercy means being weak, soft, letting anything happen. Power means strength, severity, rooting out the weeds at their first appearance. To be great is to be powerful; to be merciful is to be trampled upon.

Such is the rhetoric which is often put forth on a national level and which is implicitly believed on the personal level. The assumption is that the weed patch and the wheat field are clearly separated—and guess where we are! "We" must have a strong defense and spend ever-increasing billions on armaments, lest "they" see us as weak and unprepared. "I" am correct, so until "they" apologize, I won't speak to them.

But the story says differently. Jesus builds on the Wisdom tradition which says that it is because God is powerful that he is merciful. His might is shown not in force or destruction, but in mercy and forbearance. And there's something within us which suggests that

he is right. Like the mustard seed or the leaven, seemingly insignificant and powerless, mercy has within it the promise of greatness.

Another wise rabbi comes to my mind. A survivor of the Holocaust and a prison camp, he came to Madison and became a leader in both the Jewish and the civic community. In this sense he was powerful, but in a truer sense his power and greatness came from his sense of mercy and reconciliation so like the God he worshipped. Even though the hatred in Nazi Germany had deeply and directly affected him and those he loved, he still could speak and live a message of mercy and forgiveness.

I believe that it is possible for people to repent and change. I believe that people who seek to repent should be given a chance to do so. . . . Hatred, unbending, unending hatred is not an emotion by which I can live nor a philosophy by which I want my children and my children's children to live. Hatred does not open a road to the future of civilization. . . . Hatred, unending hatred, is not the seed bed from which redemption can grow. The chief task before mankind is still unfinished. Human beings must at long last become human and humane.
(Manfred E. Swarsensky, *Intimates* and *Ultimates*)

The readings today praise that greatness of God as shown in his mercy, his forbearance, and we celebrate because we have experienced his mercy toward us. We depend on his powerful mercy for our salvation, and we struggle to learn to be equally powerful in our mercy toward others. And in this we do need the Spirit to plead within us, to express what is yet so difficult for us, to pray and act as we ought.

Stephen C. Gilmour

17th Sunday in Ordinary Time

Cycle A

1 Kgs 3:5, 7–12
Rom 8:28–30
Mt 13:44–52

In the first reading Solomon asks God for that which the king needs most, an understanding heart to dispel his sense of inadequacy in dealing with the people. In the gospel reading, the searcher is impelled to seek a reality of priceless value, something so necessary and so great that he will give up everything for that find.

To know what I truly need and to seek for it is to learn the secret of life. To meet my own needs is to find myself, my true self in God, a self of priceless value: not what others have told me that I need, or advertising has enticed me into believing that I may need for happy living; not even what my friends or community or all the experts may suggest for me. Life is full of suggestions from others, techniques in books, personages who seem to have achieved what I lack. To know and to find what I need is an individual quest. Each is born alone, and in the last analysis, seeks alone.

Needs are unique and personal. "I need to lose weight." But what do I *need* to lose weight? "I need to be kinder and more patient." And what *must happen* for me to gain these virtues? Yes, I say with Solomon, "I know not how to begin or to finish." And yet, I must find something if I will live into myself in God.

Some of my needs may be clear to me, and meeting those needs may be difficult, yet possible. Beyond the needs that I know may lie deeper needs that I never knew existed, until I touch their empty spaces and feel the wound exposed to the light and air of consciousness. "I am desperately lonely, although I have many friends." "My career is going so well, and yet I feel so empty." "I have everything I could wish for, yet something seems to be missing." These vague gnawings are indicators, markers to deepen the quest.

"Loneliness is the poverty of self; solitude is the richness of self," May Sarton writes in *Mrs. Stevens Hears the Mermaids Singing*. "I know your affliction and distress and pressing trouble, and your poverty, but you are rich!" (Rev. 2:9a) the visionary Lord speaks through John to me. The wealth is there. How do I tap into it, draw from it?

If I reduce my needs to the most basic, I can identify with the searchers in the parables of the kingdom: nothing too concrete, yet a sense of life and presence worth the giving up of everything. An understanding heart was what Solomon requested. That was what he most needed. And it pleased God that Solomon did not ask for lesser riches, did not request less than his deepest need.

Solitude is the richness of self. The kingdom is within, more immediate and closer to me than my own heartbeat. A storehouse treasure from which the householder brings forth the new and the old, the fresh, as well as the familiar. Tolbert McCarroll writes in *Exploring Your Inner World:* "You have everything you need. You are all you need. If you are centered you will not expect anything from anyone else. You will not depend upon others and because you do not need, you are free to want and to love."

What must I give up for this priceless treasure to become real to me? All that distracts me from this single-minded pursuit. All that I am attached to, thinking that I need it, although it does not ultimately satisfy me. All that holds me back and is rooted in my own fear and resistance. The choice, moment by moment, is up to me. I am free to seek or to refuse. The pursuit of the kingdom is like a woman in the stages of divorce from her old ways. At first she is glad to be away, experiencing relief and euphoric freedom. With bitter awareness, she exclaims, "How could I have lived that way for so long?" Time passes, the hostile feelings dissipate, and she feels a bit of longing for her old home, her known securities. "Perhaps it was not all that bad," she tells herself. Tempted to return, she realizes that the marriage is over, the break irrevocable. She cannot turn back. Vulnerably she slowly begins to live into her new life. New expanses begin to unfold both within her and around her. She has turned a corner, she says, and she cannot settle for less.

Sharon Koziczkowski

18th Sunday in Ordinary Time

Cycle A

Is 55:1–3
Rom 8:35, 37–39
Mt 14:13–21

A teacher was in the faculty room, complaining as usual about the students in his class. "They are so difficult to work with. They never want to do anything extra. I have to be at them all the time to get any work out of them. I got the worst group again this year."

In the same school, another teacher, in her usual quiet way, stated a different viewpoint. "I've been so lucky with the students in my class. They always seem so eager to try something. I enjoy being with them and they even encourage me to think again about some things. I'm so impressed with their enthusiasm and interest."

The first teacher gives the same complaints every year, the second one is enthusiastic and pleased every year. And, of course, eventually they are teaching the same students!

The images we project on other people are often really pictures of ourselves. These two teachers are probably telling more about themselves than about their students. The generous and interested teacher finds students to be generous and interesting; the complaining, unhappy teacher finds students also to be less than perfect.

Today is an occasion to check our images of God. What is he like, how does he operate, what can we realistically expect from him? The readings today are powerful in their imagery and strong in their conviction that God is generous, reaching out to those in need. Isaiah speaks God's own invitation. "Come." Whatever is needed—water, food, life—is available. Not when you deserve it, not when you can pay the price, but whenever you need it!

In the Gospel Jesus concretely acts out this invitation in the story of the feeding of the multitude. The people are in need, and their need is met—not grudgingly, not half-way, but generously and in abundance. There are even left-overs for another day or another need! Paul, no stranger to difficulty and persecution, is more than confident. God's love is never absent—nothing can take it away.

In this summertime of picnics, block parties, street festivals, the image of crowds gathering and being fed might seem especially real. And we know that the hungers which are being met in these joyous events are many. The nourishment of companionship, joyful celebration, and leisure activity is food for the spirit, as necessary as anything served in plates or cups.

These are happy, joyous images of a generous God in the midst of his people. But sometimes we seem to mistrust such images. Could he really care that much about us? Can salvation be offered so easily to so many? Shouldn't we have to work harder to deserve such love? In our hearts we know that *we* couldn't be so generous, so loving, and so we can be tempted to shape our image of God to conform to our own smallness. And yet learning to place our trust in a God who is so generous is perhaps ultimately the most demanding way of life. We can't hold back, or be half-hearted about it; we have to fall head-over-heels in love with this God.

But perhaps we are afraid to admit that we are hungry, that we are in need. It might be safer not to give away so much of our heart; it might be easier to try to rely on our own abilities. We might even think that we are paying the price, doing what is demanded, and therefore have a right to salvation-on-demand from God, the great bookkeeper. Then we need again to hear the simple invitation of Isaiah—"Come, without paying and without cost . . . that you may have life." Otherwise our attitude may well become the only power which can separate us from the love of God.

Are there any really hungry people today? We have to be careful here. The disciples in the Gospel noticed the need but took no action. They asked Jesus to let the people go so that they could take care of themselves. (Sound familiar?!) But Jesus throws the ball back in the disciples' court, "Give them something to eat yourselves." Certainly we need to notice the hungers of people, but we also need to take action to alleviate such hungers. Any disciple of Jesus must share in this work.

Stephen C. Gilmour

19th Sunday in Ordinary Time

Cycle A

1 Kgs 19:9, 11–13
Rom 9:1–5
Mt 14:22–33

We live in the best of times and the worst of times. Peace groups demonstrate across the country from Seattle to Long Island, while the government relentlessly pursues Star Wars technology. Drugs and alcohol cripple millions of adults and youth; medical personnel find ways to heal the deep scars that they and their children bear. Amidst budget cuts and denial of the problem, countless homeless live on our streets moving churches, civic organizations, and city leaders to strive to meet their needs. Indeed these are the best of times and the worst of times, times of confusion and crisis.

Crisis by definition is a point of transition, a moment when the old ways of acting and solving problems no longer work and new ones have not yet been discovered. Faced with the complexity of the problems, some are overcome with a sense of powerlessness and despair. Others discover inner resources they didn't know they had, resources of courage, determination and a pioneering spirit. Today's readings recount stories of crisis. What light can the experience of Elijah and of the apostles shed on dealing with crisis?

Elijah lived in a time of political and religious crisis. Because of the influence of Jezebel, King Ahaz' pagan wife, many prophets had been killed in Israel. Elijah himself was a fugitive. Pagan customs and the religion of Baal were in vogue. At the risk of his life, Elijah had come out of hiding to demonstrate the power of Yahweh before the king, the prophets of Baal and all the people. He succeeded, but Jezebel swore revenge. Discouraged, exhausted, Elijah prayed to God to let him die. Yahweh had other plans. God sent a messenger with food and drink to strengthen the prophet on his journey to Mount Horeb (also called Sinai). Horeb was a sacred place. It was the spot where Moses encountered God, the place where God entered into a covenant with the people of Israel. Here, Elijah too encounters God. Here he receives his challenging mission. In this time of political and religious turmoil Elijah is to anoint a new king and a prophet who will be his successor. Yahweh's power will do the rest. The covenant will be restored, the people will turn to their God, but not without a major transition. God would be present in and through the struggles of this people to deliver them.

After the death of Jesus, the disciples faced a major crisis. Their leaders remembered a moment of crisis on the lake of Gennesaret. They had been alone in the boat that stormy night. Fierce winds whipped up waves that pitched the boat from side to side. They feared for their lives. Suddenly, they spotted an eerie form walking on the water and cried out, "It's a ghost!" In the midst of the storm Jesus came, telling them not to be afraid. Stunned, they remained silent except for Peter. Cautiously, he asked the vision, "Lord, if it is you, bid me come to you." Jesus replied, "Come." Perhaps it was not so remarkable that as long as he kept faith in the Lord, Peter was able to walk on water. What was remarkable is that when he doubted and began to sink, the Lord's power was still there to save him. That was the lesson early Christians learned from the memory of the story as they faced their own moment of crisis. The Lord was with them in the midst of their struggles. Jesus asked only for their faith in his presence and power to save.

As in the time of Elijah and the disciples, the Lord speaks a word to us in the midst of tumultuous times. It is our faith that will enable us to hear God's message and to do our part. We are the prophets and disciples called to spread the Good News of the reign of God by living the beatitudes today. Some are called to serve the poor; others to care for those who are elderly or ill. Some respond by directing their energies to providing housing for the homeless. Still others reach out to those who suffer addiction and to their families. All of us are called to be truthful and just in our business dealings and caring in our relationships with others, however different they might be. Together we must do our part so that God's presence and saving power will move us forward into a new era.

God speaks a word to each of us in our own circumstances. It is for us to place before the Lord the burdens we bear, the feelings our life circumstances evoke, lest they overcome us. Calm restored, our hearts will experience God's saving presence. We will be able to discern what God is asking us to do at this moment in our lives so that we might be that saving presence for others.

Barbara O'Dea

20th Sunday in Ordinary Time

Cycle A

Is 56:1, 6–7
Rom 11:13–15, 29–32
Mt 15:21–28

We Americans live with a marvelously sophisticated health care system. Illnesses of a century ago have either been eliminated or can be dealt with by medication or surgery. For the first time in human history we know the expansion of life into elder years and old age. We have the attitude that health care should be for all, nobody excepted. Yet we also know of some who receive no health care because they stay away in fear or cannot afford even minimal service.

Few things seem to be able to elicit the right feelings humans would seem to have—like a child who is malnourished or an elder ulcerated and unable to become well.

Right feeling is as important as right action when it comes to genuine health. Right feeling and right action can lead to right thinking and teaching when it comes to healthy faith and action.

The Bible selections for this Sunday focus us into a right feeling for Christian health and an attitude that yields vitality instead of disease. Salvation, like health care, is meant for all. The Latin word, *salus,* salvation, indicates that Gentile and Jew, that is, all peoples are invited to share in the medicine of God, the one who is always a wise physician. This right feeling for universal salvation was learned through Israel's dealing with dis-ease. The Temple altars were inaccessible during exile. The Word became the only medicine for life and it was cherished in synagogue and home setting. When this Word brought health, our ancestors were able to bless God, the source and author of salvational health. The ancient Jew could hand over a healthy self and a healthy community to God. He or she then partook of *shalom,* a prosperity that was healthy in peace, a healthy land and a wholesome outreach to others not of Jewish fellowship.

This *salus* and *shalom,* authentic health and well-being, could easily be forgotten and the roots of disease could easily set in. One, after all, could cling to external religiosity and a piety risking bigotry and narrowmindedness, Instead of *sanitas,* full health, a curious Latin word we reduce to mental sanity, faith could become in-sane, a mix of outward observance and niggardly nitpicking.

The Gospel shows this insanity. Galilean life could reduce women, even Jewish women, to an unhealthy state so much so that salvation would be only begrudgingly granted these "second-class" members of society.

The Gospel encounter between Jesus, a Galilean Jew, and this Canaanite woman is a startling attempt at health. This health is not only for her daughter. It is for the disciples of Jesus and the Church of Matthew as well. This woman pleads with the one we acknowledge as the Physician of life. She confesses what proper religion might forget or deny. She confesses in such a dramatic fashion that we cannot miss the point. She did him homage. She may have prostrated herself in such a way that Jesus could not ignore her even if he did not address her. Eventually a right feeling of health emerges to surprise his disciples who had wanted to get rid of her, to shock the Christians of Matthew's church and to challenge us. The woman shows that genuine health means clinging to Jesus, adhering to him, giving undivided loyalty to him and his values. Such faith yields a harvest of healthy possibility not only for her daughter who becomes well but also for us in our seeking to extirpate disease.

Even the dogs eat the leavings from the master's table, says the woman of great faith. The mission of Jesus is one that surprises our eyes and alerts us to the social sins of elitism, sexism, and narrow-doored salvation open only for the thin models of advertising. The mission task, one that espouses health, calls for a faith experience that cherishes women and men, works for justice for both, and acts to secure a healthy reclaiming of the human story of both genders. Neither his-story nor her-story will any longer do. The Gospel shocks us into universal health that makes ministry and mission fully open to all in a universally healthy church.

John J. O'Brien

21st Sunday in Ordinary Time

Cycle A

Is 22:15, 19–23
Rom 11:33–36
Mt 16:13–20

We live in an atmosphere of great personal and global insecurity. The daily news catalogues the numerous threats there are to our life and well-being: crime, toxic wastes, natural disasters. The peril of nuclear holocaust which looms over our civilization is the most formidable symbol of the insecurity of modern existence.

"Where can I find security?" many ask. Perhaps if I buy more insurance policies, I will feel safe. Maybe the answer to national security lies in larger stockpiles of weapons and more elaborate defense systems. Some see the answer only in individual terms, and work to amass a large savings account or to design a well-supplied bomb shelter for themselves and their family. Yet none of these measures really quiets the fearful heart. Somehow they are never enough to quell the gnawing insecurities of life.

Today's readings provide another perspective on this question of human security. In the first reading we see a nation facing an immediate threat from a foreign power. The Assyrians appear on the horizons of Judah. What is Judah to do? Her prime minister, Shebna, believes that military power will be the real source of Judah's protection. By turning to military alliances rather than to God, Shebna forfeits his right to the leadership of Judah, and is replaced by another. According to the prophet Isaiah, faith in God is the most practical basis of security. It is the only reliable weapon, and without it, all other policies are barren.

Such reliance on God's power requires trust in a deeper kind of wisdom. This point is made in the next two readings which probe God's plan for our salvation or security. Paul tells the Romans that God's wisdom and knowledge are inscrutable and unsearchable. *How* God will bring about the salvation of all people is not clear to Paul; the source of his consolation is a deep faith in the ways of God. He knows that God's ways are paradoxical, moving through suffering and death to resurrection from death.

In the reading from Matthew's Gospel, Peter expresses the same kind of faith. Jesus was not the kind of political Messiah hoped for by many in Israel. Earlier, in the temptation scene, Matthew has shown that Jesus will not fulfill the people's craving for security by giving them miracles, bread, and victory over their enemies. Jesus' path to security is not simple and self-evident; faith is required to recognize it. Such wisdom is given to Peter, and he expresses his faith in Jesus as Messiah. As in the first reading from Isaiah, the power to rule belongs to those who recognize the inscrutable wisdom of God as the only real basis for human security.

We have had leaders who have called us to the deeper, less immediately appealing paths to security: Mahatma Gandhi and Martin Luther King, who showed us that love is our strongest weapon for settling conflict, even if it entails suffering and loss; Anwar Sadat, who will willing to be converted to the path of peace; Pope John Paul II, who could visit and forgive the man who attempted to assassinate him. We need other such leaders who, like Isaiah, will offer our age a gripping, stirring faith. We create a climate for such leaders to emerge when, in our personal lives, we make trust in God the center of our security.

Kathleen R. Fischer
Thomas N. Hart

22nd Sunday in Ordinary Time

Cycle A

Jer 20:7–9
Rom 12:1–2
Mt 16:21–27

William James wrote, "Our minds grow in spots; and like grease spots, the spots spread. But we let them spread as little as possible; we keep unaltered as much of our old knowledge, as many of our old prejudices and beliefs as we can. We patch and tinker more than we renew. The novelty soaks in; it stains the ancient mass; but it is also tinged by what absorbs it."

Today's letter to the Romans says the same thing: "Do not conform yourselves to this age, but be transformed by the renewal of your mind . . . "

There is a choice to be made. Shall we patch and tinker, or shall we really change? Shall we choose conformity or renewal?

Jeremiah struggled with this choice. Part of his struggle is recorded in today's first reading. He had obviously chosen to be really changed; he did not conform to the thinking of the age, but to God's call. His reward? "All the day long I am an object of laughter; everyone mocks me." Jeremiah continues to struggle: "I will speak in his name no more." The struggle is resolved when Jeremiah once again realizes that the only thing worse than being a prophet would be his not being a prophet. Ultimately, in spite of the cost, Jeremiah decides to renew his commitment.

In the gospel reading, Peter struggles with really changing his expectations of the Messiah. Peter too decides that, in spite of the suffering which was now part of the picture, following Jesus was worth it.

Jesus struggled too. Peter, his follower and friend, tempts him to conform to the expectations of the people rather than conforming to his Father's will. Jesus decides that his mission is worth the cost.

And how shall our struggle be resolved? Shall we patch and tinker, accepting only the parts of the Good News which comfort us? Or shall we open ourselves to be transformed by the challenge of building the kingdom?

We know what the call to prophesy cost Jeremiah; we know what the call to apostleship cost Peter; we know that Jesus' resurrection was paid for by his crucifixion. We know, as Jesus reminds us today, that our discipleship will cost us. We must deny ourselves, we must carry our cross, we must follow in footsteps which will lead to Calvary.

The choice is perhaps easily made in moments of fervor, in times of prayer. The cost comes as we begin to live out our choice, as we begin to find we are the object of criticism, the butt of jokes. The cost brings us to moments when we say—and feel—with Jeremiah that we "will speak his name no more." The cost comes when we have, as Paul suggests, offered our bodies as a living sacrifice for the community, and some friend, like Peter, says, "What the hell did you do that for?"

The choice to be transformed by God is one which we are continually asked to re-affirm. We pay the price for discipleship on the installment plan, and each payment calls for a re-commitment to the worth of the kingdom.

We can follow the example of Jeremiah, Peter, and Jesus, or we can conform ourselves to this age. We have to decide one way or the other. Jesus did not come to patch and tinker with us; he came to transform us, and through us to transform our world into his Father's kingdom.

The cost is clear; may our decision that the kingdom is worth the price be as clear.

Carole M. Eipers

23rd Sunday in Ordinary Time

Cycle A

Ez 33:7–9
Rom 13:8–10
Mt 18:15–20

I had known Sue for many years. Even though we didn't see each other extremely often, we did stay in touch, often getting together around holiday times as well as periodically throughout the year. I'm not even sure when it was that I noticed that things were somehow different. An occasional phone call when she just didn't sound quite right. A party at which her conversation seemed a bit too sentimental and gushy. Other times when she seemed angry and abrasive, hard to get along with. At first I suspected, then I was sure—Sue was sick. Her illness was alcoholism, and it was slowly changing and destroying the person I knew.

I wasn't the only one who noticed, of course. Other friends mentioned Sue's drinking to me at times, and we expressed our concern and worry, as well as our frustration. I'd like to say I was the key person, the real friend, who helped Sue to seek treatment, but I wasn't. I kept delaying, unsure whether I wanted to risk a confrontation, and so I didn't do anything directly to help. I kept in contact, and when Sue finally sought treatment I visited more frequently than before and offered my support and friendship. But I have always wished that I had acted sooner and more directly.

For me, that's what fraternal correction would have meant—and at that time, in that situation, I wasn't up to the demands of such loving activity. It is not easy to confront another person, especially one we love and care about. It is not easy to warn another of destructive behavior without sounding like a nagging complainer or a self-righteous superior. But today's liturgy suggests that Christians are especially called to such activity.

Matthew's very practical, step-by-step advice is not just the expression of good psychological or counseling principles. It is a faith conviction which prompts such activity. The community is bound together in faith, by the life they share—and not to care about another is to break faith, to weaken that life. Matthew puts in concrete terms the commandment of love of neighbor which Paul speaks about. Ezekiel too understands the burden of speaking to the neighbor in time of need. In no case is the goal to condemn or berate, much less to come off as one who is morally superior. The goal is again one of faith, to encourage and exhort one another, to call one another to something better, to remind each other of our destiny as God's people, his holy ones.

I suspect that one of the signs of maturity is the growing ability to confront and challenge others in love. Couples and families need to learn how to do this, and there are practical skills which can be learned and practiced. People who work closely together need to grow in their ability to evaluate one another without being critically judgmental, and effective methods of team building and clear procedures of evaluation can help.

But I think that there are two factors which are necessary and which underlie such practical skills: a willingness to think more of the other person than of oneself and, second, a lived sense of Church which is convinced of our mutual dependence in the life of faith. In my case, I was probably more worried about myself than about Sue. If I said something, I might be criticized, she might be angry at me. It might not do any good (that is, I might not succeed). And at that time those things seemed more powerful than what was happening to Sue.

And without a sense of Church which is broader than our own individual salvation and relationship with God, it is hard to be convinced that the neighbor's well-being is of such vital concern. Perhaps we in the United States especially tend to view things fairly individualistically. Taking care of "number one" is important; even some charitable gestures are more generous gifts from on high than shared partnership in difficulty.

There is not for me any short and simple method which will guarantee acceptance and changed behavior in the other person (or in ourselves). But the Scripture is clear that we must struggle to learn how to put such "tough love" into practice for the good of one another.

Stephen C. Gilmour

24th Sunday in Ordinary Time

Cycle A

Sir 27:30–28:7
Rom 14:7–9
Mt 18:21–35

In Eastern religions the term "forgiveness" does not exist. There is nothing to forgive because nothing really happens to me without my choosing and my collaboration. There are no accidents, no decisive injustices, no reasons to be hurt. A simplistic way out? Not necessarily so, if approached from a different vantage point. The Eastern tenet states that that which comes my way from the external world can only affect me because I place myself in a particular situation. The key ingredient is my degree or level of awareness. If I get hit by a baseball, it is because I did not see the ball coming, and consequently did not get out of the way soon enough. If I am stung by the words or actions of another, it is because of my placement in the relationship, and my position flows from my beliefs about myself and others.

As an infant, I entered the world with unlimited trust. Helpless, I depended on others to fulfill my basic needs of food, shelter, comfort. People functioned to serve me, to take care of me. I soon realized that other people did not respond to me at my whim; I was not the center of their universe, only one part of a relational network. My desires were frustrated. I learned to manipulate or coerce them into giving me what I needed. I had to learn to wait, to accommodate myself to their concerns and interests.

As a child I drew my nourishment and protection from those around me. Often in the painful movement into maturity the child within still cries out: Care for me. Show me that I'm worthwhile. Approve of me; don't disapprove of me. In short, love me! Time and time again I ask for bread, and instead seem to receive a stone—a critical glance, ridicule, indifference. I am disappointed, hurt, angry. I want to lash back. I want to prove to you that I am somebody. Or I withdraw, telling myself that it is a cruel and heartless world.

Not one human being has ever been loved sufficiently. Like the domino effect, each person in relation to me has been the recipient of imperfect love. And each person is working to gain their own sense of being in the world. None can be for me totally and whole-heartedly. None can "sit under the apple tree with me alone." This realization can help me to give up the ways of a child and to provide a new base for my relationships with others. This fundamental truth can lay the groundwork for a forgiving posture.

What then, do I say? Do I sink into resignation? Do I not still need whole-hearted care and acceptance? Yes I do, and the movement changes if I so choose. I can shift the locus of support more and more from the external world to the world within. I can find within me the capacity to provide nourishment, comfort and protection for myself. In short, to love myself. When this begins to happen I will be able to see others, not as providers for me, but as separate entities, people with lives and histories of their own, people who have done the very best that they were able to do at every given moment. Then I can let them be, let them loose, forgive them. It is like giving them back a portion of their lives that I falsely assumed was for me. If I no longer need them to be responsible for me, then I am free to love them.

Forgiveness is most necessary for the calculating Peter in me who asks the going rate from Jesus. My bearing the grudge, harboring resentment hurts me first and foremost. In resentment a kind of fortress constructs itself around me to protect me and to ward off further attack. I walk with an invisible shield and an armored tongue. I become tense and rigid and walk as though on eggs. Much energy is used for defense. Underneath, I am vulnerable and afraid. "On the person who does evil, evil will recoil, though where it came from, he will not know," Sirach writes. Nothing is more liable to break in a storm than a rigid oak. I long for ease and relaxation, but my need to be on guard prevents letting go. If I build the wall of resentment, goodness and light cannot reach me either. Then I will truly know isolation.

Compassion is the opposite of bearing the grudge. Compassion knows that all are wounded and imperfect as I am, that rights and wrongs do not apply. With compassion I see in my neighbor's actions all of my own potential for similar injury. Compassion dissolves my separation from others and allows me to experience my common humanity with them. Thus I hold nothing against them with the knowledge that nothing is held against me. I can give before, for-give.

Sharon Koziczkowski

25th Sunday in Ordinary Time

Cycle A

Is 55:6–9
Phil 1:20–24, 27
Mt 20:1–16

In Korea a few years ago, a woman appeared in court to seek the release of a man accused of murder. What was unusual about the woman was that she was the mother of the victim. Her son and the accused had gotten into a fight, and the man on trial had shot and killed her son. The woman appeared in court not to say that this man had done nothing wrong, or that her son had gotten what he deserved, but to say that one life lost was enough, and she saw nothing to be gained by trying to make it up with a sentence of death or life imprisonment imposed on her son's murderer. The mercy of this elderly woman made the headlines.

Most of us have not seen a dear one murdered. But on the smaller scale on which we live out our days, we find it hard to let go of hurts, to forgive others or even ourselves. We calculate carefully to see that others receive only what they deserve, no more. And we feel certain that God's mercy must be like our own, that God's forgiveness and generosity toward us are also calculated carefully to fit our deeds exactly.

We are in for a surprise, today's readings say, for God has the largest heart of all. God's mercy and God's generosity in forgiving overturn all our human standards. And that is finally good news for all of us. Isaiah speaks this word of overflowing divine mercy to a people in exile. They have been unfaithful, and they are expecting only justice and judgment. Instead, they meet a faithful God who lifts them to new hope: "For my thoughts are not your thoughts, nor are your ways my ways, says the Lord."

One way to get some sense of this immeasurable generosity of God is to identify with one of the two sets of workers in today's parable. How does it feel to be one of those who has worked all day in the scorching heat, only to find that you receive the same wages as workers who showed up at the last hour? Do you think you should get more than the wage you agreed upon? Do you resent the owner's generosity? Now become one of those workers who finds that you have been paid a full day's wage for only an hour's work? Are you amazed at the owner's generosity? Does it seem foolish and a poor business practice to you?

This is what the reign or kingdom of God is like, Jesus says. In Jesus' life and teaching, God meets us with unexpected love and understanding. Our salvation is not what we deserve; nor is it determined according to ordinary human standards. It is a gift that challenges all narrowness of heart.

Christians are to help usher in the reign of God; that means that God's mercy and forgiveness must become the standard of our own. In light of today's readings we need to ask: Am I willing to offer forgiveness to my marriage partner or to other family members who have hurt me intentionally or unintentionally? Do I believe enough in the size of God's mercy to accept forgiveness for my own past failings, and stop punishing myself for them? When I use the size of God's love as the standard for my own mercy and forgiveness, I learn to rejoice in all the gifts of God, whether these are found in my own life or in the lives of others. Then I experience something of the joy of God's reign now, as I prepare for its fullness later. I learn, like Paul, that in death or in life, what counts is Christ.

Kathleen R. Fischer
Thomas N. Hart

31

26th Sunday in Ordinary Time

Cycle A

Ez 18:25–28
Phil 2:1–11
Mt 21:28–32

My mother had a trick, practiced no doubt by most Catholic mothers of her generation. I hold her blameless at this point in church history. She would say to any one of her erring children, "God will punish you." That was warning enough for me to stop contemplating mischief. Not so my youngest brother. When he was three he was maneuvering from chair to dining room table where he obviously wanted to stand tall upon the heights. My mother caught his climb from the corner of her eye as she worked in the kitchen. "God will punish you!" Moments later, a crash, a wail and then silence. From the kitchen she could see him toddle off, unhurt in all but his pride. Ten minutes of silence made her suspicious however. As she turned to investigate, he appeared at the kitchen door, water pistol dripping. "I showed God," he announced. Throughout the house our religious statues and pictures were soaked.

"You say, 'The Lord's way is not fair!'" So begins Sunday's reading from Ezekiel. "No, I will not!" retorts the second son in Jesus' story in today's Gospel. I doubt if I am the only one who admires those who speak their mind to the Lord. I even admired my three-year-old brother as he grappled with primitive images of a god whose taboo system is meant to evoke fear and trembling. In Isaiah 1:18, our God invites us to be ourselves with him: "Come, let us argue it out!" He is not put off by our rebel shout, our "No." I believe he'd rather have a vociferous argument about his competence than have us subserviently "yes-ing" him. Jeremiah, King David, the psalmists certainly had complaints and were cherished by the Lord for their honesty.

What my mother did not know and I am not always sure of, so easy is it to slip back into her homespun theology, is that God does not lurk with punishment when we wander or rebel. Punishment follows from the evil itself; it is of the nature of evil to tarnish and even destroy peace and joy. Children with cancer, earthquakes, fears of nuclear holocaust are not God's punishment, not God's will, not even God's permissive will, I venture to say. Later in the same chapter of Ezekiel as today's reading, God cries out, "I don't desire the death of the wicked person"—not even the wicked person. "I desire that the wicked turn from their ways and live" (Ez 18:22–23).

What does God desire? What is his will? What is the mind of God? Today's reading from Ezekiel tells us: Do what is just; from Paul: Your attitude must be Christ's; from Jesus: Repent. If we could ask God directly what is his mind, his will, synthesizing all the varied books and messages of Scripture, church doctrine, our own experience of God, I think the Lord might respond: "I want you to have life—free, joyful, abundant life. Turn from your wicked ways and live." This is the mind of God.

But, we argue, wasn't it God's idea that Jesus should be obedient, even to death on a cross? Didn't God want Jesus to die so that we could be saved? Never! God did not desire the death of Jesus, this innocent man who always emptied himself for the sake of God's people. St. Thomas Aquinas, centuries ago, taught that a single action of Jesus—taking a breath, eating a meal, healing the sick—could have caused our salvation. What God did want of Jesus was that this man of Nazareth totally embody the unconditional and faithful love of God for sinners and outcasts. The religious professionals hated to see God humiliate himself by such an extravagant outpouring of love and so they plotted to kill his embodiment, Jesus. Once the good news was out to the tax collectors and prostitutes that Jesus esteemed them, Jesus would not betray them, even in the face of jealousy, hostility, and impending persecution.

The mind of Christ which Paul exhorts us to have is the mind of God which Jesus himself embodied. All our Christian behavior is meant to flow from our having the mind of Christ. Like Jesus, embodying Jesus, we are invited to be so focused on the other that we are gradually emptied of our self, gradually become obedient to the Good News, gradually grow in fellowship and compassion, gradually become united in love, spirit, and ideals. We are not offered in today's readings ways of obeying law, ways of externally conforming, ways of avoiding wickedness. We are simply exhorted to enflesh the mind of Christ, to let Christ think and choose, love and pour himself out through us.

Rea McDonnell

27th Sunday in Ordinary Time

Cycle A

Is 5:1–7
Phil 4:6–9
Mt 21:33–43

The gospel parable of the vineyard is a story of smugness. As we can see from the roots of the story in the Hebrew Scriptures, the vineyard is God's people. God has planted and tended them and wants them to bear fruit. Jesus' contemporaries were not bearing fruit, and he tells his story to confront them with their irresponsibility and sterility.

The parable of course goes beyond the contemporaries of Jesus in its application, and the Church has preserved it for its challenge to people of every age. We too can easily be smug and self-satisfied, and fail to hear the word of God or accept the prophets God sends.

We can be smug as a nation. God has richly blessed us. We can turn this into pride about our prosperity and our freedoms, just as Jesus' contemporaries prided themselves on being God's chosen people. Then we begin not to notice when we fall into racism, or become consumerist, or use vast amounts of our resources for armaments. Some of our people are hungry; many are jobless. And the policies we pursue abroad are not always in the best interests of other peoples.

We can be smug as a church. We can pride ourselves on being the one, holy, catholic, and apostolic church, and forget that as a pilgrim people we are called to continual conversion. We can begin to overlook or excuse our sexism and our division into quarreling factions. Jesus was so supportive of women, and so eager to promote union in fraternal love. We can dismiss or even suppress the prophets God sends us, the way the tenants of the vineyard treated the prophets God sent them. We can cling comfortably to our traditions when the signs of the times are calling for new attitudes, structures, and projects.

We can be smug as individuals. We can feel satisfied because we are faithful to weekly worship and the financial support of the church, and forget that we are called to give evidence of our conversion to Christ by a whole life of good works. Are we deepening our trust in God and obedience to God, following the example of Jesus? Are we practicing greater forgiveness, acceptance, sharing, and service in our relationships with the people with whom we live and work? Are we responsible stewards of the goods of the earth, non-acquisitive, and contemplative of the creative and generous hand of God in all the things that touch our lives?

God continues to nurture the vineyard of his planting. The lesson of today's double parable of the vineyard is that we have to attend carefully to the kinds of fruit we are bearing, and be cautious about the sorts of stones we are rejecting.

Kathleen R. Fischer
Thomas N. Hart

28th Sunday in Ordinary Time

Cycle A

Is 25:6–10
Phil 4:12–14, 19–20
Mt 22:1–14

Time out! Where did this gospel story come from? Here's Jesus telling us that the poor guy who comes to the feast without proper clothing is thrown out. Isn't this the same Jesus who just sixteen chapters earlier says, "Do not worry about what you are to wear"?

One of the most crucial social questions of the day is "How should I dress?" We want to look good, to express ourselves through the cut, style, color and price of our garments. I can understand today's Gospel in the light of our concern for clothes, but what about "Do not worry about what you are to wear"?

Undoubtedly there is a symbolic meaning to the wedding garment. It stands for identity, and implies that the man made no effort to "get dressed." There's more to be seen in this parable though. And, there is a lot to be said for the poorly dressed man. At least he came. Those who had been invited first weren't very courteous. Can you imagine inviting folks to a wedding and having them refuse to come? Can you imagine inviting them a second time, trying to entice them with the menu for the reception? Then, imagine that they ignore your second invitation and walk away, one to get her hair done, another to a poker game. A few of the others mug you and steal all your credit cards. At this point, devastated and betrayed, maybe you'd try to talk the kids into eloping.

The king finally does get angry. He sends his servants to destroy the murderers and burn their city. We might destroy some reputations of those who had refused, and while we wouldn't burn their city, we might make it "too hot" for them to live there. So, the king has settled with them, but the issue remains, who will eat the bullocks and the corn-fed cattle? He decides to invite anyone who will come. We might go back to our list and invite next-closest friends, but I doubt that we'd hawk our celebration up and down the city streets.

That brings us to the improperly-dressed man. First of all, he must have known that he was not a first—nor even a second choice. The servants of the king had been through the town twice already issuing the invites. Our poorly-clad fellow was humble enough to accept. He was also willing to drop everything. We're not talking about a month's advance notice! One would think that the king would be delighted to have anyone come at this point, no matter how he was dressed.

We're on your side so far, wedding guest. You were humble and willing to leave your farm or business immediately to join this celebration. After all the false friends the king has had, he's got a lot of nerve questioning you. So what if you're wearing a polyester leisure suit? You came, didn't you? Come on, tell him why you didn't wear a tux. Tell him how you couldn't afford to rent one—that you've been on unemployment since you lost your job. Or tell him how you lent your best suit to someone who needed it, or that you gave it to a beggar who was cold. Tell him how you soiled it when you washed someone's feet, or that you sold your suit to buy food for an elderly neighbor. Tell him something!

But there is no answer from the guest.

At least say, "I'm sorry. Might I change?" I'll bet the king has lots of spare wedding clothes upstairs, like fancy restaurants that keep a supply of ties. Say something!

The Gospel says, "The man had nothing to say." He was thrown out perhaps, not because of his clothes, but because of his lack of response. He gave no reason, no explanation, no excuse. He made no attempt to belong, showed no desire to stay. He is asked—forcefully—to leave. There is no doubt that he will wail and gnash his teeth in anger.

His end is a far cry from the comfort and fulfillment Isaiah foretells in today's first reading. It all sounds so wonderful, but there's a catch. "On that day it will be said, 'Behold our God to whom we looked to save us!'" The rewards are the result of faith in God. You've got to believe in the host to enjoy the feast. The Israelites wanted to turn that around. "Provide all this for us, God, food and drink and victory, and then we will believe." Paul got it straight. Food or hunger, drink or thirst, victory or defeat, his strength was his faith in Jesus. Whatever happened to Paul, he had "put on Christ," he knew that God would keep his promise, and that was all that counted.

There is no dress code in Scripture, except to be "clothed with Christ." That's the only garment the king looks for. Put on Christ, and then do not worry about what you are to wear.

Carole M. Eipers

29th Sunday in Ordinary Time

Cycle A

Is 45:1, 4–6
1 Thes 1:1–5
Mt 22:15–21

A few years ago I was working with a group of teaching brothers, helping them plan their future. I asked what they thought the probable future of the church in our U.S. society might be, reflecting on the best possible thing that might happen to the U.S. church by the year 2000 and the worst possible thing. After five minutes of reflection, I asked them to call out their ideas of the best possible future for the church in the United States. After a few responses, one brother stated, "Persecution." Heads swung around to him. "Don't you mean that's the worst possible thing?" one of his confreres asked. But after the initial shock, heads were beginning to nod, knowing smiles were playing on the lips of most of the group.

What this brother meant by his startling statement that persecution might be the best possible experience for the U.S. church is not far different from what many of Israel's prophets meant when they cautioned kings and people to surrender to foreign invaders, even to be carried into exile. There is a subtle way in which, through the centuries, God's people have been lured into putting "their trust in horses, in princes," in leaders other than God, in defenses other than God, our rock, our fortress.

Today's readings are about politics and persecution. We render to Caesar a reflective, responsible involvement in politics. The Pope has asked priests and religious to stay out of office, not out of politics, for politics, as he himself shows us, particularly in the Polish arena, is the art of making the possible happen. Many Catholics in this country have offered time, energy, and talent to affect policy in a public way through elected office. All of us, however, are challenged by the Gospel and again by our bishops in their 1971 statement on social justice as constitutive of that Gospel to make the possible—a set of states united in justice and peace, truth and love—happen.

Politics as I describe it does not mean playing cards close to the chest, manipulating situations, using people. Politics directed by gospel values of truth which sets free, compassion for the weak, justice toward the oppressed, welcoming of the outcast, defenselessness in the face of hostility, will eventually make U.S. Catholics a counter-cultural minority. We have already seen the U.S. bishops publicly condemn nuclear stockpiling and first strike policy, militaristic posturing and defense spending which take monies and attention from the poor. We are hearing their voice against the god of the United States, a capitalist economy. We have watched our fellow parishioners move into deeper commitment to the voiceless, the hungry, the homeless; perhaps we have joined them. We may eventually be persecuted by our compatriots, branded communist or naive, boycotted economically, ostracized socially.

We are undoubtedly called to be as countercultural as Jesus was. In today's gospel episode about taxes, Jesus must have smiled inwardly, ruefully, for although he bested his opponents by his quick riposte, he knew that countercultural folk "get it" in the end. How they "got" Jesus eventually was on a political charge.

Who in our day tries to trap us, tries to make us bow to gods of the culture, to lull us into succumbing to "majority rules"? Who are we afraid will dominate us in the world arena? Who already dominates us? Who will save us? Can Caesar save? Can the MX missile or the Trident submarine? How God loves to destroy our expectations of where salvation lies! Who would have thought that the exile to Babylon would be Israel's purification so that she could know her Lord and Savior even more profoundly? Who could have thought that a pagan foreigner, Cyrus, would be her Messiah, the anointed one of God? Anointed in English, Messiah in Hebrew, Christos in Greek. In final days, we are always warned, we must discern who are false Christs. Who claims to be God's anointed? Does she or he live and love as Jesus did, never condemning the sinner, always seeking the lost, the lowly, the maimed, choosing the tax collector and the prostitute as friends?

The spirit of the Lord is the one who anoints Jesus to proclaim good news to the poor. There is power, Paul tells us in today's reading, power in that good news, power who is the Spirit. The Spirit of the Lord anoints us in baptism to share Jesus' mission.

We share Jesus' call to give to Caesar what is Caesar's: a countercultural critique of all that oppresses the poor—and to give to God what is God's: a wholehearted trust that as Lord of the nations his kingdom of justice and peace and compassion will come.

Rea McDonnell

35

30th Sunday in Ordinary Time

Cycle A

Ez 22:20–26
1 Thes 1:5–10
Mt 22:34–40

Some years ago, Sally Fields starred in the movie, "Places in the Heart." It was a powerful story of love of neighbor in which mutual need broke down the barriers between a poor white widow with two children and two men, one black and the other blind. Within it was another story, a terrible story of rejection and racism. In one particularly vicious scene, Moses, who had helped the widowed Sara, was attacked and beaten by the Ku Klux Klan. The Klan was determined to intimidate this undesirable black man and drive him away. Only the intervention of his blind friend saved Moses from a worse fate. All in the story were religious people. Clearly, not all loved their neighbor as themselves.

Today's Gospel has similarities to the storyline of "Places in the Heart." The time and place are different. The characters have changed. We have Jesus, an itinerant teacher, and the Pharisees and Sadducees, upright religious leaders. There is no physical violence. Rather, the leaders conspire to trip Jesus up on a question of God's law so that they might publicly disgrace him and thus rid themselves of this undesirable man. Here too, all in the story were religious people—Jesus, the Pharisees, and the Sadducees. Not all were imbued with the spirit of the Law which they discussed.

What is the greatest commandment of the Law? In other words, what is absolutely essential, what is the most important standard to live by? Jesus' answer is disconcertingly direct. You shall love the Lord, your God, with everything in you. You shall love your neighbor as yourself. What Jesus tells us is that the great commandment has two parts, both on an equal footing. He says in effect that no one can love God and hate his neighbor.

Lest we interpret Jesus' message with too narrow a vision of who that neighbor might be, the Church places before us the reading from Exodus. In the Hebrew Scriptures and in the Gospel the neighbor who has a special claim on believers is the one who lacks resources. Who are those who are not to be oppressed or ignored, but rather to be treated with dignity and justice? The word of God in Exodus is that they are the poor who lack material goods; aliens who are strangers in a foreign land; widows and orphans who have no means of support.

What does it mean for us to love our neighbor as ourselves? Things aren't so different today, or are they? It's not even easy to love oneself in a stress-filled, competitive, production-oriented society. The entire advertising industry conspires to tell us that we are not loveable unless we have the right product to make us handsome/beautiful, and own the car that turns heads, and purchase the latest, the smartest, the best of everything. Its hard to discover and respect our own real needs. Yet, we must recognize our own human needs—our deep need for understanding, for friendship, for support in our efforts as well as for basic material necessities.

The other half of the message is that we are to use our self-knowledge and healthy self-love as the standard for the way we treat others. That often calls for a change of heart. It means letting go of whatever fear or anger or prejudice separates us so that we can be sensitive and responsive to the needs of others.

Sometimes we don't have to look any further than our own families or work places to discover the marginalized in our contemporary society. Still, it is important to see the larger picture. In their "Pastoral Letter on the U.S. Economy" the bishops of our country point out that the number of people in our midst living at a poverty level is growing at an alarming rate. Who are these new poor, these neighbors who have a special claim to our love? Many are found among the elderly, among persons with handicapping conditions and among women heading single-parent households. Who are the aliens, if not the many political and economic refugees who have poured into this country from Central America, or the growing number of Asian peoples flocking to our shores?

Together we can do what we cannot do alone. Through our parishes, civic groups and social agencies we are called to participate in the life of our communities, to share our resources and to influence the structures that have the power to promote or to oppress today's poor.

Today's Gospel story is interesting if we hear it as a battle of wits between Jesus and religious leaders of his time. It is gripping, if we hear it addressed to us. It implies that whatever we do to promote the quality of life of others on the human, cultural, educational or spiritual level binds us more closely to God and to one another. That is our Christian vocation in this world.

Barbara O'Dea

31st Sunday in Ordinary Time

Cycle A

Mal 1:14–2:2, 8–10
1 Thes 2:7–9, 13
Mt 23:1–12

I had a brief encounter with a priest recently which bothered me. Obviously not in good spirits, he mumbled something about going off to a monastery. "Don't!" I said, "We need you here!" "What for?" he replied, "the lay people do everything anyway."

I ached for this man who was questioning his role. It must be devastating to put all your eggs into an exclusive-type basket, only to discover it has become rather common. It does make you wonder if your eggs have any worth.

"Ministry" used to be a very "protestant" word. It was seldom applied to what Catholic clergymen did, and never to anything lay people did. Now ministry—clerical and lay—is continually being defined and redefined, expanded and contracted, called forth and—more often than we might wish—put down.

There is a lot of ambiguity about what lay people in particular are called to do. The baptismal commitment has been reiterated, responsibility to minister to one another laid squarely on our shoulders, and yet, as we probe and search, seek and pray, we are confused by the responses we encounter when we attempt to fulfill our vocations. We are called by our baptism to minister; we are nourished by the Eucharist; we are empowered by the Spirit only to discover that these credentials are not enough. We are expected to gain "expertise," to take classes, to earn degrees—at our own expense—that we might become worthy volunteers in Father's parish. Some of us simply drop out; some of us try it and burn out. Some of us become too "expert" and find that someone has begun choosing up sides and, given the hierarchical nature of the Church, we are on the losing team.

All this is not to say that I do not sympathize with the over-worked associate or the over-burdened pastor who endeavors to share ministry and finds disaster. Some "training" programs are very effective at turning out half-cocked zealots who are shallow in faith and devoid of sensitivity to people's needs. I sympathize with the priest who has spent himself for his people and suddenly finds himself no longer wanted for hospital visits since the 20-year-old pastoral care person is much more congenial.

Ministry is a blessing. Yet, it seems that sometimes the words of Malachi have come true: "Of your blessing I will make a curse." Ministry has become another area of competition, and sometimes we're just too weary, too spent, to bother fighting to serve. So we wave the white flag at our opponents and sometimes wave good-bye to our Christian community.

Today's readings face some serious temptations of ministry. If we all—clergy and laity—take to heart the warnings they give, perhaps we could be more about serving and less about in-house arguments.

Malachi warns us that the gift of ministry—of spiritual leadership—can, like any of our gifts, become a curse. Ministry can become a curse, not only for the minister who struggles and suffers, but also for those to whom she or he ministers if we are more concerned with power and position than with people's needs. Our ministry becomes a curse on our fellow ministers when we fail to recognize their giftedness and we begin to serve personal rather than communal goals.

Jesus' warnings to the ministers of his day are even more stern than Malachi's. Our religion has to "show," but not be "showy." It is a delicate balance. Who among us would not enjoy being honored at a banquet, being given respect, and having an impressive title? Occasionally it happens, as part of the hundred-fold Jesus promised. The temptation, of course, is to begin serving in order to gain these rewards.

Then the ministry race begins; then priest and lay person are no longer colleagues but competitors. Then we begin to hide the very weaknesses which enable God to shine through us, and we begin to focus on others' weaknesses, not with compassion but with contempt.

Paul gives us, not warnings, but an example. If our ministry is to be a blessing—for us and for those whom we serve—we have to learn from Paul. He gave himself freely and shared his weaknesses and struggles openly, so that his people might come to know the love and goodness of God. He never became wealthy or politically powerful, and I doubt that a banquet was ever held in his honor, but his ministry was a blessing.

If ministers are to continue to preach the Good News, and to avoid temptations to corrupt our gifts, we need the Spirit to guide us, and we need challenge and support. If we are to be a blessing for our people, we must first bless one another.

Carole M. Eipers

32nd Sunday in Ordinary Time

Cycle A

Wis 6:12–16
2 Thes 4:13–18
Mt 25:1–13

The parable of the ten bridesmaids is one we have heard many times. Often the homily after it deals with judgment. The Lord is coming at any time—will you be ready to meet him? Will you have the morally upright life which allows you to enter the wedding hall of the Kingdom? In this reflection I would like to offer another approach. The moral approach is fine, but this parable could also give us insight into the way we see reality. After all, the events of life are no different for the Christian than they are for others. Christianity offers us a different way of seeing the same world everyone else sees.

There is a dimension to all of us similar to that of the foolish bridesmaids. We don't bring any "light" to reality. Life just happens to us. Births and deaths, joys and sufferings, successes, and frustrations swirl about us. We thank God when good things happen and we curse fate when bad things happen. Life becomes a roller coaster ride in which we are alternately victims or victors depending on the nature of the event.

In today's Gospel Jesus offers another way of seeing reality. Bring light to it. Look at it in a new light. This point could be illustrated by borrowing a story from another tradition, a story contained in the Upanishads.

> (The father said to his son:) "Place this salt in water and then come to me in the morning."
>
> The son did as he was told.
>
> The father said to him: "My son, bring me the salt which you placed in the water last night."
>
> Looking for it, the son did not find it, for it was completely dissolved.
>
> The father said: "My son, take a sip of water from the surface. How is it?"
>
> "It is salt."
>
> "Take a sip from the middle. How is it?"
>
> "It is salt."
>
> "Take a sip from the bottom. How is it?"
>
> "It is salt."
>
> "Throw it away and come to me."
>
> The son did as he was told, saying: "The salt was there all the time."
>
> The father said: "Here also, my dear, in this body, verily, you do not perceive Being; but it is indeed there.
>
> Now, that which is the subtle essence—in it all that exists has its self. That is the True. That is the Self. That art thou . . . "

John Updike in his novel *Roger's Version* illustrates Jesus' way of seeing reality when he has the lead character, Dale Kohler, say: "The most miraculous thing is happening . . . The physicists are getting down to the nitty-gritty, they've really just about pared things down to the ultimate details, and the last thing they ever expected to happen is happening. God is showing through."

Reality, for the believer, is not just one event after another. All reality, the wonderful and the painful, the awesome and the mundane, is bursting with a God who is inviting us to wholeness, to the experience of love which is best symbolized by the wedding banquet. We can see that when we look at the world in the light of Christ. And that way of looking will lead naturally to living with the moral readiness that past homilists perceived as the meaning of this parable. As Meister Eckhart wrote:

> There is nothing in God that destroys what has anything of its own. But he fulfills all things. And so we must not destroy within ourselves a trifling and insignificant good for a greater. We should bring the slight to its utmost perfection.

Douglas Fisher

33rd Sunday in Ordinary Time

Cycle A

Prov 31:10–13, 19–20, 30–31
1 Thes 5:1–6
Mt 25:14–30

Some months ago I was saddened by a newspaper article about the death of a 74-year-old man. As a young person he started life with two strikes against him. He never finished school and early on he discovered that he had no head for business. He counted among his assets love of children, deep appreciation of music, and the ability to make funny faces. Added to this, he had zest for life and a willingness to take risks. When he died last March he was a renowned chef, a private pilot licensed to fly even jumbo jets and part owner of a baseball team. In addition, he had starred in a dozen films, conducted symphony orchestras in benefit performances, and worked indefatigably for the children of the world through The United Nations Children's Fund (UNICEF). About the latter he said, "It is the single most rewarding thing I've done in my life." By the standards of today's Scripture readings, Danny Kaye was a faithful servant.

The Gospel today is about what it means to be faithful. It is the story of a master who knew the talents of his servants. He provided them with the opportunity to learn through their own experience how to develop their abilities and resources. In a gesture of trust the master gave each a large sum of money, leaving its use to their discretion. Then he set off on a journey. Years later he returned to settle accounts.

Who is faithful, that is the question. Clearly, it is the servants who took the owner's money, added to it their own talents, and produced a profit. Who is unfaithful? It is the one who let fear and anxiety paralyze him. He did not put his own talents to work, but simply buried the treasure for safekeeping. This servant didn't lose anything. He simple never did any good with it.

What does it mean to be faithful? The account from the book of Proverbs sharpens the focus. The wisdom of Israel is summarized and symbolized in the portrait of a woman who is a faithful wife. A skillful woman, she provides for the needs of her family by the work of her hands. A successful manager, she contributes to the prosperity of her household, demonstrating exceptional ingenuity. That is not all. She has a social consciousness which leads her to reach out to the poor and needy by providing for their needs. This is the Israelite who will be rewarded for her labors and praised among the people.

For us, what does it mean to be faithful? Two paradigms have been set before us. Who are we, if not God's servants? Each of us has been given talents and abilities. Clearly, it is not enough to preserve what has been entrusted to us. Like the women in proverbs and the servants in the Gospel, we are to put our gifts to use so that they may bear fruit in the service of others.

Faithfulness is an active virtue. It can be recognized in what we do. The treasure that has been entrusted to us is the vision and values of God's reign which Jesus lived and taught in the Gospel. It is for us to appreciate that treasure and to realize what it can do for the transformation of the world. It is for us to recognize our own talents and put them to work. Our task begins in the intimacy of our own households where we shape each other's consciousness and encourage the development of each one's values and talents. It reaches out beyond that through whatever the members of our household do to contribute to the physical, emotional, cultural or educational needs of others. It is especially demonstrated in what we do for the needy of our society.

When Danny Kaye died, among the wonderful tributes paid him there were a comment and a story that seemed to best describe the man. The comment which captured the radiance of his personality was that he could light up a room just by smiling. The anecdote highlighted the spirit of his commitment. Queen Margrethe of Denmark knighted the comedian. In the course of the event Kaye was praised for his film portrayal of the Danish storyteller Hans Christian Andersen and commended for his untiring work for UNICEF. To mark the occasion he was presented with a citation in which he was called "The Pied Piper to the Children of the World." The reporter recounting the story added simply "and he was." Well done, good and faithful servant. . . .

Barbara O'Dea

Feast of Christ the King

Cycle A

Ez 34:11–12, 15–17
1 Cor 15:20–26, 28
Mt 25:31–46

I remember being shocked by today's Gospel on a number of occasions. The first time, I realized that the criterion for judgment is not the Law, not sin as I was taught it, not perfection or the lack of it, but compassion. That set me free.

For a while. A few years later, I realized that instead of checking out my spiritual health by seeing how well I was keeping the Law and avoiding sin, I had a new checklist: was I feeding the hungry, welcoming the lonely, visiting the sick, attending the grieving, etc.? I marked my progress according to a new Law. I still believed my actions were saving me and earning me a place among sheep at the final judgment. So I handed over my salvation to Jesus, asking him to save me. I went about the business of compassion as best I could, trying to keep my eyes fixed on Jesus instead of on my self and my salvation. That set me free.

For a while. A few years later, I noticed that in this picture of the last judgment, Jesus separates the *nations* into two groups. He will ask the United States of America what we as a nation did for the hungry, the homeless, the imprisoned, the immigrant. I began to beg for salvation for our country. I began to realize how important a prophetic challenge is to this country, how every Christian is called to point out unjust structures again and again, called to harness personal energy and compassion into corporate compassion for the "least" among us. For a while I was frightened, burdened, angry, even strident, in my zeal to issue the prophetic confrontation to lawmakers and voters. I was not free.

The God revealed by Ezekiel is working very hard to set me free. What I learn about God, salvation, and judgment from today's first reading, this image of God as shepherd, is that God gears his saving action precisely to our need. When we are injured he binds up, when we are sick he heals, when we have lost direction he looks for us. When I am frightened, burdened, angry, and strident, he picks me up, holds me, reassures me, and sends me his son, Jesus—ruler of the nations, sovereign, powerful. I do not speak a prophetic challenge alone. Jesus, Christ, King speaks it first. It is his job description to challenge the nations, to rule the nations, to save the nations. He is king, he is shepherd.

Both images belong to another century, another country for U.S. citizens. But the ancient and reassuring truth leaps out at us. Jesus is Lord of our nation. In his justice, he provides for the poor and separates himself from those who refuse to see him in "the least" of his people. He speaks justice to the United States.

He speaks justice because he speaks compassion. I have actually heard some folks say that if black people are in heaven they would just as soon not go there themselves. Whom will Jesus gather home to himself in the last judgment? Our shepherd-king, who speaks compassion, has prepared a new nation for the sick, the imprisoned, the naked and dirty, the addict, the hungry, the vagrant, the gay, the legal immigrant and the illegal alien. We who know our own need for saving, who challenge unjust societal and church structures, who have been at home with "the least" in these days, will be at home with the least in the new nation. We call it the Kingdom of God.

Rea McDonnell

1st Sunday of Lent

Cycle A

Gn 2:7–9; 3:1–7
Rom 5:12–19
Mt 4:1–11

As we begin the season of Lent, these readings from Genesis, Paul, and Matthew direct us to reflect on the power of sin and grace in our lives. In the reading from Genesis, sin enters the world as humanity attempts to be like God in God's knowledge of good and evil. Paul tells us that, since Christ's coming, the knowledge we have of good and evil is this: we live in a world broken by sin, and a world touched by the graciousness of God. This challenges us to recognize around us the power of good and evil and to become aware of our solidarity in both.

We influence one another continually toward good or toward evil. On the personal level, we touch one another's lives in ways which enable others to become their best selves or less than they could be. The breakdown of relationships, which is the power of sin, can spread and be fueled by the smallest words and actions in a marriage, a family, a church community, an office or a neighborhood. The sin of one individual poisons the whole body and tempts others to sin. In the same way, the good action of one individual strengthens the whole body and influences others toward goodness. On a larger scale, our solidarity in good and evil is evident in the threat of war and efforts to live in global peace. Instant communication has closely linked the lives of all people. The continued goodness of all creation depends on our using carefully the material resources of our planet and calls for compassionate action toward solving the problems of world poverty and hunger and displaced populations. Whether on a personal or a global level, the sense of our corporate unity gives new importance to each act of selfishness or love we perform, no matter how small that action may seem to be.

Paul's message is the basis for hope: not just that there are both sin and grace, but that grace is stronger than sin. When we recognize brokenness and failure in our lives, when we find that we have not loved or forgiven or cared for others as we should have, we are reminded that the power of Christ is stronger than the power of sin in our lives. When our personal and family relationships seem to be torn by misunderstandings, estrangements, and quarrelling, Christ's power of forgiveness is stronger than these divisions. When we see nations and peoples divided by the drive for power and centuries-long conflicts, we can continue to work with hope toward world peace. Since Christ's coming, the power of grace abounds, and the Genesis story of the entry of sin into the world is not the last word.

This call to conversion, compassion and hope applies to our own Church community. We are sometimes scandalized to recognize the presence of both good and evil in the Church, to find conflict, failures and sin in our parish community. We recognize that we are human, and therefore part of the Genesis account of sin's continual entry into the world. We need to also notice all of the acts of love, forgiveness and caring which occur in the Church, reminding us that God's grace is at work among us. We are called to extend our worship into those acts of love for one another which reflect the true meaning of the Eucharist as the living out of a unity and solidarity of love in the body of Christ which brings hope to a world broken by sin. We want to be delivered, especially the various temptations not to be ourselves.

The readings relate the themes of good and evil to the experience of temptation. Humanity is tempted in the garden and falls. Jesus is tempted and stands up against his tempter. The temptation in both cases is to be something other than what we are called to be. In the Genesis account, God breathes into human persons the breath of life and they become living human beings; but they want to be like God, knowing good from evil. In Matthew's account Jesus is tempted to be other than he is, to become a flashy Messiah, satisfying people's desire for miracles and power, rather than a suffering servant who redeems through the paradox of cross and resurrection. True to himself, he chooses the road of the suffering Messiah.

Kathleen R. Fischer
Thomas N. Hart

2nd Sunday of Lent

Cycle A

Gn 12:1–4
2 Tm 1:8–10
Mt 17:1–9

I'd like to suggest that we think about where to look for the Lord. If we hear the invitation, if we want to answer the call as Abraham did, where should we be looking to find him?

Today's readings suggest an answer to me, and perhaps surprisingly the answer is *"not on the mountain."* The event on the mountain is the exciting part, the unusual part, the striking part; the disciples get a glimpse, get an idea, of the Lord's glory. But the point is that this is indeed unusual; it is not the norm. Jesus leads them up the mountain, but he also leads them back down. Peter's suggestion to stay up on the mountain, to build booths there to enshrine the event, is not well received.

The event of the Transfiguration is set in the Gospel just after Jesus has spoken about his suffering and death, just after Peter argues with him about that. Now the apostles get a glimpse of the Lord in his glory, almost to encourage them, sustain them, so that they might continue on the path which leads to Jerusalem and death. And no sooner do they come down from the mountain than Jesus encounters very directly the harsh reality of a young boy hideously possessed by a demon.

There is a great temptation, both as individuals and as a Church, to settle in, to build tents up on the mountain, to prefer to stay up in the air, away from the level ground where people really live. As individuals we sometimes hear it expressed as "I don't want to get involved." As a church community, we sometimes hear it expressed as "the Church should stick to things about God and not get involved in politics."

A little over a hundred years ago, many people were indignant at those Church leaders who spoke out against slavery. The Church should be talking about God, about Jesus, but not about a political and economic issue such as slavery—even if slavery did have to do with how we treat one another. Mountaintop theology, abstract and general, was okay, but religion which got too involved with people's real here-and-now lives was often rejected.

Today we hear similar complaints whenever religion comes too close to real-life issues. The so-called conservatives might well want the Church to take a strong, public and specific stand on prayer in the classroom, sexual morality or pornography—but not on nuclear weapons, capital punishment, or gun control laws. So-called liberals might approve the Church's statements on atomic warfare or Latin American struggles but feel that abortion or sexual morality are personal and private.

The temptation is there to deal only with abstractions, to think that religion has mostly to do with saying prayers and taking care of myself and God. Sometimes the temptation is even to think that Lent is mostly about how I can make myself better as an individual. The temptation is to remain on the mountain, hoping for a startling vision of the Lord in glory, thus missing the day-to-day life off the mountain, missing the Lord as he speaks to us in the events and people of ordinary life.

Today's liturgy indicates that we need to look for the Lord in our ordinary day-to-day life, in the struggles we daily undertake, and in the people who are around us. The family which struggles to stay close together, the parents who are trying to do what is best for their children, young people who are searching out where their life is leading them, are not just engaged in mere human activities. They are doing things which are deeply religious. And it is in these things, off the mountain and down in the plain of real life, that they can look for and find the Lord.

Stephen C. Gilmour

3rd Sunday of Lent

Cycle A

Ex 17:3–7
Rom 5:1–2, 5–8
Jn 4:5–42

The Samaritan woman left her water jar, went off into town (running, I'm sure) and told the townspeople, "Come and see someone who told me everything I ever did!"

He hadn't of course. There was much about this woman's life which Jesus didn't talk of, but her exaggeration was beautiful, and one which anyone who has been accepted and forgiven in his or her deepest weakness can readily understand.

Jesus had not recounted everything she had ever done, but he did let her know that he was aware of all her "husbands." I imagine this fact of her life was not only what bothered her most, but what the others gossiped about most. This was perhaps the one thing which made her an outcast among outcasts. Now she has met Jesus, and gently, not embarrassing her, he lets her know that he knows this troublesome detail of her life. He lets her know that it is, in fact, only a detail. She has worth in spite of her failed relationships—perhaps even because of them.

We know Jesus is incredible; his love and acceptance of this woman only illustrate it again. The Samaritan woman was quite unusual herself. She had every right to be suspicious of Jesus and his motives. She comes right out, though, and asks him why he is bothering to speak to her. It seems as though between being a Samaritan, a woman, and the wife of some five husbands, her self-concept wasn't exactly thriving. Once she caught on that she and Jesus weren't communicating on the same level, she trusted him—and more, she believed in him.

In one way we could say, "What did she have to lose?" Maybe she was calloused by rejection and humiliation. Still, she was immediately honest with Jesus. That, no matter what previous hurts she had experienced, opened her to hurt again.

What was it about Jesus that made her risk? What was it about him that gave her the courage to admit what perhaps she had never admitted even to herself? How was it that this woman, an outcast, a "sinner," perhaps a cynic as well, went running back to town to give witness to Jesus?

A miracle perhaps. The same kind of miracle that is often recounted in movies: man has a horrible past; meets woman; they fall in love; reluctantly he confesses his previous life, certain he will lose her because of it; she smiles and admits that she's known his sordid adventures all along and it doesn't make any difference.

Love is miracle enough; love which accepts failure and weakness is almost unbelievable. Paul says it in today's reading, "It is precisely in this that God proves his love for us: that while we were still sinners, Christ died for us."

If you have ever had the experience of loving someone unconditionally, you know that nothing that person says or does or fails to do can alter that love. You can be hurt, even devastated, but always you choose to love again. I'm not sure most of us ever experience that kind of loving. There are so many roles we must fulfill, so many expectations we have of each other, that our loving becomes enmeshed in coulds and shoulds and ifs. If we find it difficult to love unconditionally, still more difficult is it to believe that we are loved that way. We judge others' motives by our own and if our own motives are less than pure, we naturally suspect that others have similar hidden agendas.

We end up crying out with the doubting Israelites, "Is the Lord in our midst or not?" We wonder, as they did, if this awful journey will ever get us to the promised land. We too remember past securities and wonder if we weren't better off before.

The Israelites thirsted; the Samaritan woman thirsted. We thirst: for renewed faith that our journey makes sense; for renewed belief in the unconditional love of God; for someone who will meet us at the well and, by accepting us as we are, bring about our conversion. We thirst for the miracle of love.

Paul says, "The love of God has been poured out in our hearts." God's love can quench our thirsts; God's love gives us the ability to quench the deepest thirsts of our brothers and sisters. We, like Moses, can touch the rock of a heart grown bitter and open it; we, like Jesus, can meet people at the well and surprise them by our understanding. We, like the Samaritan woman, can admit the unfaithfulness in our lives which leads us to see our real thirst, and to witness to him who quenches it.

"The love of God has been poured out in our hearts." And once we drink, we can pour for others.

Carole M. Eipers

4th Sunday of Lent

Cycle A

1 Sm 16:1, 6–7, 10–13
Eph 5:8–14
Jn 9:1–41

To understand today's readings we must reflect on light and darkness, sight and blindness. The readings present the meaning of Jesus and Christian existence to us in terms of these experiences.

Marius von Senden's book, *Space and Sight*, expands our awareness of what it means to see. When Western surgeons discovered how to perform safe cataract operations, they operated on dozens of men and women of all ages who had been blinded by cataracts since birth. Von Senden recounts some of these cases. As one twenty-two-year-old girl first focused her gaze on things, she expressed more and more gratitude and astonishment and repeatedly exclaimed: "Oh God! How beautiful!" We have a similar experience of discovery when we turn on the light in a darkened room. In the darkness we stumble and grope, unable to distinguish between objects and space. The light reveals things in their true identity, proportions, and place.

The religious thinker Teilhard de Chardin frequently said that Christianity is not an additional burden of observances and obligations added to our life. Rather, it bestows significance, beauty, and new light on what we are already doing. Christ is the illumination of our existing world, and faith in him enables us to see that world truly. One of the ways Christ saves us is by revealing who God is and who we are meant to be. Jesus shows us God as forgiving, loving and faithful, welcoming the sinner and the lost. And he shows us that humanity itself is possible, through the power of a heart converted and renewed in him.

True sight is really insight into who Jesus is and how his vision transforms the landscape. John's Gospel is full of people who are looking for salvation: the Samaritan woman at the well; Nicodemus who comes to visit Jesus in the darkness of night; the crowds who are fed by Jesus. We are also looking for salvation, for the healing of our broken loves, for release from our loneliness, for righting of the injustices of our world. Those who stop looking because they have begun to see are like the man born blind: they come to believe in Jesus. Such sight is a gift; to receive it we have only to open our hearts to Jesus, the light of the world.

This light is not meant for ourselves alone. "Live as children of light," Paul says. "Light produces every kind of goodness and justice and truth." We are meant to bring the light of Christ to the darkness of one another's lives and of our world. One example of a woman who did this is Fannie Lou Hamer, one of the great leaders of the Black freedom struggle. Born into a family of Black sharecroppers in the Mississippi Delta, she engaged in a nonviolent struggle for the rights of the Black and poor. Many of her projects met with apparent failure, but she endured great hardship and persecution without bitterness. She is remembered for proclaiming the Word through songs like:

> This little light of mine, I'm gonna let it shine . . . Let it shine, let it shine, let it shine!

Her life is one reminder that God's light of love and justice continues to shine even in the midst of the most terrible darkness. We are called today to believe in that light and bring it to others.

Kathleen R. Fischer
Thomas N. Hart

5th Sunday of Lent

Cycle A

Ez 37:12–14
Rom 8:8–11
Jn 11:1–45

How often have I cried with the grieving Martha, "Lord, if you had been here my brother would never have died!" If you had been here, Lord, that accident would never have happened. If you had been here Lord, I would never have lost my job. If you had been here, Lord, things would have gone much better.

Whenever I have heard this Gospel read, Martha sounds "sweet"—sort of making a backwards act of faith. I hear her blaming Jesus. "Where were you when I needed you? You could have helped, and you didn't."

Lucky Martha. Her brother's life is restored; her faith in Jesus is confirmed. I suppose that, knowing the end of the Lazarus story, I expect happy endings too. Yet, I'm often left muttering, "Lord, if only you had been here!"

In the first reading God says, "I will open your graves and have you rise from them. . . ." It must have been easy for Ezekiel to believe God's promise when those dry bones came to life. Lucky Ezekiel; another happy ending.

What about those of us who don't get happy endings? What about those of us who are left with dead brothers and dry bones? Where is the God of miracles, the Lord of Life, when we need him?

"Your brother will rise again," Jesus assures Martha, but it doesn't seem to help. "I know, I know, he'll rise again in the resurrection on the last day." That doesn't help her much now. Her brother is dead and she is hurting. Can't you do something *now*?

Lucky Martha. Jesus does do something—something wonderful. And he prays to his Father, "I know that you always hear me, but I have said this for the sake of the crowd that they may believe that you sent me." Welcome to the crowd—the crowd of those who wanted to believe but whose skepticism made them seek proof. We are the crowd of today, onlookers at the raising of Lazarus. It happened so that we, too, might believe that our loving Father sent Jesus, and that his word can be trusted. But what is the message for us as we sit amid dead brothers and dry bones?

St. Paul gives us a clue in the second reading. "If the spirit of him who raised Jesus from the dead dwells in you, then he . . . will bring your mortal bodies to life also. . . ." There is life . . . and there is life. The flesh has to be enlivened by God's Spirit. The focus then of the Lazarus story and the dry bones tale is not those who are physically dead, but those, like Martha and Ezekiel, who struggle to live and to believe while surrounded by death.

The Gospel tells us that Jesus wept and that he was troubled in spirit. Could Jesus have doubted that his friend would know eternal life? Or could his tears have been caused by the doubters—those who questioned his love for Lazarus? "He opened the eyes of that blind man," the crowd muttered, "Why could he not have done something to stop this man from dying?" Perhaps Jesus cried because they looked for love to be proved by miracles. Perhaps he cried because they had misunderstood the message of his healings.

A friend of mine wanted to pray a prayer of healing for me. I thought of the words from Ezekiel: "I will open your graves and you shall rise from them. . . ." My friend's prayer made me realize that I am entombed because I choose to be. I am afraid to be healed of past hurts because if I let go of the pain, I'm not sure what I'll have left. I guess I really believe that dried bones are better than nothing at all, that grieving over the dead is easier than facing my fellow mourners and comforting them.

To be healed, to rise from our graves, to revitalize our bones means letting go of what Paul calls our "flesh"—our selfish nature. Jesus is not a good-luck charm which, when properly worn, will ward off deaths. He is simply a friend, a companion in our griefs, who calls us to go on living—living unselfishly. He calls us, empowers us, to open our graves of self-pity that our sufferings might lead to compassion.

To celebrate Lent is to reaffirm our belief in Jesus' resurrection, and our own ultimate rising. We know as Martha did that we will rise again on the last day. That won't help us now, though, unless we learn to accept the little deaths along the way and practice rising from selfishness to compassion.

Yes, Lord, you are here, and my brothers die anyway; yes, Lord, you are here, and yet I find myself surrounded by dry bones. Because you are here, Lord, I am a survivor. Yes, lucky me!

Carole M. Eipers

Passion (Palm) Sunday

Cycle A

Is 50:4–7
Phil 2:6–11
Mt 26:14–27:66

Today's liturgy leads in to one of the most solemn and rich weeks of the liturgical year. We are celebrating the most awesome mysteries of our faith—the passion, death and resurrection of Jesus of Nazareth. We can ask ourselves a whole series of questions, for example, Do these events impinge in any way on my life? Do I want them to? What is their meaning for my life? How can I discuss what they mean in my life?

If I slow down and try to get in touch with the feelings I might have as I approach Holy Week, what do I discover? Dread? Confusion? Avoidance? Anticipation? Reverence? One thing cannot be denied. A crucifixion is not a pleasant affair.

The readings today place us in the context of Jesus' saving mission. There was a job to be done. Jesus became man out of love, in order that we might be free. He has a purpose which gives meaning to his actions and his choices. Perhaps when we were young we took the time to consider our lives as a whole— what career we would choose, what lifestyle or partner we would choose. Too often, however, that's the end of it. We can get caught up in the demands of living and rarely or never take stock of the greater context or horizon of our lives. Do I allow myself to be called to reflection? Is my life directed by an intentional goal, or do I just allow life to happen to me, reacting rather than acting?

In the first reading, Isaiah acknowledges his gifts, and sees that the job he is called to do flows from those gifts. He is docile. He opens himself to *listen* to the message of Yahweh—a message that is mediated every day through the events and persons in our lives. He is going somewhere. He has a sense of ultimate direction and meaning. This, in turn gives meaning to the rejections, the disappointments, the sufferings of life. We see Isaiah here in a situation of extremity— something with which we are all familiar. He resolves to follow his goal and "sets his face like flint." In a limit situation, we may feel alone and abandoned, but we are told that we are *not* alone. Christ was not alone in his extremity. The Scriptures offer us lots of company in our misery. They offer hope.

In the reading from Philippians, we are invited to take on the very attitude of Christ. In order to speak his message, he was willing to empty himself, to become a slave. It all seems too ridiculous outside of the context of his mission and message. He did not cling to his title, his position, or the esteem of being God. Those things seem to pale in the light of his mission to love us, and make it possible for us to be free. It is an exalted calling, yet ours is not so very different. Each of us is called to proclaim some message. It may not be a message from a podium, or a microphone, or a pulpit. It may not even take the form of words. It might reside in my presence to others, in the works of my hands, in a kind word or a compassionate glance. But we cannot be free, we cannot be who we are meant to be alone. Each of us has a key that permits another to be opened. We do have a power over each other—the power of love— which allows another to blossom in the sunlight of God's love. This is how we come to be persons of wholeness and integrity. This is the core of the goal, the mission, the direction of our lives as Christians.

There is sorrow and difficulty along this road, as well as joy and peace. But we need, above all, to *know what we are about*. We need to be going somewhere, to be aiming at something. Without this thrust of choice and meaning, it becomes difficult, if not impossible, to bear the vicissitudes of life today. Each of us has a job to do here. At times, this may be crystal clear. At other times it may elude us in confusion and doubt. But with Isaiah and with Christ, we need to pray for the grace of insight, for the grace of courage, for the grace of perseverance.

Matthew's gospel focuses on the betrayal of Judas. At every turn, in today's readings, the characters face adversity. Yet the paradox confronts us. Jesus' humiliation was transformed into exaltation. Isaiah has faith that ultimately, he will not be put to shame. Jesus' death is transformed into resurrection. At one extreme, this presents a counterpoint to indifference, to cynicism. At the other extreme, it challenges us to allow our own lives to be transformed, or at least to trust that, in the long run, our sorrow will be turned to joy. The good news of our existence, that is to be given to others, will not be proclaimed nearly as effectively if we do not know what it is, or if we do not trust that, if we listen, we will discover it piece by piece as we live.

As we walk the way of the Passion with Christ this week, let us try to appreciate the gifts of freedom and love that are ours because of Christ's mission, and to see in him the contours of our calling to love and liberate our brothers and sisters—nearby and across the globe.

Elizabeth A. Dreyer

Easter Sunday

Cycle A

Acts 10, 34. 37–43
Col 3, 1–4
Jn 20, 1–9

Easter is the very heart of our faith. All of today's readings call us to joy and celebration, for the word of light is spoken into our broken, suffering situation. God raised his suffering servant after his good life, his trials, his apparent abandonment. The disciples struggle to believe it; it is too good to be true. Perhaps we also struggle to believe and understand the meaning of Jesus' resurrection. Today is a time for reflection on how Jesus' resurrection creates hope for our present and future existence.

Christians are promised that their own resurrections will be patterned on that of Jesus. And the biblical evidence regarding Jesus is that he has been raised to a new mode of eschatological existence. Such an eschatological existence must be described by way of negative analogies: it is not subject to our dimensions of space and time, nor is it subject to sin and death. While the resurrection narratives differ in details, the accounts stress that it is Jesus himself who is seen, but a Jesus who has been radically transformed. Resurrection is an experience of continuity in the midst of change.

Resurrection, then, does not mean escape from this material creation, but its ultimate transformation. God does not intend to destroy what he has created; God is present bringing it to fulfillment. The world as we know it will not pass away or be annihilated; rather, it will somehow be transformed and changed into the city of God. Moreover, the power of resurrection is not reserved to some future age, but is now at work in our lives. Faith in the resurrection changes the way we live out the ordinary details of our lives.

What will be destroyed has only passing value; what is to be transformed retains its importance. Belief in the resurrection as an event of identity in the midst of change sustains a life of love, for it underscores the lasting value of all individual things and persons. It is the basis of a deep reverence for all of life. Christian love often consists of simple actions that seem insignificant: efforts to make a patient more comfortable, a home visit with a parishioner, the tedious household tasks of a parent. But the Christian disciple decides here and now for life or death, and Christian love is the sign that we have "passed from death to life" (1 Jn 3:14).

The resurrection also brings hope to our personal existence. Every healing is a partial resurrection. The psychologist Carl Jung shows us how this pattern of death and new life can be found in the experience of human growth. He describes the stages on the way to individuation or personal maturity as experiences of death and rebirth: the child leaves the womb, the adolescent enters adult life, the adult moves through the crises of middle age to true selfhood, the person leaves this world in death. At all these stages we find that God's transforming power is at work in our present, giving promise to our future.

Reflection on the resurrection as transformation enables us to deal creatively with all the negative elements of the world. The Latin American liberation theologian, Jon Sobrino, describes the biblical hope in the transformation of the person and history as a hope against death and injustice. Since death has been conquered by life in Jesus' resurrection, we can continue to work with hope against poverty, hunger, violence, and war. Faith in the risen Jesus is belief in the present and future transformation of existing creation, the release of its beauty hidden by the presence of sin, evil, and suffering. Easter is indeed occasion for joy and celebration, for it is the basis of our hope and courage.

Kathleen R. Fischer
Thomas N. Hart

2nd Sunday of Easter

Cycle A

Acts 2:42–47
1 Pt 1:3–9
Jn 20:19–31

The readings today speak of faith, and a lot of credit is given to those who are willing to believe without seeing. Peter encourages the people to believe in Jesus Christ even though none of them has had the opportunity to see him in the flesh. In the Gospel, the Lord praises Thomas for believing, but singles out even more those who have believed without seeing. What can all this talk of faith and believing mean for us today?

Belief, in a generic sense, belongs to the human condition. It is an activity that goes on everywhere all the time. Scientists believe the experiments of their predecessors, and base new discoveries on them. Mathematicians do not re-invent the logarithmic table every time they sit down to do their calculations. Children believe their parents. We all believe a certain amount of wisdom from those who have lived well. A traveller believes that what the map-maker has recorded is accurate. These examples of belief are eminently reasonable, and life could not move forward without belief of all kinds.

Religious belief differs from these examples, but it, too, is reasoned, and from some perspectives, also necessary to living. Bernard Lonergan defines faith as "knowledge born of religious love." What does this statement mean?

In the Christian tradition, the starting point for faith involves a personal relationship with Jesus. Christianity is not an ideology, or a system of propositions. At its core, it is simply about a person, and that person is Jesus Christ. As in all personal relationships, the presence of love is a gift. One does not sit down and *decide* to fall in love with another person, or with God. It is given. It is the same with faith. None of us *decided* that we would believe. We all know persons who would like desperately to believe, but just can't see reality in that way. The gift is offered, and some of us are blind to the offer, some see the possibility of faith, but refuse to respond, while others respond with indifference or with enthusiasm. We all know the story of the sowing of the seed.

But the love between us and Christ is the cornerstone of faith. The knowledge that is faith comes forth from, and is shaped by religious love. Faith makes it possible to have a kind of knowledge that cannot exist without religious love. Pascal tells us that "the heart has reasons that reason does not know." Love produces a knowledge that involves making judgments about what is or is not valuable in life. It involves placing meaning on certain things, and seeing other things as meaningless, or perhaps as less important than others. Once we are touched by the gift of loving God, faith is there as part of the gift. Faith gives us the power to judge what is truly worthwhile, and to act on this knowledge.

Many writers have referred to the "leap of faith." Most of us may have experienced this, but may not have thought about what it actually means. It becomes obvious in a discussion with a non-believer. The leap is not irrational, but does go beyond reason. To the eyes of love, to faith, the world is changed. It becomes an expression of God's own generous gift to us. Our experience and our history become the means by which we discover who God is. Human existence is sacred, and will come to its fullness at the end of time. The material world is good, but it is not the whole of reality. Suffering is seen as a purification, a preparation, a sharing in the cross. Evil is to be overcome with good. Every act of every human being has the potential for infinite value.

The woman or man of faith is one who strives, out of love, to know God (*fides querens intellectum*). She or he is one whose goal is self-transcendence, which involves receiving the Spirit of love consciously into our hearts (Romans 5:5), hearing the Word of God preached by the Christian community, and keeping it, and thus being brought face-to-face with God for all eternity.

As a by-product of this faith born of love, we may experience a growing sense of being rooted, of peace, of confidence in our knowledge, born of faith. This does not mean that life ceases to be a struggle, or that doubts will never assail us. But it can give us a perspective on reality, and rules out the possibility of being completely at a loss in the face of life's vicissitudes.

The life, death and resurrection of Jesus is the impetus to the believer. It is by these events that we know that our faith and trust will not be in vain. The Word incarnate and the Spirit of love go forth and "will not return to me empty." Faith is a knowledge that cannot be completely exhausted by explanation. There will always remain a hint of the "madness of God."

Elizabeth A. Dreyer

3rd Sunday of Easter

Cycle A

Acts 2:14, 22–28
1 Pt 1:17–21
Lk 24:13–35

Whenever I teach the Gospels I love to invite people to try to know and experience Jesus as a very human being. For the most part, these adult learners are grateful to understand Jesus' human development, his growing in wisdom and grace even as he aged. We resonate with his anger, his frustrated tears, his joy in the Spirit and in little children, his compassion for widows and lepers. To know him as human is to love him humanly, with more warmth and intimacy than we would have dreamed.

However, since most of us also cherish dreams of our perfection and since he is our pioneer into the perfection of risen life, we would expect that Luke might have cleared up Jesus' irritation with the disciples on the road of Emmaus. "What little sense you have!" Jesus' resurrection, however, did not make him less human but more perfectly human. It seems that a very important part of profoundly human relationships is sharing feelings honestly, of caring enough to confront. Peter bluntly confronts his compatriots in the first reading because he cares deeply about their repentance and salvation: "You even used pagans to crucify and kill him."

Confronting does not mean telling off. My experience, however, is that most of us confuse the two and would rather err through too much gentleness than too much severity. I question if such gentleness is love. Perhaps the most important distinction between telling someone off and confronting is the experience of a previous caring relationship. I can easily tell off a bus driver, whom I will never meet again, but I owe my family and friends more than an explosion of temper. Feelings of anger can indicate a deep concern, and a loving relationship will keep me at least minimally alert to the one I am confronting, his experience, or her immediate feelings.

Jesus offers us a model of confronting care in the Gospel. First he approaches the disciples and then begins to walk along with them. If he "approaches" he must have been walking toward Jerusalem and thus meets them face to face. He turns from his direction to walk in their direction. He asks them to share their experience: "What are you discussing?" They are in distress and they honestly show him their turmoil and dashed hope. Again, Jesus does not interpret their experience for them but asks them to clarify their statement about all the "things that went on these past few days." "What things?" Jesus inquires.

Jesus wants to listen carefully to *their* interpretation. He gives them a chance to spell out not only their experience but their feelings about it, the meaning they find in it (or the lack of meaning). He establishes a relationship by his attention to their experience (briefly, for gospel stories can only be shorthand versions of how Jesus initiated relationships). Then he shares his feelings with them. Not content just to express his frustration with them, he immediately begins to remedy their dullness. Far from being put off, hurt or angry by his confrontation, they are exhilarated.

Jesus approaches and meets them face to face. Confrontation is a face-to-face event. Passive aggressive behavior might indicate that I am angry but it usually clouds the atmosphere, increases unnamed tension, accomplishes nothing. Jesus changes his direction to walk along with them. If I risk confronting someone, I risk changing my direction, my opinion. To "walk along with" calls for my time, energy, and attention. This relationship will change me, even as I ask the other to change.

I respectfully ask for the others' experience of a situation and ask for clarification. I hear it as best I can, open, attentive to the other. Then I express how I feel, what I have seen or heard, what concrete changes I hope for. I stay with the other until I am sure that I too am understood. Far from being put off, hurt, or angry, the confronted person often realizes my care, appreciates the risk I took. I am invited to "stay," to share "the meal"—in other words, our relationship is cemented and deepened.

This Lucan resurrection appearance is yet another story of Jesus' love for his friends. We do not live in friendship by our own power. The risen Lord is with us when we need to approach another directly, honestly, caringly. He seats himself with us, blesses us and breaks open the bread of truth with us. Whether we are confronted or do the confronting, may we recognize the risen Lord teaching us how to love well.

Rea McDonnell

4th Sunday of Easter

Cycle A

Acts 2:14, 36–41
1 Pt 2:20–25
Jn 10:1–10

In a memorable episode of "All in the Family," Gloria and Mike plague Archie with a riddle. There has been a terrible accident, and a young child has been hurt and seriously injured. Rushed to the hospital, the boy is prepared for a necessary operation, but the surgeon who has been called in suddenly says, "I can't operate, that's my son"—yet the doctor is not the boy's father. Archie is at first puzzled, and suggests a case of mistaken identity. If not, was the doctor a stepfather, and not the real father? Was the son adopted? Unsuccessful in these attempts at a solution, Archie is at first annoyed. He is ultimately furious when the answer is revealed—the doctor was the boy's mother!

Clearly our image of something, even an unconscious image, shapes our thinking and even limits our understanding. Archie's image of "doctor" was so strongly masculine that the otherwise obvious solution to the riddle could not be imagined. The image had in a sense taken control and assumed an almost unquestioned identity of its own.

The image of Jesus as the Good Shepherd has been extremely popular in Christianity and general piety. It is important to look behind this commonly accepted image, to see what it really conveys. Is there more to it than we might at first expect?

In one sense this is a comforting image—the good leader who lovingly provides for his flock, the one who even puts his life on the line for their sake. In contrast to the oft-heard, "My name is Mike, and I'll be your waiter this evening," here is someone who calls us by name, not for business profit but for our own sake, because he loves us.

But we have to be careful lest the image be too soft, too sentimental or romantic a characterization, both of the Jesus who "was made to suffer," who "brought our sins to the cross," and of us, his followers, who are called to "reform," to "follow in his footsteps." The Scripture portrays a power here, an overwhelming strength which enables him to endure his own unjust suffering in union with us who are not innocent.

Neither can the shepherd imagery in these texts sustain an interpretation of docile sheep-Christians, blindly following designated leaders. The Pharisee-leaders are not listened to or followed by the man born blind (in the verses preceding today's gospel selection); they are poor shepherds and deserve to be rejected.

The texts are not a plea for tranquil subservience, but a call to authentic leadership, based on personal relationship and characterized by loving service. Without these qualities, leaders become subject to condemnation as thieves and marauders. All leadership in the Christian community is judged not on some intrinsic worth due to position or authority but by its faithfulness to Jesus, the only true gateway to the pastures of life.

This challenging aspect of the sheep/shepherd imagery also extends to all believers. Unlike those who have gone astray, believers must change their lives and follow the authentic Shepherd. The letter of Peter clearly admits that suffering is not unique to the Shepherd; enduring amidst difficulties is also a mark of the faithful follower.

A question always appropriate to ask is "where am I in this passage?" Usually we envision ourselves as the sheep with Jesus as Shepherd, but we could also consider ourselves in the shepherd role. As baptized people, each of us has received the gift of the Holy Spirit and is called to follow in Jesus' footsteps, to bring life in its fullness to others.

Stephen C. Gilmour

50

5th Sunday of Easter

Cycle A

Acts 6:1–7
1 Pt 2:4–9
Jn 14:1–12

What do you do when you encounter a stone in your path? There are a variety of ways to handle it: you can see it, but ignore it; you can skirt around it; if it's not too big, you might kick it out of the way or kick it along the road playfully; if you are distracted by other things, you might stumble over it. A stone in our path might be troublesome if it causes us to fall; a stone in our path might be welcome if we are attempting to cross a stream and remain dry-shod; a stone encountered during the leisure of a beachwalk might be picked up, examined, and pocketed as a treasure.

How do we respond to the living stone who is the Lord? There are a variety of ways to handle him as well. He can be ignored, or skirted around; he can be kicked out of the way, or used to help us across troubled waters. The living stone who is Jesus can be the cornerstone upon whom we build the entire structure of our lives, or he can be a stumbling block who gets in our way.

"A stone which the builders rejected that became a cornerstone." Who would use rejected material to build with? Children would. Adults are fussy when they build; they want "the best." Children sit and wait for the rejects: the scraps of lumber, the bent nails, the "slugs" of metal, even the marvelous sawdust. It doesn't matter to children if the material is guaranteed or supposedly indestructible, for, to use Shakespeare's phrase, "the play's the thing." They have as much fun with the process of building as with the product. What is important to children is their plan, their dream, the sound of the hammer and the wonder of what a saw can do. It doesn't seem to matter if the fort they build will last or if the chair they make will be comfortable. In fact, they might not even finish; they might find something else they'd rather do together. Children are not so much about attaching wood as they are about cementing friendships. Tomorrow they will build anew, or turn their homemade chair into a rocket and travel to the moon.

"A stone which the builders rejected that became a cornerstone." Who would use rejected material to build with? The homeless would gladly accept imperfect lumber to house their children; the hungry scavenge for bread in our trash cans; the poor perceive our cast-offs as treasures. The stone which the wealthy builders rejected is life for children, for the homeless, for the poor.

"The stone," Peter says of Jesus, "is of value for you who have faith." Often it seems that we can find much better, far more durable material to build our lives around than the words of Jesus. Our cornerstones are inscribed: "Power," "Wealth," and "Success." These cornerstones loom large in our lives, while the living stone who is the Lord becomes merely a pebble in our shoes.

"I am the way," Jesus says, the way to build. Jesus did not construct great churches, nor even a monument to his father. But he told us what he was building: the kingdom of God. He showed us the stones with which to build that kingdom: forgiveness, healing, compassion, peace. We've found stones to throw instead: grudges, revenge, rejection, violence.

The early Christians we hear about in today's passage from the Acts certainly had their troubles. There was preaching to be done, there were people to be fed, disputes to be settled, divisions to be healed. Stumbling blocks? They could have been of course, had the community not made Jesus its cornerstone. Perhaps the skeptics and cynics tried to convince the seven men who had been chosen that there were certainly more significant things for them to do with their lives than to be distributors of bread. But the seven must have remembered that Jesus said "The greatest among you will be the one who serves." Rather than stumble over those words, they chose to build their lives around them.

Jesus is a "living stone" and the community he builds is one of people, not things. "I go to prepare a place for you," he promises, assuring us that we need not build an everlasting dwelling here. We need not worry about things; we have only to learn the way to build the kingdom. And Jesus is the way.

How do we respond to the living stone who is the Lord? There are various ways to handle him. Perhaps there should be a stumbling block at the entrance to our church, or a cornerstone which we are forced to bump into. It might remind us that Jesus has to be more than a pebble in our shoes if we are ever to find that place he has prepared for us.

Carole M. Eipers

6th Sunday of Easter

Cycle A

Acts 8:5–8, 14–17
1 Pt 3:15–18
Jn 14:15–21

In seeking the meaning of "Spirit" for our everyday life, we discover this kernel of truth emerges—Spirit is power. Unfortunately, the word "power" often has a negative connotation in our usage, referring to exploitation, manipulation, greed. Power is associated with the rise of dictatorships, political scheming, one-up-manship.

The three readings speak of either the promise or the conferral of the Spirit, and always in the context of power. In this transmission something happens to the recipients. What, we ask ourselves, is this experience of the Spirit coming to people? What changes? What is added to people's lives?

Jesus speaks of giving another "Paraclete," a legal term meaning "helper," "mediator," "advocate." The presupposition is that we are not complete, not capable of living on our own, cannot speak in our own behalf. Our consciousness leaves us with insufficient, and sometimes unreliable, tools for tending to the garden which is our very selves. We attempt to live out myths which, instead of bringing us contented and satisfying lives, leave us disillusioned and disappointed. Rather than feeling ourselves powerful over our own destinies, we feel helpless and trapped—at the mercy of circumstances and forces that we neither bargained for nor know how to bargain with.

The back cover of Gary Snyder's book of poetry, *Turtle Island,* reads, "All however, share a common vision: a rediscovery of this land and the ways by which we might become natives of the place, ceasing to think and act (after all these centuries) as newcomers and invaders." Is not the position of the newcomer one of powerlessness—not knowing what to do or where to go? Is not the attempt of the invader to acquire power—external domination over the environment and its people? Is not the human journey, both inner and outer, that of becoming a native, at home, whole, together with all sentient and non-sentient creation?

Jesus speaks of not leaving those who are in touch with him orphans—comfortless, desolate, bereaved, forlorn, helpless. He speaks of letting himself be clearly seen by people and making himself real to them. This is the power of which he speaks, in giving the Spirit.

This power threatens the invaders of the earth, those whose systems promote grasping and acquisitiveness, those who feel no roots in nature or in their own inner nature. Not for nothing did the first Christians gather in circles of disguise. Not for nothing did the apostle Philip address an outcast nation. Not for nothing did Peter intimate that those first Christians would suffer unjustly. The power of the Living Spirit threatens, but it cannot be extinguished. This resource cannot be exhausted, but, paradoxically, replenishes itself as it is given away.

Sharon Koziczkowski

7th Sunday of Easter

Cycle A

Acts 1:12–14
1 Pt 4:13–16
Jn 17:1–11

1. What does it mean to be intimate with someone? What characterizes intimacy? Jesus and the Father are intimate, we learn from today's exegesis. How did that happen? How did Jesus, who grew in wisdom and age, also grow in grace? Reflect and share.

2. What does it mean for us to be intimate with the Father or with Jesus? How have you grown closer to the Father and/or Jesus over the years? Reflect and share.

In my experience, intimacy begins with an attraction. I notice someone who is good or beautiful. It does not matter whether the person is the same sex or not. Sometimes I place that person on a pedestal, sometimes I get tongue-tied in the person's presence, withdraw a bit out of awe that can, at times, feel like fear. As the pedestal person becomes more real to me, admiration remains but I become more comfortable, more trusting, more aware of our mutuality as the person responds to my attraction. I fall in love. At this point, psychiatrist Scott Peck writes, we become not only attracted to but "invested in and committed to an object outside of ourselves" —in our discussion here, a *person* other than ourselves. Love deepens between us and I am stretched, opened. "The experience of real love . . . involves an extension of one's limits"

When intimacy will develop in a mutual relationship, and I make a decision to invest my energy in our relationship, I discover new wellsprings of energy. When I commit myself to another, I am mutually received and experience a deep sense of belonging. "In love" gradually becomes love. Scott Peck defines love as "The will to extend one's self for the purpose of nurturing one's own or another's spiritual growth." Peck's definition looks a lot like Erik Erickson's stage of generativity in his famed eight stages of human development. Nurturing is a key concept for both theorists.

We turn to our Sunday readings and find Jesus at his most nurturing during his last supper: with the first community waiting for the Spirit who would make them generative toward the whole world, "even to the ends of the earth"; and for a later generation of Christians suffering persecution with a love so mature that they could lay down their lives. The source of Jesus' and his disciples' "will to extend themselves," we are told explicitly in our first two readings, is the Holy Spirit. When Jesus uses "belonging" language in the Gospel, the implied source of unity is the Spirit.

Jesus not only celebrates his intimacy with the Father in his last supper prayer but he also invites each of us to enjoy the same intimacy with himself and with God. He prays that we might have life, the eternal life available right now, that comes from knowing God and the one whom he sent, Jesus. To "know" meant, for Jews like Jesus and John the evangelist, much more than to apprehend intellectually. Truth can be very satisfying to the mind but it alone is not the substance of "eternal life." For Jews, knowing means experiencing, having such a deep, intimate union with another that they use the same word for sexual intercourse: "Adam knew Eve and she conceived." We are invited to know God and Jesus right now—and intimately. No need to wait for union in heaven. Jesus invites us to life, in abundance, to love and to union now.

We are invited through all the stages of human intimacy to the closest union with our God and Jesus. God is so distant, transcendent, awe-inspiring, judgmental, even fierce. Jesus is so divine, has it all together; we stand in awe not only of his miracles but also of his perfect humanity.

In the second step toward intimacy, the pedestal is replaced by admiration of a real God as manifested in the Old Testament, a real Jesus whom we find in the Gospels themselves. As we read the Scriptures directly, we become far more comfortable, more trusting of a tenderhearted, gracious God; of Jesus with human emotions of joy, disgust, irritation, fear and fury, with human confusion and doubt. As Jesus and God become real for us, we are not only attracted, we are in love. We begin to invest ourselves in the relationship through habits of scripture reading and prayer. We become committed and move in deepest love to that "will to extend ourselves" in order to nurture others.

Finally, intimacy is mutual. As God and Jesus become more real to us, we can be more real with them. We begin to experience how attracted they are to us, how they admire us, delight in us. They have invested themselves and will continue to pour their energy (literally, *dynamis* in Greek, a name for the Holy Spirit) into relationship with us. They are committed to us forever.

Rea McDonnell

Pentecost Sunday

Cycle A

Acts 2:1–11
1 Cor 12:3–7, 12–13
Jn 20:19–23

How does the Spirit speak, and what are its manifestations in our world today? We may even ask ourselves: Is he hiding behind the widespread distrust of Church and political authority? Is he lost under threat of a failed economy and possible nuclear disaster? Is the Spirit hostage of crime, violence and fear? Is the Spirit manifest in mass media and from the pulpit? Is our time so different from that of the First Pentecost? Are the gifts of the Spirit so explicitly described by Paul present in and applicable to our world today?

We have a curious way of responding to speech. We say things like: "That *touched* me." "I felt *moved.*" "The speaker *left me cold.*" What kind of communication actually can change the fabric of another person? Perhaps we can learn thereby something of the Spirit.

When Jesus promised the Spirit, he made it very clear that it was a Spirit of Truth. In truth, the Spirit is present; wherever truth is spoken, the Spirit resides.

Now truth is difficult to come by for various reasons. One, there does not exist any one single "truth", possessed by one individual. Truth is many-faceted, as varied as individuals and cultures. Truth is not the possession of leaders, who channel it down to the fold. "Do not corral the Spirit," Paul writes. Truth dwells a particular way in each individual and in each community.

Second, truth is not a servant, but demands service of us. Truth will not allow itself to be manipulated for long to serve anyone's ends. Truth often comes in conflict with our conscious designs and desires.

Third, truth is not always pleasant and flattering. Sometimes it appears dark, and out of fear we wish to hide it, resist it, compromise it. If truth be painful to admit, however, admitting it can also bring us into a right relationship with ourselves, with each other, and with our world. Admitting truth, far from being a humiliating experience, can be the occasion for healing and restoration.

The basic enemy of truth is fear: fear of losing something; fear of giving up what we think we prize; fear of what others will think of us; fear that we cannot withstand the consequences of speaking the truth.

Truth is not a marketable commodity. More often it is a disruptive force, whose enemies are legion. "Don't act as though the truth doesn't exist because it is not heard," Daniel Berrigan recently told a gathering of Pax Christi. "Don't conclude that because you are not heard, you must stop yelling."

Where, then, is the Spirit? It resides in truth, however and by whom truth is spoken. Truth alone moves, stirs, touches people in lasting and satisfying ways.

Sharon Koziczkowski

Trinity Sunday

Cycle A

Ex 34:4–6, 8–9
2 Cor 13:11–13
Jn 3:16–18

Who is God? If you ever had to answer that question in your own words, what would you say? Could you imagine a homilist some Sunday morning coming out into the congregation with a microphone like a roving reporter asking the question: "Who is God for you?" Or imagine a rare quiet moment when your family was all together. If you were to ask each one, "Who is God for you?", what kind of an answer do you think you would get? What kind of answer would you give?

Matthew Fox, a contemporary Dominican theologian, believes that our notion of God has become shrivelled up, that we need to recapture the sense of God as Creator of the whole universe, source of its harmony and order. He speaks of One who is beyond all that we are capable of imagining, yet One who is lovingly associated with the whole creation. For him, as for St. Paul, God's Spirit still works in all and through all, continually bringing forth new development, new life.

The author of Exodus offers another image. He describes God's self-revelation to Moses. Moses has gone up to Mount Sinai early in the morning as God had instructed him to do. Standing before God, he listens as the voice of the Lord says, "Yahweh, the Lord, a merciful and gracious God, slow to anger, rich in kindness and fidelity . . . forgiving." Preachers have often focused on the mysterious name of Yahweh, speculating on its interpretation. It is a bit humorous that biblical scholars have never been able to pin down its meaning. Perhaps that is the best kind of name for One who is beyond all our categories. What is unfortunate, however, is that we often overlook the rest of the description. The God who revealed himself to the people of Israel is a wonderfully relational God. Just think of it, our God is a God of tenderness and compassion, One who cares about and suffers with us. Do we pray to a God who is kind and faithful and forgiving?

There is yet another description of how God has been made manifest in today's Gospel. In the story of the encounter between Jesus and Nicodemus, Jesus is presented as the Son of God sent into the world so that the world might be saved. It is as if creation weren't enough for God: revealing himself to Moses and the prophets weren't enough. Once again God's people were wandering, confused. The God of compassion tries again, sending the Son to be with us, to manifest in a human way that God is indeed a great lover of humanity. Jesus fulfilled his mission without regard to personal cost. His love for the Father and for all his brothers and sisters was so great that it led him to accept death on a cross.

Thus has God been seen over the centuries according to Exodus, John, and a contemporary theologian. Within that tradition who is the God you've come to know in your heart and in your understanding? Is your God great enough, loving enough, close enough? That is a crucial question. Your answer will reveal much about you and about your understanding of what relationship with God entails. For you and all of us are created in God's image.

If God is the source of the entire universe, then all of us are part of a bigger picture. If God's Spirit permeates all, we are related to all of creation, especially to that part of it entrusted to us, the planet Earth. It is ours to promote harmony and order in nature and to oppose whatever contaminates or destroys the environment without which we cannot live. There has been abundant evidence that chemical waste, air pollution, and insecticides used in agribusiness destroy people. For the love of our Creator and for the love of our children for generations to come, it is the responsibility of our generation to do our part to restore the balance in nature.

Jesus was sent not to condemn, but to save. He spent his life spreading the reign of God on earth. To his followers he promised the gift of the Spirit that they might continue his mission in the world. It is ours to spread the reign of peace and justice in our times. It is ours to promote harmonious relationships and to oppose violence in family life, in the workplace and in the world. Those who treat others with justice, respect and love are contributing to the order and harmony in the world and honoring the God who made us.

How we live reflects what we believe. As we grow in our relationship with God, our lives are gradually transformed into God's likeness. Take some time this week to look at the mirror of your life, then answer the question, "Who is God for you?"

Barbara O'Dea

Corpus Christi

Cycle A

Dt 8:2–3, 14–16
1 Cor 10:16–17
Jn 6:51–58

The Eucharist is a mystery. This celebration of Corpus Christi is an invitation to encounter the mystery and to enter into it. It will always remain a mystery. The question, "How can this man give us his flesh to eat?" will go unanswered. The fact that real food and real drink are shared and life is given is what is experienced by entering into the mystery. For centuries the bread has been broken and shared, and new insights into the meaning of the Eucharist continually surface.

When a eucharistic minister anywhere in the world holds the bread of life and says, "Body of Christ," it has ramifications for all of the universe. It means that God chooses to satisfy our hunger by nourishing us with his own life. It means that a community of believers have gathered to celebrate and to share the bread of life together. It means that the physical and spiritual hungers of our world are present and encountered at this eucharistic meal. It means that the world will be touched and changed because these Christians will share the living bread with those in need. Ideally, the Eucharist means at least these things.

The first reading, the remembrance of the desert period, reminds us that we need to feel hunger in order to know that we need nourishment. The desert theme will recur with Jesus' temptations. It recurs throughout history and in our lives. It seems that we need deserts to make us aware of our hungers and the hunger of others. Whether the desert introduces Christians to a hunger for affirmation, beauty, security, food or love, it teaches that hunger is painful and that we are dependent on God and on one another. Widows know the desert of loneliness, young people the desert of confusion, and parents the desert of anxiety. These too, are hungers, and in these deserts it is helpful to listen to the words, "Do not then forget the Lord your God who brought you out of the land of Egypt." (Deut. 8:14) It is possible to bring all the various kinds of hunger to the Eucharist. God's continual faithfulness gives us reason to trust that our needs will be met.

We are all nourished by the Body of Christ, but Paul's words in the second reading refer to the deeper reality of communion with one another. If we share in the one loaf, broken for us, we become a single body. If we are eating and drinking the same life-giving bread and wine, we are becoming the same body of Christ. Union with Christ and with one another intensifies through the Eucharist. Intimate fellowship binds together those who share at the table of the Lord. The intimacy between the vine and a branch creates close union among the branches, "I am the vine, you are the branches." (John 15:1) New awareness of union with each other and how to live it out is growing in Christian communities today. The understanding of our bonding in Christ makes essential a ministry of care of one another in love. Neighborhood groups, Bible study groups, school volunteer groups, peace groups, and many others can become Christian communities when they develop an awareness that they are bound to one another through sharing the bread of life.

The Gospel announces that the living bread is the source of life for the union of the "single body" and the transformation of its members. Jesus insists that the bread be eaten so that people will have life— Christ-life. This communion of life between Christ and the Christian transforms the body. The Gospel is a call to live with his life. The one nourished becomes the nourisher. The receiver of Christ-life becomes the giver of Christ-life. This is the way in which the body contributes to the "life of the world." As the Christian community goes forth from the eucharistic celebration, they are the Eucharist for those they meet.

Believers need to make sense out of what happens at the "breaking of the bread" which they experience again and again. They come with their human hungers and participate in a communal action through which they are nourished by the living bread. Sharing the bread unifies them with others in the community. Together they are the body of Christ. They go forth with life and strength and power from eating and sharing the bread, to be as Jesus was in the world—compassionate, healing, life-giving.

Christians care for one another by babysitting, visiting one another in the hospital, consoling one another in time of death. Often they reach out to give life to a stranger. We need to grow more and more in awareness of our call and our responsibility to take steps to liberate the oppressed, to change evil societal structures, to feed the forty percent of the human race who go to bed hungry. We are, after all, the Body of Christ upon this earth. There is no other body of Christ.

Clare Wagner, O.P.

CYCLE B

1st Sunday of Advent

Cycle B

Is 63:16–17, 19; 64:2–7
1 Cor 1:3–9
Mk 13:33–37

Another Advent. Another Christmas. Somehow, after 2000 of them, it loses its "spectacularness." Even after 20 Christmases or 39 or 59 or 89, Christmas doesn't have the same impact it used to have. Aside from loss of belief in Santa, have we lost some other beliefs as well?

Perhaps we have, Isaiah suggests. "Why do you let us wander, O Lord, from your ways?" It's his fault that we're in the personal and global messes in which we find ourselves. God has hardened our hearts. Jesus has come and it hasn't made much difference in our lives or in our world. Along with losing belief in Santa, we've misplaced our trust in the goodness of God, and our faith that Jesus is the Messiah. No wonder Christmas means so little. We have kept the rituals, but lost the reason. Christmas is another empty celebration, like throwing an anniversary party for a couple who are no longer in love.

"Would that you might meet us doing right" we think wistfully with Isaiah. Somehow, in our busy everyday lives, the thoughts of "doing right," of "being mindful of God's ways" become wishful thinking, if we think those thoughts at all.

When Lent begins, we are signed with ashes and reminded of our origin and of our impending death. When Advent begins, perhaps we should be signed with clay and reminded that God is the potter. Advent should be a time of softening the clay, of gentling us—a time of allowing God to wedge us, to knead us until we are re-formed into the image of his Son. Christmas would be far more than tinsel and toys if we had all become new incarnations of God-with-us.

Clay is nothing without the potter. Unless he works it, molds it, has a vision of what it will become, it remains a formless mass. The potter can do nothing without the clay. His vision needs raw materials in order to become reality. We need God, that is clear; God needs us, Jesus made that clear in today's gospel story. We are "the servants in charge, each with his own task." The words spoken by Jesus are addressed to us, "Be constantly on the watch! Stay awake!"

Be constantly on watch for the potter's hand reaching to mold you; be sensitive to his touch. Stay awake so that you might be responsive to his desires. Trust the potter even when he destroys what you were in order to begin anew. It would be ludicrous for the clay to suggest that it knows better than the potter what it should be. Even servants who are left in charge do not re-write the Master's wishes. They have a sense of subordination to the larger vision. They are constantly on the watch, not because they fear that the Master will "catch" them, but because they are anxious to see him again, to let him take over. There is uncertainty in being left in charge. They are willing, but long for the total security of the Master's presence.

There you have it. Advent in a nutshell. We are lumps of clay who have been left in charge of the Master's work. We are, as it were, both clay and potter. Constantly being formed anew by God, we, humble clay though we are, are bidden by the Master to help form each other as well.

"I am" the lover says to the beloved, "putty in your hands." We are all molded by those who are significant in our lives. Friends strengthen us when our clay has grown thin; they reinforce the potter's design. Others try to shape us into something we're not, and we're "bent out of shape." Some use what we thought was a beautiful vase for an ashtray. Once in a while someone attacks us and punches holes through our design and we find that clay can bleed. There are those who, while left in charge, remember the Master's design and they speak his words to heal our sagging spots. Their gentle, strong touch is reminiscent of the Master's own. If we become too hardened, their breath relaxes our rigidity and we are moldable again.

So we have come to another Advent, and the season greets us with reminders. We are clay, God is the potter; we are in charge of building the kingdom here, but we are not the Master.

Whether it's our 20th or 39th or 59th or 89th Advent, we are still being formed and the potter's hands reach to shape us anew that we might become, not meaningless Christmas ornaments, but embodiments of the meaning of Christmas, vessels of the Spirit of Jesus.

Carole M. Eipers

2nd Sunday of Advent

Cycle B

Is 40:1–5, 9–11
2 Pt 3:8–14
Mk 1:1–8

When I was a child, my parents took my brother and me to an Easter egg hunt in a public park. They pointed out to us the boundaries we were to observe, and off we ran in search of eggs. I don't remember how far beyond the parameters we wandered, but I do remember turning to look for our parents and realizing that we had lost sight of them. I will never forget the terror of being lost, of trying to find our way back along the path we had come, of wandering and crying until a helpful adult led us to a policeman who helped us find our parents.

Most of us have probably had the experience at one time or another of being lost. We may have literally wandered in the woods, taken a wrong turn, lost our sense of direction, or we may have experienced a more figurative kind of disorientation in a difficult dilemma or personal crisis. God's chosen people shared this experience in their desert wandering and in the loneliness of exile in a foreign land. The experience of wilderness, desert, wandering is a universal one.

The word addressed to us in today's readings is the ancient word of consolation: there is a way out. God has always shown his people "a way"—out of the wilderness, the desert, the land of exile. Someone has always appeared to lead, to point out, to shout, to mark out or to *be* "the Way." The age-old message is: "Someone is coming. . . ."

When the Baptizer made his announcement in the wilderness, the people responded—perhaps out of curiosity, perhaps out of relief or anticipation, perhaps to hear more about this Someone who would soon come. But the word was not merely consoling; something was demanded of them. The prophet always speaks a word that requires more of us. The prophet's lone voice is heard; its message is haunting in its promise and its demand. But the promise and demand of the one who is announced, who *is* the Way, will be even greater.

Like the Jews at the Jordan, we sense that the consolation of Jesus' coming to us is only one facet of the way. We are somewhat apprehensive of this One who is to come, who comes again and again to summon us to change, repentance, new beginnings. But instinctively we sense that he is to be trusted—this Lord who comes to us sometimes in power, sometimes like the gentle shepherd. And we are told that where God leads, there is ultimately righteousness and peace.

Our own leading out may be out of personal crisis. Or perhaps we may be led into a more creative, purposeful direction in our lives. The way may be shown us to more responsible choices or more authentic service or to a deeper knowledge of our personal identity. The wilderness may be a situation beyond our own control or it may be of our own making, but we are drawn to the One who beckons.

While we must be cautious not to be too literal, the imagery of apocalypse in 2 Peter is especially striking to us in our age of nuclear awareness. We sense that our own cultural and societal "wildernesses" engender a special yearning for new heavens and a new earth as well as for peace and righteousness. We sense with a special urgency our need to follow where Jesus will lead us, despite the personal demands upon us. We deeply desire to experience the glory of God which is promised for all humanity to see.

The popular musical setting of Matthew's Gospel, *Godspell,* opens with the moving, distant voice of the prophet singing: "Prepare ye the way of the Lord." The attention of the audience is caught, perhaps by the haunting melody. Or, perhaps it is attracted by the ancient promise that resonates deeply within each of us: "Someone is coming . . . there is a way. . . ."

Joan R. DeMerchant

60

3rd Sunday of Advent

Cycle B

Is 61:1–2, 10–11
1 Thes 5:16–24
Jn 1:6–8, 19–28

The other night I caught a story on national news about the cordless telephone. I was alerted to it because Christmas '83 had found a friend of mine searching the stores for a cordless phone she could afford for her very active husband. Too expensive, was her sad verdict. She may have been spared a dud. Hidden on the base of such phones, since the government forces such disclosure, is the announcement that privacy is not guaranteed. That lack of privacy, anyone's ability to tune in on a cordless phone conversation even with an ordinary radio, was the focus of the news story.

Now it is Christmas. The downtown streets and shopping malls ring with familiar, joyful, yet hectic noises. If we had ears to hear we would be able to tune into a myriad of other sounds and conversations that fill the air waves. In today's reading, Paul instructs us Christians on how to fill the sound waves: rejoice always; never stop praying; constantly give thanks. Stop for a moment and reflect on the voices present but unheard in the room with you right now. If you had a radio you could tune some in. Would anyone be rejoicing, praying, thanking?

An impossible task Paul sets before us? Not at all. Paul continues his message with a prayer that God make us holy and whole; "He who calls us is trustworthy, therefore *he* will do it." In another letter, to the Romans, Paul tells us how *God* does the rejoicing, praying and thanking constantly. God pours out his Spirit in our hearts, a Spirit who continually cries, Abba, Father, a Spirit who joins our spirit. When we don't know how to pray, Paul continues, the Spirit speaks out of the depths of our hearts with unutterable groanings. Since prayer is such a hunger for us, and since our responsorial song, the *Magnificat*, promises that our God has given every good thing, let us focus on the Spirit and how the Spirit prays continually within us.

Our Gospel today is about John who baptizes with water; a few verses later in the narrative, John tells us that Jesus will baptize in the Holy Spirit. Jesus can baptize us because he himself was baptized in the Spirit. The early Church always applied the words of Isaiah to him: The Spirit of the Lord is upon me because the Lord has anointed me. To be baptized means, literally from the Greek, to be immersed in. When, in the Gospels, Jesus moves from his "hidden life" in Nazareth, arriving at the Jordan to be baptized, the Spirit comes upon him in a new birthing, a re-birth into a new and generative way of life. Throughout the Gospels then, we see Jesus immersed in the Spirit, driven by the Spirit, let by the Spirit, rejoicing in the Spirit, handing on the Spirit both in his death and in his resurrection. The Spirit is his life-link with his Father and his impetus to a life of mission and ministry.

We are baptized in the Holy Spirit. For some of us that has meant a new awakening in our adult years, a conscious surrender to the power of God at work in us. For all of us, however, the Spirit was poured out in our water baptism. We, like Jesus, were anointed as prayers and ministers in the power of the Spirit. Some of us may not have taken hold yet of the Christ who took hold of us (Phil 3) in our baptism. Now is the acceptable time!

We are immersed in the Spirit who continually prays, rejoices, thanks our Abba, whether we are conscious of the Spirit's prayer or not. When we take time to reflect, to pray, we are tuning into the Spirit's prayer from our very depths. There can be no such thing as a "bad" period of prayer because even if we are distracted or resistant, upset or sleepy, the Spirit prays within us when we do not even know how to pray. Stop a few minutes again and listen for the Spirit's prayer within you. Try to hear the Spirit's prayer in the others of your group, as the Spirit fills the sound waves with joy and gratitude, with groans and "Abba." The Spirit is our life-link with our God.

The Spirit also missions us to proclaim good news and freedom, to heal the broken-hearted, to announce the Lord's favor. The word that we proclaim is a healing, wholing and holy-making word. It is the Word Jesus who heals, makes holy and makes whole. "He who calls us is trustworthy, therefore *he* will do it." We who hunger for holiness and wholeness, for a life of prayer, for a life of intimacy with God can rejoice and be grateful, for "the hungry he has given every good thing."

Rea McDonnell

4th Sunday of Advent

Cycle B

2 Sm 7:1–5, 8–12, 14, 16
Rom 16:25–27
Lk 1:26–38

After astronauts left highly sensitive seismometers on the moon's surface, it was discovered that each month, as it comes closest to the earth, a faint shiver passes through the moon. No one knows exactly why this is so, or what it is within the moon that responds to the earth. It is an intriguing image, however. If the mere presence of one physical body to another can have this impact, what possibilities are there for the impact of God's presence in our lives?

Personal presence is a powerful reality to consider from almost any perspective. So much of who we are and who we can become is affected by our relationships to one another. Knowing this, attempts to ponder the personal presence of God seem almost beyond our imaginations. But today's readings give us some insight into what can happen when God touches the lives of human beings who are open to the divine presence. We realize that God's presence frequently reverses human expectations. What is asked of us—and done for us—can not only run counter to what is anticipated; it can go beyond our wildest dreams.

Following his many royal accomplishments, David decided to build a dwelling place for the Lord. The message communicated to him in response was that not only should he not build the house, but the Lord would instead be the builder! And the Lord, who claimed responsibility for David's numerous successes, would build a house made not merely of luxurious cedar. God's dwelling would be in David's descendants, in a future dynasty that would never end.

Later, Luke tells us, it becomes clear that God intended to dwell within the human race. Who would have expected the dwelling of the Most High to be within a young Jewish woman in the insignificant town of Nazareth (a town considered so lowly that it was despised by Jesus' contemporaries)? The "lasting throne" promised to David was to be—irony of ironies—in human flesh! We begin to see that nothing is a barrier to God's reversal of the anticipated: neither the plans of royalty, nor the hopes of generations of Jews, nor even, as we note in Elizabeth's unexpected pregnancy, the advanced age of a barren woman.

And so, we are confronted again with the question: what would it be like to really open ourselves to this presence in our lives? What surprises might God have in store for us? David's acquiescence to the prophet's communication enabled the fulfillment of the promise of a more durable and magnificent "dwelling" than even Solomon could build. So, too, with Mary's acceptance of a word that challenged her understanding of life's possibilities, empowering her to bear the Savior of the world, the promise of David.

What would God emplant in us if we lived open to the mystery of God's fruitful presence: What seed would be born of the divine initiative? What wild, undreamed-of possibilities could be actualized in us? What new life could be generated within us, our families, our communities, our world? As we await the celebration of the coming of God-with-us, we are reminded today that the presence of the Lord is no less real for us than it was for David or for Mary. It is the same mystery, as Paul writes to the Romans, given to us to bring to birth the miracle of new promises and new possibilities. It is the same lasting goodness of which the psalmist sings. All that is required of us is the same receptivity to this presence that is asked of all who suspect that there are no limitations to what God can—and will—do with us.

Joan R. DeMerchant

Christmas Day

Cycle B

Is 52:7–10
Heb 1:1–6
Jn 1:1–18

It is easy to idealize Christmas. Store windows and TV advertising give us plenty of assistance, offering images of gift giving, family reunions, and love around the fireplace. Everyone talks for weeks in advance about "the holidays."

The fact is, the Christmas season is a difficult one for many people. Family reunions resurrect old family problems. The loneliness of the already lonely is heightened by images which represent everyone else as together and happy. And the day-to-day struggle of living goes on right through Christmas.

There is a kind of wisdom in the classical Christmas stories from which we might learn a more realistic approach to the Christmas event. The Little Drummer Boy is a poor child, scratching his head to figure out what he can give the Christ child for Christmas. Amahl, in *Amahl and the Night Visitors,* is a crippled child living with his mother. Dickens's *Christmas Carol* portrays another poor family, the struggle to put a meal on the table, and a father who has to work on Christmas. O'Henry's *Gift of the Magi* is the story of a man and woman who love one another enough to sacrifice the most precious possession each has in order to give a gift to the other. The irony of the story is that the man sells his watch to give the woman a gold brooch for her beautiful hair, and she cuts off and sells her hair to buy him a gold chain for his watch.

In the situations described in these stories, we can see more of the shadow side of life, the limitations that beset us all, the struggle of existence. Yet each is a story of joy. In each story, new life is experienced right in the midst of difficulties, as people make the most of their situations, give and receive simple gifts and services of love, and find themselves mysteriously touched by God's graciousness.

The birth of Jesus is the earliest of these stories and the inspiration for the rest. The only reason the cave or stable in which Jesus is born seems idyllic is that we are not in it. Being warmed by animals is better than nothing, but it does not come up to central heating or even a modest campfire. Being the object of a deadly search by King Herod and his men hardly promotes feelings of security in this young family so far from home. Yet, without any of the difficulties removed, this is a basically happy scene. These people love one another, are grateful for what they have, and find their security in God rather than anything else.

The birth of Jesus does not immediately transform the face of the earth, but it is light in darkness, as John's prologue tells us. It is new life. It is God speaking to humankind in a Son. If the event is not the immediate transformation of the face of the earth, it is at least the seed of a transformation, a parable spoken to us in the midst of all the limitations, sufferings, and struggles of our lives. Real joy is possible in our world, but it does not usually come with the removal of all our problems. It comes in the midst of our problems, when in patience and hope, and with small gifts of love to one another, we allow God to give us an experience of new life. To be realistic about Christmas is not to expect some miracle that will suddenly change everything, but to know that when we change our attitudes and our actions in the spirit of Jesus, we will see the light dawn in our darkness.

Kathleen R. Fischer
Thomas N. Hart

Feast of the Holy Family

Cycle B

Sir 3:2–6, 12–14
Col 3:12–21
Lk 2:22–40

It seems strangely minimal to set aside only one day to focus on the family of Jesus. And it seems equally strange that we know so little about his family. The family is such a strong and universal human institution that we might expect to hear more about his family in Jesus' life. But his family, like most of ours, is the backdrop against which the whole of his life is played out. We can probably get the best sense of what Jesus' family was like by looking at the kind of life it generated in him.

There are a lot of opinions, of course, about the impact of families on individuals. On the one hand, we are told that much of who we are and what we do mirrors our family's genetic configuration and influence. At the same time, equally forceful voices advise parents to relax and remember that children are ultimately responsible for their own choices and actions. Most of us, however, probably approach our family lives together more out of instinct than out of an operative philosophy about family. We remember—consciously or unconsciously—our own experience of family and try our best to improve upon that for our own children and grandchildren, nieces and nephews.

However we suffer through or choose to live out our family lives, we know there is a power in this human bondedness that can destroy people or give them life. We hold up examples of the enlivening power that families can have. We talk about people we know who come from "really good families," or we respect families who stick together through tough situations. We have our own personal images of "ideal" families, or we may admire a single parent who has raised responsible children and maintained a sense of family wholeness. Most of us have a kind of nostalgia for family life as we would wish it to be and a special regard for family strength maintained despite adversity. Note, for example, the number of popular TV sitcoms that center on families in their growing variety of configurations.

We recognize, as well, that families can be destructive and that their destructive influence can linger over a lifetime. Most therapy and counseling strive to undo damage done in poor family relationships. We know that we can inflict the deepest pain on one another in families, whether that is done physically, verbally, or in the passive withholding of desperately needed love and respect. The power of evil that can envelop families or familial relationships is probably most dramatically expressed in such perverse bonds as the Charles Manson "family" of the 60s or the violent Mafia "families." We know, perhaps from personal experience, that people can use and abuse, manipulate and hurt one another, no matter how close they are.

At the heart of what we hold as Christians is the belief that in Jesus, God's redemptive power touches life "from the inside." And that reality includes our being together as family. Today we raise up our hope and conviction that this life-giving power can transcend our weakness, our pain, our mistakes and even our pathology as we struggle to dwell and grow together. We affirm that in our efforts to make our families a locus of strength and vitality, God is "on our side." Sometimes we're amazed at the hints of this gracious power in our families, as we observe one another develop against frequently insurmountable odds. We watch, for example, as people grow and mature in family configurations that bear no resemblance to those familiar to us. Or we know of families that battle to overcome patterns of abuse or struggle against illness or addictions or a variety of losses. We celebrate gratefully and humbly the healing of incredible hostilities or the bridging of lengthy separation of members absent from family circles for years. And often we suspect that an Other has enabled us to get peacefully and lovingly through another day or year together.

The burden is on us, of course, to "activate" this power. Today's readings tell us how we must regard and treat one another. Family bonding involves hefty measures of kindness and patience, of forgiveness and putting up with each other, of gratitude and love. We could add to Paul's list from our own experience of working at being family.

Finally, what we pursue in the intimate bonds of our personal families, we are challenged to duplicate in the larger families to which we all belong. All of us—even those of us who have no immediate families—are members of our parish family and of the family of God's people, the Church. And in the last and greatest circle of connectedness, we are members of the human family. Today we celebrate the enormous power unleashed in and through us which enables us to live together in strength and wisdom and grace.

Joan R. DeMerchant

Epiphany

Cycle B

Is 60:1–6
Eph 3:2–3, 5–6
Mt 2:1–12

Today we celebrate in a special way the epiphany, the manifestation or showing forth of the Lord to all peoples. This is a joyful feast because it reminds us of the faithful presence and love of our God for us. Our God is one whose presence overcomes all powers of sin, alienation, and disharmony among peoples.

In the first reading, the author provides us with a visionary poem spoken in praise of Jerusalem, which is seen as the "City of the Lord" (vs. 14c). We could also understand Jerusalem in this context as a symbol of the people Israel, those who have been covenanted by God, who are his chosen ones, his beloved. In verse 2, the image of "darkness covering the earth and thick clouds the people" reminds us of the covenant experience of Israel on Mt. Sinai, whereby God invited his people to enter into a special relationship with him (Exod 20:18, 21). Although Israel is not the greatest of nations, although the people periodically fail in their covenant relationship, still the Lord loves them and is always faithful. The vision provides the hope that Israel, because of the faithful presence of God, will eventually triumph. "Nations will walk by your light."

In the reading from Ephesians, the author proclaims that this visionary hope of Isaiah is now fulfilled in Jesus. Because of the Incarnation and the faith of the early proclaimers of the Good News, Jews and Gentiles are now invited to share in the fulfillment of the promise as the New Israel. No one is excluded from a share in the saving presence of God.

Matthew's gospel has sometimes been called the "Jewish Gospel" because of the author's concern to show Jesus as the fulfillment of God's promise to the people Israel. Toward the end of Chapter 1, Matthew has told us that Jesus is Emmanuel, that is, God-with-us. God, whose presence was manifested in the Old Testament in fire and clouds, in mighty winds and in gentle breezes, now manifests his presence in his Son Jesus, Emmanuel.

In our reading from Chapter 2, we see that Jesus is born in Bethlehem, the city of David, the proper birthplace for the new king of Israel. As in the vision of Isaias 60, all nations, symbolized by the astrologers, come because of the light they have seen (the star). His birth ushers in the final age—the time of the final and total manifestation of the presence of God.

Frequently, in reading or listening to this story, we get caught up in the details and forget the true meaning of the story. As "God-with-us," Jesus calls us to a new way of thinking and acting. Although Matthew says Jesus is of the kingly line of David, he certainly does not conform to the usual expectations of kingship. Indeed, he tends to turn upside down the usual expectations about kingship. He consistently refuses, elsewhere in the gospels, to accept the power and prestige, the wealth and deference usually associated with kingship. Our Emmanuel calls us to different values. Even in this story, the cross begins to appear. Jesus is a threat to Herod, who will soon set out to eliminate him. Strangers seem to recognize him before those who should have been more alert to his coming.

And so with us. Is Jesus truly Emmanuel for us? Where do we find God-with-us in our world? The Fathers of the Second Vatican Council reminded us that Jesus is present in many different ways. He is present in his word, the word of scripture which must be read and listened to with a realization that this is God speaking to us today. Jesus is present in the church, his body. He is present in each of us, as we share in his life. He is present in the sacraments, and in a special way in the Eucharist. He is present in all of creation, because since his Incarnation and Redemption, all of creation is being drawn into oneness with him.

Let us focus on one of those presences: his presence in us. Traditionally we have called this presence "grace." Grace is a share in God's own life. Through baptism we are incorporated into that divine life—we share in the very life of God. As some of the early Fathers of the Church have said: "God became man (human) so that man (humanity) might become God." What an awesome and wonderful reality! In a real sense, this feast of the Epiphany should be a time of great thankfulness for us. Not only do we celebrate the Incarnation and manifestation of Jesus, God-with-us, to all peoples, but we also celebrate his continued presence in each of us. We are the continued epiphany of Jesus in our world because we share in the very life of God. So let us rejoice for our God is with us. Let us nurture his presence within us and pray that his presence will be ever more manifested in our world.

Kathleen Flanagan, S.C.

Baptism of the Lord

Cycle B

Is 42:1–4, 6–7
Acts 10:34–38
Mt 3:13–17

The Jungian approach to this Sunday's Gospel means taking the figures of John the Baptist, the Spirit, and Jesus and asking how those figures live within each one of us. What in me is like the John the Baptist presented in this story? What in me is like the Spirit? What in me is like Jesus?

In reflecting on this I found these three figures to correspond to three moments in the conversion theory of Rosemary Haughton. In her classic, *The Transformation of Man,* she says that much of our time goes into "formation." We try to form ourselves into better people. That means doing many good actions. Perhaps we do all manner of loving and caring things for our family. Perhaps we join a society which helps the poor. We educate ourselves, we sacrifice for others, we pray. But they are all things we plan to do. "Transformation," the creating of ourselves anew, the "taking off the old self and putting on Christ," is not something we can plan. Transformation, a radical change in being, a radical vulnerability to grace, can only happen when life falls apart, when formation is shattered, when we don't feel as though we possess the answers. When life falls apart, we have the possibility to become new in Christ. Transformation, however, does not automatically happen because of a life crisis. Life can fall apart and it can simply make us bitter. Transformation can occur if we look back at the crisis (this cannot happen during the crisis) and we see grace. We see a new direction, a new possibility of relationship beyond ourselves. Oftentimes the language which gives us the ability to recognize grace comes from the previous formation. Transformation is not a once in a lifetime event. We are often forming ourselves and then being transformed.

Let's apply the thought of Haughton and Jung to today's Gospel. John the Baptist is the formation time of my life. Remember, John does many things to make himself a better person. He leads an ascetical life. He fasts. He prays. But ultimately he knows someone else outside of his lifestyle will save him. What within me is like John? What do I do to "form myself" as a better person? In that formation, am I, like John, waiting and willing to hear truth from another?

Our Gospel story gives us a "crisis event." We hear that the heavens are torn apart and the Spirit descends. When have "the heavens" of my life been torn apart? When have I been confused, doubting everything about my life? When has my life been dark and my soul vulnerable?

Finally, our Gospel has the transformed, the person converted totally to God and to others—Jesus. What in me is like Jesus, like one who relates to God not as an abstract power to be avoided or used, but as Father, as a person calling me?

To help your congregation reflect on this process within themselves, perhaps this story could serve as an example. Elizabeth Christman in her novel *Ruined for Life,* tells the story of a young woman, Neal Connor, who lives a year as a volunteer worker in a poor ghetto. She goes there with a good Catholic education and with a real desire to help people. Her education, her loving family, her willingness to reach out to others is her formation. In her year as a volunteer she does much for those she serves, but as a character, her personality is very consistent with what she was when she first volunteered. She is someone with a generous heart but sees the poor as unfortunates whom she does things for. However, one day she is viciously and brutally attacked by someone she thought she had helped. Everything she thought she valued and stood for fell apart. But after the event, as she got in touch with the Spirit working within her, she recognized herself as one with the poor. She shared their sense of powerlessness. She could see from their point of view. Yet she only recognized the grace contained within the crisis because of the "language" of her formation.

Let's pray for the internal discipline to form ourselves into better people as John does. And let's pray that the moments of crisis in our lives will transform us into a people open to the Spirit of Jesus.

Douglas Fisher

2nd Sunday in Ordinary Time

Cycle B

1 Sm 3:3–10, 19
1 Cor 6:13–15, 17–20
Jn 1:35–42

In this brief (two paragraph) selection from John's Gospel, we have the words "look" and "see" six times. "Seeing" is important throughout John's Gospel. But he does not always mean the same thing when he uses that word and neither do we. Let's "look" at three possible meanings of "see" and then make some connections to the journey of faith.

Two different types of "seeing" go on every time my wife and I watch a baseball game. I am a fan of the "avid" variety, while my wife goes to games because of my interest. When she looks out on the field, she sees the fielders, batter, runners on base, someone warming up in the bullpen. What I see is a double steal possibility with runners on first and third or a possible squeeze play because the hitter on deck is a lefty and the pitcher warming up is lefty so the team at bat wants to get a run in any way they can to avoid having their lefty hitter face the lefty in the bullpen. I see the right fielder playing shallow, so I know there will be a play at third if the runner on first tries to go to third on a single. My wife and I are seeing the same game but we are seeing in entirely different ways.

Now let's turn to today's Gospel. The two disciples of John see Jesus but respond in a rather impersonal way. "Where do you live?" They have Jesus in front of them and all they want to know is his address. It is like looking at a baseball game in which the bases are loaded and the score tied and saying "Where does the third baseman live in the off-season?" John, however, sees in an entirely different way. He "stares hard" at Jesus and sees who Jesus really is: "Look, there is the Lamb of God." He gives a title to Jesus which shows that John sees not only a man before him but the meaning of that man.

Reality can be that way for us. We can just see what goes on around us: the laughing, the crying, the loving, the dying and on and on. Or we can see what it all points to. We can see God at work, not in a far off place, but right here among us. Elizabeth Barrett

Browning gives us an example of this second type of seeing:

Earth's crammed with heaven,
And every common bush afire with God;
But only he who sees, takes off his shoes. . . .

There are still more depths to what looking and seeing can mean. Looking can go beyond mere observation and it can go beyond intuiting meaning. Looking can mean involvement with another—it can mean a relationship. When Jesus saw Simon, he "looked hard at him and said, 'You are Simon son of John; you are to be called Cephas.'" When Jesus sees people he enters their lives. He calls Simon by name and he changes his name. Jesus is so involved with the person that the person is changed. Jesus' looks are commitments to people.

It is this last way of seeing which is ultimately saving. In the play "Equus," a psychologist discovers that he needs to see more than his patients: "I need—more desperately than my children need me—a way of seeing in the dark." In religious terms we would say that he needs a relationship with Jesus which is a light in the darkness. We need a companion for a journey in darkness, and our faith gives us that companion in Christ. Looking at Jesus, on the deepest level, means a union with him.

Bringing this homily full-cycle, let's go back to the disciples of John. Their initial seeing produces the impersonal "Where do you live?" But Jesus takes this superficial sight and brings them further than they ever intended to go. Diarmuid McGann points this out in his book *Journeying in Transcendence: A Jungian Perspective on the Gospel of John:* "They want to know where he lives, a rather impersonal response. He invites them to vision, enlightenment. The invitation leads to staying with him and that leads to seeing and the seeing gives way to witnessing and following."

No matter what kind of seeing we are doing now, we have a God who is beckoning, calling us to look deeper and deeper, until we look so deep that we can exchange glances of love with the Lord.

Douglas Fisher

3rd Sunday in Ordinary Time

Cycle B

Jon 3:1–5, 10
1 Cor 7:29–31
Mk 1:14–20

The Gospel story of Jesus walking along by the Sea of Galilee is a story of leaving and following. Simon and Andrew leave their jobs and follow Jesus. James and John leave their father Zebedee and follow Jesus. These appear to be "once and for all" moments if we just look at today's Gospel. But when we put this story in the context of the entire Gospel we know that Simon and Andrew fished again. We can presume that James and John remained loving sons to Zebedee. In like manner, are there times when we are called to "leave" in order to follow Christ?

Simon and Andrew leave their occupation—fishing—to follow Jesus. Are there times when we are called to leave our occupations to follow Christ? This could be a "once and for all" leaving, as people have done who worked in factories which make nuclear weapons, or others who have left jobs which involve products harmful to society. But are there other times when we stay in our job but step back from it to follow Christ? For example, it could be that a person has a job he/she loves and he/she is making great career strides within the company. But suppose in that company some employees are being treated unjustly. Perhaps they are underpaid or treated shabbily. If we take today's Gospel seriously, that person should "leave and follow Jesus" not by quitting the company but by addressing the injustice. This might be unpopular and risky. It might mean leaving the success track. But it might be a modern day invitation to follow Jesus. I know a priest who was on the clerical success track. He was obviously "going places" in terms of power within the diocese. But he also recognized great injustice in the way our Church refuses to empower women. He remains a priest, but "left and followed Jesus" in terms of speaking out on this matter. He no longer makes great strides in terms of career but he takes the Gospel to heart.

James and John leave a relationship to follow Jesus. We can apply this to our lives by asking, "Are there times when we must confront a loved one with truth?" An example is a person (John) I know who had a friend (Tom) who obviously was drinking too much. They were good friends who shared many good times. John knew that if he confronted Tom about the drinking, Tom would be furious. Their good times might end because Tom might never want to associate with him. But John had the courage to "leave and follow." He stepped beyond the usual limits of their friendship which included silence about Tom's drinking. And Tom was furious. John's risk paid off, however, when Tom eventually sought help. That could be a modern day application of James and John leaving their normal relationship with their father to follow Jesus. Does your commitment to Jesus, which involves a commitment to love and truth, mean a change in a relationship to another?

Another "leaving and following" occurs in the Gospel in the first paragraph when Jesus says, "The kingdom of God is close at hand. Repent, and believe the good news." Jesus is asking us to leave the ways of sin and live in the ways of the kingdom. Are there any sinful ways we are tied to which Jesus is inviting us to leave? In our own hearts we can examine things we do which are sinful which Jesus asks us to end. We can ask that same question on the societal level. Many of us believe that the nuclear arms race is sinful. But day after day we create more and more weapons of destruction for "security." Perhaps we can "leave and follow" by taking part in the political system to end the arms madness and attempt to live by the ethics of the kingdom, the peace of God.

"Leaving and following" Jesus means a life commitment, but that commitment is lived out in the small "leaving and following" which is offered to us in practical, everyday circumstances. Let's pray for the courage of Simon, Andrew, James and John. And let's pray that whenever we are called to leave something, it is only to go "after Jesus."

Douglas Fisher

4th Sunday in Ordinary Time

Cycle B

Dt 18:15–20
1 Cor 7:32–35
Mk 1:21–28

The responsorial refrain accompanying Psalm 95 in today's Eucharist may also be used to begin a community's celebration of the liturgy of the hours either in the reflective reading hour or in the celebration of morning prayer. The latter liturgy refers to this refrain and Psalm 95 as "the invitatory." This response to Deuteronomy 18 retains its connectedness with the liturgy of the hours as an invitation: "If today you hear his voice, harden not your hearts." The psalm invites this assembly back to its origins. These are desert origins; these origins are not always inviting in the ways media hypes invite people. The psalm harkens this Church back to God's invitation. The divine invitation leads a godly people away from consumer allurements and the hostilities of evil.

Like the fisherman in Seamus Heaney's poem, "Casualty," Christians can find themselves "swimming towards the lure of warm lit-up places, the blurred mesh and murmur drifting among glasses in the gregarious smoke." This does not seem to be what we, as Church, are called to. If today you hear God's voice, harden not your hearts. Hear instead the harkening to prophetic life. The vocation to be prophet is a charism, a gift from God to help fashion charity and God's reign.

The prophetic call came to Moses, the one who is murderer and desert leader, the one who encounters God on mountaintop, the one who tries to escape the call and the one who is lionized in Deuteronomy as divine mouthpiece for the second law. The prophetic call came to Jesus, the good news of God, the one who called to conversion of mentality and mores so that he might establish God's reign through a brutal cross death. The prophetic call came to the disciples of Jesus so that Christ's Church might be *sacramentum et exemplum*, sign and example (St. Augustine), so that Christian disciples might avoid *accedia*, the dangerously stale, worn-out blahs feared by desert-dwelling and medieval Christians.

The prophetic call may be a compelling urgency for some Christians who respond by lifelong, liminal life style for peace and justice, veracity and simplicity. But is it not a quality the entire local assembly is called to figure into its fabric?

What is this prophetic call for us as Church? Deuteronomy indicates that the call engages people so that divine truth may be conveyed. This occurs less through abstract truth and more through the witness of prophets to be interceding, suffering with and dying for the community. The call works its way into the personal commitments and undivided hearts of those who discern rightly and experientially.

The call enables married and single, celibate and family people to keep balance, to remain free from existential and eschatological worry and fear. A prophetic Church keeps some balance. On the one hand, it does not become totally absorbed in egocentric self-absorption and concern with status pecking order. On the other hand, it does not succumb to a fanatical asceticism in which some are better than others. A prophetic community respects all members and devotes its energies to the Lord and God's reign.

Lastly a prophetic Church listens to its wounds, the carping redolent of Massah and the hurts echoed at Meribah. Its teaching is humble and gentle because its authority and power come from the deepest wrestling one can engage in—how to recognize the reign of God in the crucified One and the cross-bearers in its midst.

Why do we, as Church, heed the call inviting all members to be somehow prophetic?

What is at stake is God's reign, God's co-creating with Church in order to knit creatures of all cultures and their cosmos into a planet worthy to be mirrors of God and destined to be a homeland whose sod and soil are rich for salvation. Today's Gospel shows a Jesus recognized by the powers of darkness. The demonic spirit shrieks that it knows who Jesus is, the Holy One of God. A prophetic Church tries to turn that around. It tries to be a mouthpiece for Christ's identity to be known and loved. It works to muzzle and shut up the loud shrieking of creatures and cosmic creation. It does this by proclaiming not the fanatic amazement that comes with cures but the prophetic witness of the great prophet, Jesus, the crucified Son of God who is Lord and Messiah. It shows gentleness, a crucified Jesus and deep feeling instead of overpowering, arrogant conquering and muzzling of the spirit of prophets.

John O'Brien

5th Sunday in Ordinary Time

Cycle B

Jb 7:1–4, 6–7
1 Cor 9:16–19, 22–23
Mk 1:29–39

"You can't eat the orange and throw the peel away—a man is not a piece of fruit!" These words of Willy Loman in *Death of a Salesman* are a modern counterpart to the words of Job we hear today. Economic ruin and poverty bring Job's contemporaries disillusionment and anguish. The experience of human suffering is poignantly personal. Being without funding and health still brings people to ask if God is punishing them, or if the dreams of life are vacuous!

One cannot but wonder about the global suffering—the acid rain, the threat of nuclear harm, the famines, seas rife with what nations discard. In Miller's play, Charley says this of Willy: "Nobody dast blame this man. A salesman is got to dream, boy. It comes with the territory."

Our post-holocaust world dreams up various antes. Elie Wiesel's pen plays out three possibilities. The first is that of courageous speaking out. In *Zalmen, or the Madness of God*, the rabbi speaks: "We proclaim ourselves free from false promises, from vows taken under duress. . . . And I say and I proclaim to any who will listen that the Torah here is in peril and the spirit of a whole people is being crushed. . . . And all the sufferings . . . for nothing." The second is that of divine deception. In *The Trial of God*, three rabbis indict God for allowing God's children to suffer the fate of a pogrom. The Jewish community turns to Sam, one they judge to be a tzaddik, a Just, someone who can intercede on their behalf. "You are God's only defender, you have rights and privileges: use them! O holy man, we beg you to save God's children further shame and suffering." But Sam is Satan and has deceived the community. He says: "So—you took me for a saint, a Just? Me? How could you be that blind? How could you be that stupid? If you only knew. . . ." Finally, in *Ani Maamin, a song lost and found again* (Ani Maamin means "I believe"), God sheds tears when observing the suffering of his creation and people.

Job speaks out his own misery, his troubled night, his days being swifter than a weaver's shuttle. Suffering seems to leave him without hope. No platitudes can assuage his anguish. What can be made of ancient and modern suffering, anguish and illness? Christians can speak courageously and protest. Christians can be brought to deception and disillusionment. Christians can put faith in a crying God who is touched by human plight and who cares. Human lament, a threnody still played out on the melancholic strings of the violin, can be met by divine tears, God's right feeling.

God's authentic feeling seems to be writ large in Jesus as he is depicted in this summary section of Mark's Gospel. This Jesus, of divine origin, engages the demonic. He cures Simon's mother-in-law by laying hands on her and raising her up. The fever breaks. Out of brokenness comes wellness. She is raised up and begins to serve. Mark reports that all brought their ill to him as well as those under demonic influence. But Jesus is not deceived, blind or stupid! He enters into a lonely place to be absorbed in prayer. Through his solitary bonding with God Jesus preserves right feeling; he retains his right identity. He is able to move on to proclaim that oppression, illness and senseless suffering are not victors. He, the good news, one coming to announce the reign of God, is the gradual unveiling of God's answer to Job's pleas and plaint.

We can see a pattern in this short episode. Jesus engages Simon's mother-in-law. His response is compassionate healing. Her response is to serve. This triggers regional response throughout Galilee. In turn, this enables the Christian community of Mark to act in similar fashion; trust in the crucified Son of God enables a Markan Church to proclaim good news and to heal.

The call for us is similar as we live out our Christian vocation in this time. We gather to pray, to hear this word for our personal, group and global troubles. Jesus' word compassionately heals and raises us up. We then serve by offering praise and thanks for the mighty works of God done in our midst, especially for the sick and disabled. But our prayer keeps us genuine; we do not gloat over our boon fortune as we ignore the bane plight of others. Through our attention to the sick and disabled, our anointing and pastoral care for the ill, our advocacy for those whose voices are unheard or whose sounds have been stilled, our action for justice and peace, in various ways each Christian and the whole assembly extends good news and broadens the horizons of God's reign.

John O'Brien

6th Sunday in Ordinary Time

Cycle B

Lv 13:1–2, 44–46
1 Cor 10:31–11:1
Mk 1:40–45

Today's readings center on the theme of outreach to the outcast. The selection from the Book of Leviticus describes the experience of the outcast himself. He must live alone, cut off from the life of the community, without hope. The lot of the outcast is loneliness and separation from the human supports which make life bearable. In the passage from Paul's letter to the Corinthians Paul concerns himself with our attitude toward those who are different from us. We are not to seek our own advantage; rather, we should make the well-being of others our concern. This is the way to imitate Jesus. The reading from Mark sets this example of Jesus before us even more forcefully. Jesus is moved with pity by the plight of the leper; he reaches out with a healing touch to those rejected by society. This theme of outreach to the outcast prompts reflection on two questions: 1) What is my attitude toward those considered outcasts in our society? 2) How do I myself share in the experience of being an outcast, and so stand in need of Jesus' healing touch?

In the accounts from Leviticus and Mark, the leper is the primary example of those who fail to measure up to a society's standards of beauty and wholeness. The leper represents the person we set apart or cut off in any way because we consider him or her flawed. In order to hear the message of these readings we must be concrete about who the lepers are in our own lives. The contemporary leper may be the one who is homely, fat, mentally ill, or an alcoholic; she may be the teenager who becomes pregnant before marriage, the homosexual, or the hippie; the leper may be the black sheep in the family who is seen as a failure by the rest of its members, or the person of a different racial or ethnic background who moves into a neighborhood. Who are the modern lepers we cut off from our support and acceptance?

Once we recognize who the outcasts are in our lives, we are ready to hear Jesus challenge us to reach out to these people. Jesus' cure of the leper in this passage from Mark is not an isolated incident. Jesus makes it clear that he has come to save just such people. He heals ten lepers (Luke 17:11–19) and eats at table with sinners and tax collectors (Luke 19:1–10). In the parable of the lost sheep Jesus tells us that God's mercy is like that of a shepherd who would leave ninety-nine sheep in the wilderness to search for one stray sheep (Luke 15:4–7). The lost sheep, like the leper, is a symbol of one who is cut off from the community, alone and without resources until someone reaches out to it. The good news is that Jesus came to bring salvation to such outcasts.

We are meant to imitate Jesus in this outreach. When we give a party, he says, we are to invite the poor, the crippled, the lame and the blind (Luke 14). In other words, Christians are to bring Christ's love and healing to those whom society has rejected. Our standard of acceptance is not society's criterion of beauty and wholeness; it is Jesus' concern for the poor and needy. Jesus' judgment does not follow society's standards; rather, it is directed against those who, considering themselves virtuous and saved, look down on others.

Sometimes the person we throw away and reject is ourselves. Outreach to the outcast, then, means willingness to hear Jesus' healing words as directed to ourselves or that part of ourselves which we find hard to accept. The leper in us may be some past action which we cannot forgive or forget. It may be a physical feature or a limitation in energy, knowledge, or skill that we must accept. Perhaps it is our failure to measure up to the Christian ideal, to love and forgive others. When I am willing to acknowledge the outcast in myself and open that part of me to Jesus' healing, I will begin to understand the meaning of his saying that he has not come to call the just, but sinners. Then I will also be ready to reach out to all other outcasts with the same love and acceptance Christ offers me.

Kathleen R. Fischer
Thomas N. Hart

7th Sunday in Ordinary Time

Cycle B

Is 43:18–19, 21–22, 24–25
2 Cor 1:18–22
Mk 2:1–12

" . . . we address our Amen to God when we worship together."

The literal meaning of the word *Amen* is "It is firm." As it is used by Paul in today's second reading, it is an affirmation of faith, a faith which brings the Christian community together to worship, to celebrate as a community of believers.

All of the scripture used in today's Eucharistic Liturgy speak to us about faith; the faith necessary to accept the directions of Isaiah—to forget the things of the past and to embark upon something new—and the faith necessary to believe in the power of the Lord as illustrated in Mark's gospel.

Because the word faith is a common one, especially to members of the Christian community, it is a word which rarely stimulates reflection. Faith is something we seem to take for granted and something for which we seem to take credit ourselves.

Faith is a gift, a gift of the power of God himself, a gift which is neither acquired nor earned. Faith is a gift freely given and one which must be freely received. Our response to that gift of faith is one of co-operation. However possessive we are about our faith, we must acknowledge that it is because of God that we are privileged to possess it.

But faith is a gift which, like the seeds sown by the sower in the gospel parable, can grow only if we seek to nurture it, if we seek to deepen our understanding of it and if we seek to generate it to others.

On a very basic level, any of us who have ever planted a flower or vegetable seed are aware of the nurturing, understanding, and generating process.

Human persons by their very nature seek growth on all levels—economic, social, intellectual, emotional, and political. This fact we accept as a normal and fundamental part of living. However, many members of the Christian community, although striving to grow on the levels which were mentioned, do not strive to grow spiritually or religiously. Often Christians are quite content to possess an understanding of our faith which is adolescent, at best, and frequently juvenile.

"I had eight years of Catholic School," or "I went to a Catholic high school," or "I had to take a theology course in college." These responses are common and, more often than not, imply that "I know all I need to know" and "I believe in God and in Jesus, therefore why do I have to learn anything more?"

In our complex democratic society would any of us be content, or even survive, if all we knew about our government and our politics was what we were taught in a junior high school civics course?

In any of our fields of work, would any of us be content, or even survive, if all we knew about our job were the basic instructions given to us when we completed initial training?

In the routine operation of a household, would any of us be content, or even survive, if all we knew about operating a home was what we knew when we first started on our own?

To any of these questions, the answer would be an immediate no. Why then do we assume contentment, or survival, in things spiritual or religious when we have not actively sought a deeper and more complete understanding of our faith?

Isaiah points our minds and our hearts in a future direction. Mark tells us that through the physical sign of healing the people came to believe, and Paul tells us that our Amen is a firm commitment, initiated by God who has placed his Spirit in our hearts.

In each of these examples we are confronted with a dynamic situation, not a stagnant one. Each of these examples challenges us to grow to nurture, to understand and to generate so that through him we may more fully address our Amen to God when we worship together.

James P. McGinnis

11th Sunday in Ordinary Time

Cycle B

Ez 17:22–24
2 Cor 5:6–10
Mk 4:26–34

Today's readings are incredible! Our experience of nature makes the words of God from Ezekiel seem ludicrous. God takes a tender shoot from the top of the cedar tree, sticks it on a high mountain, and it thrives. If I tried that, I'd end up with a dead twig stuck in the ground. God goes on to say he will bring low the high tree. I can trim branches off, but I can't guarantee the tree will live. I could also wither up the green tree; in fact I've done that, but I have found it beyond my power to lift high the little trees or to make withered trees bloom.

The Gospel reading plays havoc with nature's laws as well. What farmer would not love to have Jesus' story come true? "A man scatters seed on the ground. He goes to bed and gets up day after day. Through it all the seed sprouts and grows without his knowing how it happens." Next thing he knows, it's harvest time. No fertilizer, no pest control, no weeding, he just scatters the seeds and reaps the harvest. It's a farmer's dream, but far from the reality of producing a good yield.

Then Jesus turns nature upside down one more time. The mustard seed does not produce the largest of shrubs. It's product is small and rather frail, hardly big enough or secure enough for the birds of the air to nest in.

After reading Ezekiel and Mark I want to shout. "Things just don't happen that way! I have planted seeds and I know the care it takes to make them grow. I have lavishly nurtured withering plants and saw them die in spite of it. Who are you trying to kid, prophet? Do you think we're that gullible, Jesus? What's the point?"

The point of God's promises and Jesus' parables is that, first of all, they are both known to exaggerate. They do not exaggerate in the sense that braggarts exaggerate to inflate their images, not as dishonest people exaggerate in order to manipulate others. The kind of exaggerating God does is the sort we do when we are in love. Words are inadequate to express what we feel, what we hope, what we promise, and yet we use them anyway. We promise the "moon and stars," we speak "forevers" in our effort to expand language to fit the depth of our experience. And God, greatest lover of all, limits himself to human expression and hopes that in the prophet's hyperboles we recognize and come to believe in his love and his promises which cannot be contained in ordinary speech.

Jesus' parables are the exaggerations of enthusiasm born of commitment to the Father's Kingdom. When we commit ourselves to an organization or to an ideal, we are prone to exaggerate too. We see, in our first fervor, not just the group or the cause, but the potential for working together, for accomplishing a goal. Jesus gives us the story of the sower scattering seed and the mustard seed, not as a con-man aiming to have us invest in something worthless, but as a loving brother eager to share his vision and to set exploding in our minds the infinite possibilities he sees for us to make our world a better place.

Ezekiel's prophecy and Jesus' parables remind us that God's love and promises and the promises of the Kingdom are too marvelous to be contained in words. They also remind us that the Kingdom of God does not always follow the laws of nature, nor those of society, nor even the pattern of our everyday experience. Jesus' teachings were constantly upsetting common beliefs and practices, and those who live the values of the Kingdom surprise us by being gentle in the face of violence, generous in the midst of a greedy world. They, like the mustard seed in Jesus' parable, don't act the way we would expect them to.

What is the greater miracle, to see a cedar shoot stuck on a mountainside grown into a great tree, or to see a person forgive rather than strike back? What is more wonderful, to see a withered tree bloom again, or to see a withered person come back to life because someone has loved and healed him? What is more outrageously magnificent, to see a mustard seed grow to house the birds of the air, or to see a family grow in love to accept unwanted children into their home? When we witness love in action, when we experience the reality of God's Kingdom among us, then today's readings seem understated rather than exaggerated.

Paul gives us the clue to understanding all of today's readings when he says "We walk by faith, not by sight." The readings are incredible only if we have not been building the Kingdom. They are incredible only if we have failed to trust God's promises enough to close our eyes and dream the dream of our brother, Jesus.

Carole M. Eipers

12th Sunday in Ordinary Time

Cycle B

Jb 38:8–11
2 Cor 5:14–17
Mk 4:35–41

A leading financial concern has run a television commercial promising "clout" to those who possess its plastic money credit card. Another promises that even if you are not recognized, doors will open and acceptance will be yours if you just own their card. Still others promise you instant happiness with the buy now-pay later approach to life.

Credit cards and economic clout have become the major symbol through which we validate our existence and gauge our happiness. We have come to equate *who* we are with *what* we possess. Psychologist Erich Fromm asks a rather disturbing question: "If I am what I have, but what I have is taken from me, what then am I?" The answer is all too obvious: nothing. The meaning of existence and the dignity of each person comes to be defined in terms of dollars and cents.

Is it any wonder that the discontent of so many in the land is no longer quiet but quite vocal? Are we still surprised by the groanings of so many concerning the emptiness of earthly bread? The head of the corporation or the average businessman struggles to "make it." Yet very often such "making it" demands our ultimate concern. Our friends and family have become strangers. We lack a spiritual center.

What are we to do? We can't tear down General Motors, give up our jobs, or empty our bank accounts. That would be irresponsible. Our readings offer some insights into our pressing individual and communal plight.

St. Paul in his second letter to the Corinthians reminds them of the need for a proper *vision* or *focus* for their lives. The energy, talent, and zeal of Saul would now be used by Yahweh-Jesus to build up the Body of Christ. Paul's eyes were open to the immense treasure of God's love poured out in Jesus. The love of God is the treasure hidden in earthen vessels. The same Spirit which raised Jesus is at work in us.

What specifically does this mean for our growth in Christ? It means quite simply and radically that we are to become other Christs. The same Spirit which animated Jesus' ministry motivates our Christian vocation through baptism. We are free and liberated to die to self-centeredness and self-preoccupation so we can be for others. We begin to live a new life. It is not so much that happiness is found in grasping and controlling, but rather that we have been grasped and lured by the love of God. The gift of the Spirit is not something we earn as much as something we learn to accept. This allows us to accept ourselves and others. We have nothing to prove or compulsively seek after.

This new vision and new existence brings happiness and the *new creation*. Jesus is the New Being through whom *all* creation has hope of new life. Jesus as the New Being reveals what true human existence is all about: a loving relationship with Yahweh as Father. Secondly, Jesus is the person for others. In both movements of love, vertical and horizontal, we are challenged to extend ourselves and grow in the Spirit. This is not easy and much pain is involved. We have to relinquish old values, routines, agendas and securities. We have to make room for others and let Jesus be the center. The need to make room and let go of the well-traveled path always causes anxiety. Yet very often it is only in looking back that we realize how much we have grown in our pilgrim faith. We look back not to pause and admire the view but to get a healthy sense of the work of the Spirit and the encouragement and hope for tomorrow. This talk of the new creation and new being by no means excludes suffering, sin, and the cross.

The book of Job is one of the most eloquent encounters with the shadow side of reality—evil. We know well the war within us over wanting to do the good, yet the weakness of our spirit. We read each day how much the old world and sinful selves and structures hold sway. The new creation is in the making, so we must continue to endure the tensions and sufferings of the present until it comes to perfection. Out of the whirlwind of our daily lives we seek to listen to and experience the power of God's care.

In the Gospel of Mark, Jesus announces the kingdom and confronts the mystery of evil in its individual, social and cosmic forms. Jesus preaches the good news and heals the sick, challenges those in power to repent and reminds the cosmic forces that they are under the hand of Yahweh. Jesus does all this not to put on a show but to challenge his audience to faith. In these words and works those who would come after him are challenged to see the hand of God. There will be opposition and even death but the kingdom will triumph because God is faithful and keeps his promises.

William F. Maestri

13th Sunday in Ordinary Time

Cycle B

Wis 1:13–15; 2:23–24
2 Cor 8:7, 9, 13–15
Mk 5:21–43

These readings invite us to reflect on one of the deepest mysteries of human existence, the problem of evil. Evil touches our lives in many forms. The readings mention some of these: disease, poverty, pain, and especially, death. The widespread experience of evil raises two questions for us: (1) Where does evil come from? and (2) What can we do about it? Let us see what light today's Scripture brings to these two related issues.

The reading from Wisdom makes it clear that pain, suffering, and death are not God's creation. God wants us to be whole and happy. This is captured well in Jesus' words to Jairus' daughter: "get well and live," as well as in the statement which summarizes his whole purpose: "I have come that they may have life, and have it more abundantly" (John 10). God's gift to us is life. But along with life he has also given us freedom. We are free to love or to hate. Here lies the source of evil in the world. It comes from the misuse of human freedom. Paul's letter to the Corinthians spells this out concretely. When we have more than we need, while disregarding the needs of others, we are deepening the power of evil in the world. So the poverty and hunger we see around us have human causes. They result from sin.

Our answer to this first question, "Where does evil come from?" already suggests a partial solution to the problem. We are called to establish justice in the world. Our first response to evil in life should be to eliminate its existence wherever possible. Paul suggests one way. If communities learn to share with one another from their abundance, no one will have to go without. In proposing this kind of mutual sharing, Paul is not asking us to make heroic sacrifices. He asks only that we follow Jesus' example by responding to those who are in need.

There are other ways to struggle against evil besides that which Paul describes. We heal the pain of loneliness by reaching out to others in friendship. We unburden the discouraged by offering them our support. We heal the suffering of the handicapped by providing jobs for them. When we try to eliminate the prejudice that keeps people from equal opportunities, search for new cures for disease, or form networks to promote world peace, we are sharing in Jesus' work of conquering the evil in life.

However, all of our best efforts cannot touch the evil which we fear most. Our own death and the death of those we love remain the greatest manifestations of the mystery of evil in our lives. Here the story of Jesus' raising of Jairus' daughter takes us to a deeper level of reflection. If we had only our own human resources in the fight against evil, we might soon despair. But in Mark's account we are reminded again of the power of Jesus to heal and overcome death. We share in this power through faith. If we believe in Jesus, even death loses some of its force in our lives. We fear death most because it brings an end to all that we are and have hoped for. It destroys all that we have built individually and as a people. Faith in Jesus assures us that death is not the end. Our attempts to establish justice and conquer evil are transformed and completed in Christ's power.

Kathleen Fischer
Thomas N. Hart

14th Sunday in Ordinary Time

Cycle B

Ez 2:2–5
2 Cor 12:7–10
Mk 6:1–6

"Before I begin I would just like to say that I hope that I will be able to confide in you completely, as I have never been able to do in anyone before, and I hope that you will be a great support and comfort to me."

These words were written by Anne Frank, the young Jewish girl who, with seven other people, was literally forced into hiding for two years during the Nazi occupation of Holland. Anne's description of how they lived in a two-room dwelling in constant fear and isolation, imprisoned not only by the terrible outward circumstances of war, but also inwardly by themselves, made me intimately and shockingly aware of what I believe to be one of the world's greatest evils: any attempt to imprison and silence the beauty and uniqueness of the human spirit.

And yet, at the same time, Anne also made poignantly clear to me the ultimate strength of the spirit because she never gave up! For, despite the fact that she was totally isolated, her hope and need to be heard and understood found its expression in a young girl's diary.

It seems to me that we are a lot like Anne in her need. Aren't we all in need of someone to understand us—someone to love us simply for who we are? Someone who, George Elliot says, "can give us the inexpressible comfort of feeling safe with them—having neither to weigh our thoughts or words, but pouring them all right out, just as they are, chaff and grain together, certain that a faithful and friendly hand will take and sift them, keeping what is worth keeping, and with a breath of comfort, blowing the rest away."

If this is, in fact, a need which we all share, the obvious question is why does it seem so difficult to fulfill? What is it, do you suppose, that we do to each other that causes us to hide from one another out of fear and mistrust? What was it that our Lord's neighbors did to him in today's Gospel that made it impossible for them to know him?

As I thought about this, I was reminded of an experience that I had a few months ago. I was at the house of a friend who had invited me to a summer barbecue. And, given the fact that it was an informal gathering, I decided to dress casually; nothing outrageous—a plain green shirt, a pair of jeans, and some gym shoes.

Well, everything was going along beautifully until I was finding my way through the buffet line and, just as I finished loading my plate, I began to hear the murmurings from a group of older women I didn't know. "You see the one over there in the green?" one said. "Believe it or not, he's a priest." "Where?" shouted the other one. "My God, are you blind as well as deaf?" said the other. "Right there with all that food on his plate." And, as I walked by, the first one said, "Here, right here. He's a priest," to which the other one yelled out, "He's a priest? Dressed like that? No wonder everyone's leaving the Church!"

Well, I had three reactions—two were immediate, which I can't share with you. The third came several days later. It was a feeling of pity—a pity which comes from the realization of what we do to each other, the way we judge the worth and dignity of a person on the basis of a preconceived notion of the way we "think they should look or dress or live." The way we presume, on our ignorance, the power of determining who is acceptable or unacceptable, both in our communities and ultimately in the sight of God.

This is precisely the same presumption on which our Lord's neighbors judged him in today's Gospel. This is precisely the same presumptuous power which led to his crucifixion—the presumption that they knew what the Messiah was supposed to look like, dress like, and live like. On that basis, they presumed the power to judge him.

Perhaps this is the same presumptuous power our Gospel warns us against in today's readings: the presumption that we know what a good mother, father, priest, or person is supposed to look like, and, on that basis, presume the power to judge each other out of our own ignorance—a power which can only be presumed by the One who knows our hearts.

Terrance S. McNicholas

15th Sunday in Ordinary Time

Cycle B

Am 7:12–15
Eph 1:3–14
Mk 6:7–13

The readings today speak to us of the need for basic trust. The renowned psychiatrist Erik Erikson indicates that basic trust is the first and most crucial step in the development of a healthy personality. If the child does not experience his or her environment as secure and worthy of trust, lasting personality damage will result. In order to grow we trust. The *decisions we make* in terms of trust have far-reaching consequences for our individual and community lives. We know well that trust involves risk as much as freedom demands responsibility. Without a willingness to risk and experience pain we never grow. It took a great deal of courage to trust and risk for Abraham to follow the call of Yahweh, for the disciples to leave their nets and follow that itinerant preacher, for Mary to say her yes of faith to the Word. The Christian story is one of trust, courage, and risk-taking. Therefore, let us examine three aspects of trust offered by the readings: *Whom* do you trust? *What* do you trust *in*? And finally, *Why* do you trust?

In our first reading we encounter a rather strange, yet very modern figure named Amos. Amos is a herdsman and tiller of the soil by trade. God calls him to preach to Israel of its impending doom. Amos preaches against the social injustices of the time with a call to conversion and reform. Also, he challenges the desire of the Israelite king to build a competing shrine of worship at Dan and Bethel to replace Zion. The result is predictable. Amos is denounced as a political traitor and, worst of all, a "prophet for hire." Amos responds that he is no professional prophet but a man of the earth whom the Lord called to preach. Even in the face of "religious" denunciation and political threats he is first and foremost one who *must* speak *God's* word. If suffering false accusations and rejection are the consequences, so be it.

The story of Amos parallels the history of the Church and our own as well. For when we (the Church) stand up to the "principalities and powers" of this world we must expect rejection. When as Christians we witness to the needs of the poor and the oppressed, opposition comes to us. It is painful to challenge our "generous self" to respond to the needs of others. It calls for courage and risk-taking to trust in the Lord rather than the wisdom of this world. *Whom* do you trust? For Amos it is the Lord and his word. For the Christian living today the answer is the same though the form may be different: Jesus is Lord and through him we have light and life.

Our second question is: *What* do you trust *in*? For the people of Amos' time it was military and political alliances, shrines of worship, or some self-righteous notion of divine election and exemption from moral responsibility and covenant-justice. In the letter of the Ephesians we witness a community that is hoping in the Parousia or second coming of Jesus. The unfortunate element in their hoping was their blindness to present needs. Our reading is a reminder that we are to hope and trust in the present and future activity of Christ. The community is the place, event, sign, and sacrament of the graciousness and justice of God.

Today we find ourselves asking the same question as the Ephesians—*What* do we trust in? No doubt some will say the GNP, our personal wealth or power, or some technological advancement. Yet, what we are called to trust and hope in is our election into the Body of Christ. This is the great mystery of God's love revealed in Jesus. And what is even more wonderful is the realization that the whole creation is called to newness of life in the Cosmic Christ.

Finally, we come to our last question: *Why* do you trust? Ours is a cynical age. We have been stung by our leaders who breached the faith. Lately, we have little stomach for trusting. Why get fooled again? The Gospel of Mark offers an answer. We can trust because at the root or ground of our trusting is the covenant of Yahweh-Jesus. The same God who creates and recreates is also the one who revealed the Really Real as gracious and with-us through the Spirit. We can travel through our everyday existence with confidence because One has come to show us the way. Jesus tells the disciples to take none of the expected things for their journey. They are to go under the providence of God.

Jesus expects of us the same. We agreed through baptism to travel light, dependent on God's providence and the good will of the community. We are expected to reach out to the stranger, the alien, and child in today's world which is often unfriendly and hostile to these least of our brethren. For it is in our midst as stranger, alien, unborn, and neglected that we once again touch Jesus.

William F. Maestri

16th Sunday in Ordinary Time

Cycle B

Jer 23:1–6
Eph 2:13–18
Mk 6:30–34

We are far from the days of Jeremiah and the days of Jesus, during which sheep and shepherds were part of the landscape, and from regions of the world where they are still the majority in the livestock population. Still, the language of sheep and shepherds remains alive for us, draws us to itself, in spite of our weaker connection with the wooly flock and the ambivalences we may feel about being described as such a flock. It is a language carrying connotations of care and leadership, especially in the Church. This weekend's Scriptures can lead us into a reflection on those "shepherding" realities—realities we also refer to as "pastoral," that adjective which describes both the countryside in which sheep graze, and the care of the people of God.

Jesus' pastoral call, in today's Gospel scene, is a call from a people yearning for guidance and healing. He was, we are told, moved by these yearnings, and chose to move closer to them rather than remove himself, as he had begun to do that day.

We who hear the story could also choose to remain distant from the people. But in proclaiming this Word we proclaim that we, too, are the people who yearn and long and hunger, and whose yearnings and hungers are understood by Jesus the reconciler. In retelling today's Gospel story we invite one another to dwell in the experience of the people gathered by the side of the lake, to know ourselves as loved. In entering into the story as the people whose yearnings moved Jesus' heart, we learn the Christ who is our shepherd, our strength, our salvation, and learn again how to receive his love.

Christ our shepherd is also Christ our peace, who shows forth in his life, in his death, in his rising to new life, not only who he is but who we are, or who we can be. Caring for us, he invites us to participate in the shepherding of others: in retelling the Gospel story today, we also proclaim that we are Christ's body, that we share in his mission.

This is something we often forget when we hear sheep/shepherd stories: the Gospel invites us to know ourselves as objects of care and shepherding, but also as subjects, as participants in the shepherding action of Jesus Christ, the one who reconciles the separated, who shows forth in his person the God who is integrity and justice, the God who returns exiles to their homeland. We who hear the story could draw close to the people, but remain distant from Jesus. Instead, we can enter fully into the scene and view ourselves as part of Jesus. For we who are people of God are both "the flock of Jesus' pasture" and "the Body of Christ."

Today's readings can help us to reflect on realities of leadership in our lives and challenge our perceptions and assumptions. Most of us probably view ourselves as either sheep or shepherd: our thoughts and opinions about leadership, whether inside or outside the Church, then become, inevitably, thoughts and reflections about "the other." The problem of leadership becomes "their" problem—either because "they" are so difficult to lead, or because "they" are bad leaders. Think, for a moment, of your own perceptions about church leadership. Are they fraught with "we" and "they," shepherds and sheep?

In today's Gospel Christ calls us all to acknowledge him as shepherd. He calls us all, as well, to participate in his mission, in his identity as shepherd, though we may live out that mission in many different ways within the Church and elsewhere. We have all been reconciled by him, baptized into him. Every time we remember and proclaim this, we remember and proclaim that we are both the flock, gathered from the ends of the earth, and a people in mission, called to gather, to teach, to heal—to be Christ in a world full of hungers and yearnings.

Jane C. Redmont

17th Sunday in Ordinary Time

Cycle B

2 Kgs 4:42–44
Eph 4:1–6
Jn 6:1–15

Today's first reading and today's Gospel present two interesting "feeding" stories. The first takes place in time of famine; the second apparently after a very long walk. The stories are about people who were really hungry. And not just a few folks either. Baal-shalishah is asked to feed "a hundred men"; the disciples are asked to buy bread for over five thousand people.

It is difficult for us to identify with large groups of hungry people. Most of us have never experienced famine, nor even traveled all day without taking a snack along. We tend to stockpile our food against the day of shortage. I doubt we would sleep very well if we had no more on hand than our daily bread.

Our family has had occasions which might be distantly related to today's stories. I have made a small roast, a few potatoes, and company drops in. No time to bewail the size of the roast nor the number of potatoes. Hospitality rules, and the family holds back feigning fullness and looking forward to raiding the refrigerator after the company departs. The company eats enough; the family snacks later. But today's stories pose more difficult problems.

First of all, there is the "feeder's" problem. There's no logical way to assume that twenty barley loaves and some fresh grain will satisfy the hunger of 100 men. There's even less reason to believe that five barley loaves and a couple of dried fish could begin to touch the hunger of over 5,000 people. The temptation of the feeder is to say, "What good is my little bit among so many?" There was also reason for the feeder to wonder, "If I give up the food I have, will I myself starve?" There was no refrigerator to raid later on. The risk was very real.

As I was reflecting on today's feeding stories, I got a call from a friend of mine who is a good example of a "feeder" in our world. Dennis is an orthopedic surgeon who spends several months each year donating his time and medical expertise to treat suffering people in Third World countries. I have seen photos of his patients in those countries, and know the miracles that his care and compassion have worked. I have also seen photos of the many others whom he could not treat. How easy it would be for Dennis to say, "What good is the little I do among the thousands of suffering people?" How easy it would be for him to choose not to go to these countries at all. Ignorance of the suffering could be so much more comfortable than the knowledge of so many needs which go unanswered.

There are people in our world who are "potential feeders." They have a few loaves, a couple of dried fish, but they hang on to them. Our society has convinced them that their loaves and fishes are possessions which make them better than others. Rather than use what they have to serve others, they spend their lives in futile efforts to multiply things for themselves. Society can convince us that we have worked hard for our loaves and fishes and we're entitled to them, no matter who is starving or in need. In fact, if everyone worked as hard as we do, they would have earned their own loaves and fishes.

The second unique difficulty that was apparently overcome in today's Scripture stories is the crowd's reaction to the meager offerings. Can you imagine the hundred famine-ravaged men saying, "Forget it! Keep your lousy barley loaves. We'll wait 'til the caterer arrives with a seven course dinner for all of us"? Could you imagine the 5,000 hungry men in the Gospel saying, "We don't care for dried fish"?

That did not happen, of course.

Can you imagine people laughing at my friend Dennis's efforts in poor countries and declaring his work inadequate and therefore useless?

That does happen, of course.

Sometimes it is easier to be a part of the hungry crowd than to be the guy who has only a few loaves and fishes. The crowd gets sympathy if nothing else; the poor fool who contributes what little he has to offer often gets ridicule and contempt.

The old motto, "It is better to light one small candle than to curse the darkness" is not very popular these days. It seems far more fashionable to curse the darkness, to bemoan the terrible conditions in our world or our parish or our community. It is even more acceptable to walk around bumping into walls and denying that it's dark at all. Today's readings call us to believe in the power of one small candle—or a few loaves and fishes—to make a difference. If we withhold our gifts, or mock the seemingly paltry efforts of others, we just might miss a miracle.

Carole M. Eipers

18th Sunday in Ordinary Time

Cycle B

Ex 16:2-4, 12-15
Eph 4:17, 20-24
Jn 6:24-35

In the beginning, God created us hungry. Today's readings invite us to focus on this reality; how else will we understand the meaning of food? And how else, besides reflecting on our many hungers, will we, as the contemporary hymn invites us to, "look beyond the bread we eat," and see Jesus the Lord, the Bread of Life?

Sometimes all we know is our own hunger. It may be the physical hunger of the crowd of people who needed to eat before they could hear the Good News—the hunger which rumbles in bellies and is so strong that it masks the other hungers we carry within us. Or the hunger we know may be one of those "others"—the hunger for intimacy, for harmonious community, for God's healing, for God's word. Sometimes we cannot even name this kind of hunger, but feel it in a vague uneasy way. The people in the Gospel story knew they wanted to be fed, but did not know at first how deep the hunger was. It takes us years, sometimes, to understand the hungers which God has placed in our hearts and souls, and to understand that we are most deeply hungry for that same God.

Today, we take time to acknowledge the hunger, and it is with an awareness of that hunger that we say "Amen" to Jesus who is for us Bread of Life. To know how deep are our hungers is to know how powerful is the gift of his word and healing work.

Jesus comes to us as bread. And we who say "Amen" to "The Body of Christ" as we are offered the Eucharistic bread are saying "Amen," as St. Augustine wrote, to our own reality, "Amen" to the fact that we too are the Body of Christ. That is part of Paul's message. His words in the Epistle are not a simple moral injunction but a statement about transformation and revolution rooted in his belief about the power of Christ. In Christ our bread of life, for whose word we hunger as much as for bread, the world has already begun to be transformed. Our lives, Paul reminds us, participate in this transformation, because we are his body.

Jesus is our bread of life, "broken that we might become bread for the world." We, the hungry people, the still broken people, are also the church, servant of the world, those who in Jesus' name and in the power and grace of God try to bring food to the hungry, whether in body or mind or spirit or heart.

It is harvest time in many parts of our country—a fruitful time to reflect on hunger, not simply as a physical need to be fulfilled—though we cannot ignore the need around us, in our own community and in our world—but as a reality with many levels. From this meditation, we can move into an understanding of the many meanings and levels of food, and of Jesus as our food, Jesus the fulfillment of our hunger. If we move through this meditation we will be led to feed those who hunger—for food, for friendship, for the word of God—out of solidarity and gratitude, not guilt.

We remember our times of hunger, we stay hungry, we learn the meaning of our own hunger and the hungers around us: so solidarity is born, and moves us to feed the hungry. We remember how we have been fed, we keep the memory alive of the times when God nourished us in our need, we celebrate Jesus our Bread again and again in our Eucharist: so thanksgiving, gratitude (the meaning of the word "Eucharist") is born, and overflows into our lives, and moves us to share the bread from our tables and the bread of God's word.

Jane C. Redmont

19th Sunday in Ordinary Time

Cycle B

1 Kgs 19:4–8
Eph 4:30—5:2
Jn 6:41–51

Today our attention focuses on the great gift of the Eucharist. The questions that I would like to pose to you in relation to today's Gospel are, where in our world today, nearly 2,000 years after the last supper, does our Lord bring us together to celebrate the gift of himself? And, can this gift be celebrated only at Mass, or can it be celebrated elsewhere? Or perhaps, the most important question of all is, if in fact we do celebrate the Eucharist, how do we do it?

In my own attempt to answer these questions, it has been helpful for me to read and re-read a poetic piece by R. Voght entitled simply, "Eucharist."

He was old,
  tired and sweaty,
Pushing his homemade cart
Down the alley,
  Stopping
  now and then
To poke around in somebody's garbage.
I wanted to tell him about EUCHARIST
  But the look in his eyes,
    the despair in his face,
    the hopelessness of somebody else's life
    in his
    cart—
  Told me to forget it.
So I smiled and said "Hi" and gave him
EUCHARIST.

She lived alone
  her husband dead,
  her family gone.
  As she talked at you—not to you,
    Words, endless words, spewed.
So I listened and gave her EUCHARIST.

Downtown is nice,
  lights change from red to green
    and back again—
  Flashing blues, pinks, and oranges;

I gulped them in,
Said "Thank you, Father" and made them
EUCHARIST.

I laughed at myself,
  "You with all your sins
    and all your selfishness—I forgive you
    I accept you
    I love you."
It's nice, and so necessary, too, to give
yourself
    EUCHARIST.

Tired, weary, disgusted, lonely,
  Go to your friends,
  Open your door,
Say "Look at me" and receive their
EUCHARIST.
My Father, when will we learn
  You cannot talk EUCHARIST—
  Cannot philosophize about it—you DO it!

You cannot dogmatize EUCHARIST
  sometimes you laugh it,
  sometimes you cry it,
  often you sing it,
Sometimes it's wild peace
  then crying hurt.
    Often humiliating
    Never deserved.

You see EUCHARIST in another's eyes,
  Give it in another's hand held tight,
  Squeeze it with an embrace.

You pause EUCHARIST in the middle of a
busy day,
  speak EUCHARIST with a million things
  to do
  and a person who wants to talk.
For EUCHARIST is as SIMPLE as being on
time
    and as profound as sympathy.

I give you my supper.
I give you my sustenance
I give you my life,
I give you me.
I give you EUCHARIST

Perhaps, the best way to celebrate Eucharist is, as Voght suggests, by becoming Eucharist for others!

Terrance S. McNicholas

20th Sunday in Ordinary Time

Cycle B

Prv 9:1–6
Eph 5:15–20
Jn 6:51–58

One line in today's reading from Paul to the Ephesians leapt out at me. "Be filled with the Spirit," he says, "addressing one another in psalms, hymns, and spiritual songs." I envisioned myself setting "Honor thy father and thy mother" to music and chanting it to our twelve-year-old son. It made me laugh the way some of the old Fred Astaire and Ginger Rogers movies used to do.

If you look at those old movies in a totally objective manner, they are ridiculous. Man and woman meet for lunch or have a conversation or whatever, and suddenly burst into song and end up dancing down the street. That's just not how life is among sober, mature adults.

A couple of times, though, I watched an Astaire-Rogers movie and I didn't laugh. The song and dance made sense. Looking back, I guess my reaction depended on two things: how deeply I was involved in the story, and with whom I was watching it. If I was really involved in the story, it seemed like the song was the only thing that made sense right then. If my fellow viewers were equally involved, we could share our belief. If they weren't, then inevitably someone would make a joke of it and the whole movie would seem ridiculous again.

"The Sound of Music" is a more "religious" example. When the Mother Superior began singing "Climb Every Mountain" it could easily be dismissed as "out of character" for a Mother Superior, and silly. Yet, those who felt the emotions of the story and identified with the characters took the song very seriously. In Maria's confusion, what else was there to say? And could it have been said more beautifully?

I think Paul's advice to "address one another in psalms, hymns, and spiritual songs" can strike us as pretty silly too. Even if we don't dance down the street, even if the Word we bring is spoken, not sung, sometimes the reaction is, "That's not how real life is! You're ridiculous!" And, sometimes, the fear of that sort of reaction can prevent us from ever speaking the Good News at all.

One time I failed to speak the Good News was when I was taking a Hospital Ministry course. I was on my assigned rounds with my "Chaplain" badge pinned proudly on my white jacket. I entered the room of a young football player who was recuperating from knee surgery. His room was crowded with four or five friends who had come to visit. "This is not the time nor place for any of that religion stuff" I told myself, and entered into their friendly banter. Before you could say "Fred Astaire and Ginger Rogers" the young man had pulled a Bible from his bedside drawer and began explaining to his friends and to me how the passage from Isaiah about "steadying all trembling knees" had strengthened him during his ordeal. What I had thought would seem ridiculous was the only thing that made sense to him. His friends could have laughed, but they obviously were too involved in this young man's story, and his faith had made sense to them too.

That visit changed me. It gave me the courage—not to sing and dance—but to speak my faith. It gave me the courage to risk being told, "That's ridiculous" on the chance that someone might say, "That's the only thing that makes sense to me too."

Like Fred and Ginger dancing, speaking the Good News requires practice. We don't need lessons in oratory, though; we need practice in living our beliefs. Then when we sing and dance our faith, it will ring true—and not appear as an empty show. It takes practice in sensitivity too, the kind of sensitivity which Jesus had. He understood people's readiness for faith. He had compassion which allowed people to grieve and to express their human emotions. He understood that timing could mean the difference between turning someone off for good—and converting them.

I guess, like my experience of the old musicals, whether the Good News makes sense depends on two things: how deeply you are involved in the story of our God and of Jesus, and with whom you are sharing the experience. If we speak our faith we run the risk of being laughed at as irrelevant, but we also open the possibility of giving others the courage to speak their faith.

Fred could always count on Ginger, but we who speak the Good News run the risk of dancing off alone, and that can be painful and humiliating. But, though we may seem the fool momentarily, ultimately each of us has a partner. They call him "The Lord of the Dance."

Carole M. Eipers

21st Sunday in Ordinary Time

Cycle B

Jos 24:1–2, 15–17, 18
Eph 5:21–32
Jn 6:60–69

Today's reading spoke clearly to me of freedom of choice, particularly in how I could interpret the familiar, and oftentimes painful, Ephesians' passage. Yet, we are encouraged to do our own hermeneutics with Scripture just as our ancestors did. Our life experience is no less valid or meaningful—and is an integral fibre in the total fabric of our journeys.

There is a four-part theme to today's readings, one that can be applied to each one of our lives, no matter how diverse: choice/crisis/mutual deference/risk-taking. How we initially *choose* to use this pattern makes all the difference.

When I read the word "submission" in Ephesians, the old hackles went up again. And I had a choice to make: to react in my traditional manner to the exclusive, sexist implications, or to step back and see it as part of a theme that went far beyond my reaction. In choosing the latter, I was stretched and enriched.

If we look at the placement of this passage, we note that it is preceded by Joshua 24, and Psalm 34, which speak of both the choice God offers us in discipleship as well as the attentiveness he offers in times of crisis. The passage that follows (John 6) highlights the crisis of faith that inevitably arises for us all, and the risk-taking that comes in proclaiming our faith in Jesus.

When Joshua stated that " . . . as for me and my household, we will serve the Lord," it was a radical decision for a society that worshiped many gods. Yet it was a decision based on the providence of a God who was totally faithful in all his promises to his people. Is our decision today to follow Jesus less radical than Joshua's? Think about that. The fertility gods of our ancestors were more obvious, perhaps. But we do have our idols, as well. More subtle, more sophisticated, but just as powerful: success, money, material goods, the image we present before others. To publicly state—and live out—the decision that you and your household will serve the Lord is no less risky for us than it was for Joshua. Rejection, scorn,

humiliation are oftentimes the price we pay for this "radical" lifestyle in a scientific and technologically-oriented world.

"The Lord is close to the brokenhearted . . . He hears them when they cry out and rescues them." In our human journeys, pain is present at different stages. Psalm 34 has always imaged for me the little child who cries out in pain, hunger, distress—completely unabashed! How often we become "adultified" with our pain, unwilling to cry out even to our God in the privacy of our prayer. Yet we long to do so. Our God welcomes that cry. Just as a mother/father soothes and comforts their little one, so too does our God long to comfort/rescue us.

The willingness/ability to expose our gut feelings comes only out of the experience of an intimate relationship. For me, that is what Ephesians is saying. To submit, to defer to another, *is not a passive relinquishment* of ourselves, but rather an *active, free choice* to *include another in our life.* And the riskiest part of this inclusion is that, in a truly intimate relationship, our total self is seen and experienced by the other person. All that we keep hidden and undercover now becomes visible. And this is where the *submission* enters in. For if we are loved, and love intimately, then we *actively permit* our God/friend/lover to care for us—and that caring sometimes involves painful realizations about ourselves.

I believe that Peter was at this juncture of his faith journey when he took that giant leap in proclaiming his faith in Jesus as God's holy one. Many of his brothers and sisters in Christ were experiencing a crisis in their faith as well. Peter *actively permitted* Jesus to direct, and be instrumental in, his life. No easy decision for Peter—or for us today. Yet, the blessings from this decision include a model for us in our other relationships. To love as Jesus loves us is not easy nor, I believe, possible, without his spirit and life within us. And even then it's tough work!

Many years ago, our next-door-neighbors decided to plant two tiny saplings next to each other. They thought they would both have a better chance of a more fruitful life if they became entwined rather than "going it alone." Today, the result of their decision graces their yard in the form of a 40-foot silver maple(s). And it has provided for me a constant reminder of *mutuality,* that respectful deference to another by *choice* that complements and enriches far beyond singular endeavors.

Our God invites us into a relationship of mutuality with him, freely chosen, and promises us if we make this decision, he will honor it always. Trust yourself to yield to his invitation.

Elizabeth Ann Walsh

22nd Sunday in Ordinary Time

Cycle B

Dt 4:1–2, 6–8
Jas 1:17–18, 21–22, 27
Mk 7:1–8, 14–15, 21–23

When my brothers and I were young, we had a fascinating board game called "Taxi." The box it came in proudly stated that "Taxi" was "the game with rules made to be broken." The game pieces were tiny taxicabs, and the object of the game was to win by breaking the rules which governed the number of passengers you could carry and the speed at which you carried them.

I haven't seen a game of "Taxi" around for decades and I think I understand its unenduring quality. As my brothers and I played the game we found the lack of rules, or the acceptance of lawlessness, frustrating. There was no way to control the other players. I would delight at speeding my overloaded taxi around the board, but it made me angry when my brothers got away with similar moves. Winning was all that counted; there were no consequences for wrong-doers. The fun of the game, supposedly, was that there were no rules; the result was that we created our own rules, or we quit the game.

We all need freedom; we also not only need, but seek limits. Whether we join a club or an organization, or get a new job, we ask explicitly or implicitly, "What are the rules?" Yet, when the rules are clearly set before us, we tend to pick and choose which are to be kept and which can be broken.

A Baptist friend of mine religiously follows her church's law which forbids smoking. She just as religiously breaks the card-playing prohibition every week when she joins her poker group. Her subset of Baptist rules makes card playing forgivable but condemns smoking. Her choices work for her, but cause difficulty when she joins other Baptists whose subsets of rules condemn cards and accept smokers.

I suppose it would be fine to create our own subsets of rules which determine acceptably breakable laws from those which are to be kept if we were isolated individuals. But our God, with a twinkle in his eye, mixes us together with our need for freedom, our desire for limits, our wanting to know the rules and our deciding to break some of them, and then he says, "Now I've got a community!" Maybe God didn't figure that with all those strange ingredients he put together an interesting phenomenon would develop: folks who are better at picking and choosing rules for others to follow, rather than just following the rules themselves.

Life can be as uncertain and confusing as a game of "Taxi." There is the fact that cheating, lying, and manipulation often bring wealth and power and fame; lawlessness does seem to win sometimes. There is the fact that our society has legalized certain types of killing, and then our conscience begs us to break the law in order to protest. There are times when it seems that, in life as in "Taxi," the rules were made to be broken.

"What are the rules to this game of life?" we find ourselves asking again, wondering if perhaps someone has changed them. God, having designed the game and the players as well, did not leave us without rules. God gave us laws so that we might enjoy the game and play it well. But today's readings about God's laws can confuse us even further.

The reading from Deuteronomy warns us not to change God's commands; in the Gospel, Jesus accuses people who keep the law of disregarding God's commands and clinging to human tradition. The temptation is to make our own rules again; to pick and choose laws rather than to reflect on the Scriptures and try to figure it all out.

Jesus says the spirit of the law is greater than the letter of the laws. He does not advocate lawlessness, but he does condemn legalism. We can get caught up, like the Scribes and the Pharisees did, equating the law of the land with the Law of the Lord. We can claim to be committed Christians when in reality we are cultural Catholics who have adopted society's norms for morality rather than God's norms. Committed Christians are sometimes called to break the law; criminals are motivated to do the same. How can we know for ourselves what God asks? It takes more than knowing the rules. It takes prayer, reflection, and sharing with other people of faith, an appreciation of tradition, and the ability to translate the values of Jesus not only into contemporary words, but into contemporary action.

Jesus said it all boils down to one law: Love God and love your neighbor. He asks us to keep the law ourselves, but also to forgive those who don't keep it.

And that makes Christianity about as popular as "Taxi." A lot of folks don't buy it; and some just quit the game.

Carole M. Eipers

23rd Sunday in Ordinary Time

Cycle B

Is 34:4–7
Jas 2:1–5
Mk 7:31–37

He was an old man whom I met while deep sea fishing in Florida. I met him on an overcrowded boat while awaiting further instructions from the captain. Almost immediately it became apparent to me that he was extremely hard of hearing. My first clue was when he shouted to me, "What's your name, son?" "My name is Terry," I responded. To which he shouted back, "What?" To which I shouted again, "Terry!" "Oh, Larry," he yelled, "nice to meet you! Tell me, Larry, do you like to play golf?!" "No!" I shouted. "Great," he shouted back, "maybe we can get together and play nine holes!"

Well, needless to say, our conversation went downhill. His embarrassed wife signaled him to be silent. For the next four hours he sat quietly trapped inside himself. He was literally unable to share himself with anyone on that boat simply because of his inability to hear.

Imagine the isolation he must have felt. Imagine the tremendous frustration. Imagine the horror of knowing yourself to be a good and loving person and, for one reason or another, being unable to share your love and goodness with others.

My fear is that we are much like this man. I fear that, like him, you and I, despite the fact that perhaps we are capable of hearing, are in danger of being entrapped inside ourselves. I fear that, unlike this man, we are simply content with our own inability to respond to each other as we know we can and must, simply because we choose not to hear.

I mean, let's face it, you and I believe ourselves to be Christians, but do we communicate this belief to others by the way we respond to them? And if we don't—why don't we? What is it that we are not hearing, if in fact we're really listening?

In response to this question, I suggest that perhaps what we are not hearing, or even listening for, is the voice of our Lord in the voices of one another. For instance:

Do we hear the voice of our Lord in the tears of our pregnant teenage daughter, begging us to allow him to become transfigured in our hearts so he may forgive? Or do we hear only our pride?

Do we hear, in the cries of the poor, our Lord begging us to allow him to be transfigured in our hearts so that he may provide? Or, do we hear only our own selfish needs?

Do we hear, in the anger of those whom we find most difficult to love, our Lord begging us to allow him to be transfigured in our hearts so he may heal? Or, do we hear only our pride?

I suggest to you today that, perhaps, like my friend, we too are hard of hearing. I fear that, like him, you and I, despite the fact that perhaps we are capable of hearing, are in danger of being entrapped inside ourselves. I fear that, unlike this man, we are simply content with our own inability to respond to each other as we know we can and must, simply because we choose not to hear.

I suggest to you today that, perhaps, we are in need of a cure similar to that described by Helen Keller:

> We walked down the path to the well-house, attracted by the fragrance of the honeysuckle with which it was covered. Someone was drawing water and my teacher placed my hand under the spout.
>
> Suddenly I felt a misty consciousness as of something forgotten—a thrill of returning thought; and somehow the mystery was revealed to me. I knew then that W-A-T-E-R meant the wonderful cool something that was flowing over my hand.
>
> That Living Word awakened my soul, gave it light, hope, joy, set it free! There were barriers still, it is true, but barriers that in time could be swept away.

Terrance S. McNicholas

24th Sunday in Ordinary Time

Cycle B

Is 50:4–9
Jas 2:14–18
Mk 8:27–35

"But you, who do you say I am?" Jesus' question to Peter always echoes in my mind and heart as a question to *me* after I hear today's Gospel. The story of Peter's call, with Jesus' direct, burning question, invites us to speak *to* Jesus rather than *about* him: to hear him, and to talk back, in the second person—"you, Lord," not "he." Who am I for you? How much do I really mean to you?

Today the question echoes even more deeply, for James's epistle expands and deepens the question. Do you realize all that I am? Do you understand who I am? To proclaim Jesus as Lord, James reminds us, is to proclaim him—and strive to know him—in his fullness. To proclaim Jesus as Lord is to proclaim God's absolute commitment to the human race and God's identification with us, including the most poor among us, the most "undesirable," the most desperate. We cannot have faith and set ourselves apart from those who are God's own—who are Jesus' own—who are our own. James calls us to be as intimately involved with the human condition as God is, the same God who became flesh for us in the one we call "Lord."

"Who do you say I am?" The question burns still more strongly: to proclaim Jesus as Lord is to proclaim him crucified. Peter's profession is linked immediately—lest Jesus' followers forget, lest the early Christians of Mark's community forget, lest we forget—to the Passion. To say "you are Lord" is to embrace Christ's way. His way is the way of the cross, the way of grace but not always of gracefulness. In saying "you are Lord," we come to understand that abundant life always involves death of one kind or another. It is at this point that we—that I—always begin to cry, "yes, Lord, but I don't want to change!" Oh for the easy graces, the constant consolation in prayer, the learning without effort, and growth without suffering, and faith without doubts, and the dulling of the challenge of faith! Oh for Jesus-the-easy-answer instead of Jesus-the-Way . . .

But Jesus-the-easy-answer is not Jesus. And Jesus-the-Way does not only show forth, in his way of the cross, that on the path to abundant life there will be death. He also reminds us that in the midst of pain, rejection, death, are the seeds of resurrection—not because Jesus-the-easy-answer will appear and magically heal the broken heart, immediately banish all illness, force the warring parties to sign the peace treaty. But the day we come to understand that Jesus has entered and embraced the realities of sin and death is the day we understand that he has helped us to see them for what they are, and renounce them, and denounce them. In experiencing the depth of brokenness with Jesus, we experience the call to mend the brokenness.

Last December, I attended what has become an annual service commemorating the life and martyrdom of the four American church women who were killed in El Salvador five years ago. Rarely have I seen these realities of call and cross, death and risen life, proclamation of Jesus' lordship and care for those weakest and most oppressed members of his Body, so interwoven with one another, all at once. "Here I am, Lord," we sang, remembering that the four women had spoken and prayed those words. We heard excerpts from their letters about the people among whom they worked. Many of us wept, for their death, for the deaths of so many of the people they served, for fear that we too might be called away from Jesus-the-easy-answer, to the way of no ease which they embraced. But the Church was alive with resurrection: yearly our numbers grow at the memorial service; more of us, not fewer, sing "Here I am"; we gathered not simply to weep, but to proclaim our hope in Christ and commit ourselves to serve his people who suffer. The death of four women who said "you are Lord" are bringing forth life.

We will not all say, "you are Lord" in the same way. The Scriptures do not point us, or push us, toward a particular task, but toward a person, Jesus-the-way. They urge us to become people who, like the Servant in Isaiah's song, like Jesus himself, enter the difficult mystery, rely on the strength of God, and hope against hope. They urge us to answer Jesus' question "Who do *you* say that I am?" with our lives.

Jane C. Redmont

25th Sunday in Ordinary Time

Cycle B

Wis 2:12, 17–20
Jas 3:16–4:3
Mk 9:30–37

Today's reading from Wisdom is a vicious one. People are plotting to destroy "the just one." Instead of listening to this good man, taking his words to heart, examining his truth, they turn on him. "The Jews," we think, "they did it to Jesus. They plotted and planned and they killed him." Yes, and some of them killed the prophets too. Anyone who challenged their way of life, anyone who had the audacity to suggest reform, was destroyed.

Christians plotted too. They too turned on their prophets and annihilated or excommunicated those who questioned, or who spoke of conversion or renewal.

We all do it, I guess. "Let's get the good guy" or woman. It's a more subtle conspiracy; it's not written or spelled out like today's reading. The result, though, is the same. The just one is killed: physically or mentally or emotionally or spiritually, somehow we do him in.

Why is getting the just one such great sport? First of all, we want to discredit that person. If he or she is questioning, probing, intimating that we are not perfect, we don't want anyone taking that message seriously. Second, there is the common opinion that if we debase someone else, we look better; if we condemn, we are somehow justified.

We have been taught, or have learned through experience, to be cynical and somewhat suspicious of good people. We are on guard, watching for ulterior motives. We tend even to discourage our friends from being too good. "Don't be naive" we warn those who trust; "Don't be a sucker" we warn those who forgive; "Give it up" we declare to the peacemaker. We discourage them, partly of course because if they are trusting and forgiving and peaceable then we might feel compelled to be so also. The term "do-gooder" has become, ironically, a derogatory term.

Christians, we assume, are "good guys." However, to paraphrase an old saying, "You and I are the good guys. And I'm not so sure about you." In the end, we all tend to say, "I am the just one."

Who then is the "good guy"? In today's letter from James, the writer says that the wise person is the good person. He spells it out for us: the wise person is "peaceable, lenient, docile, rich in sympathy and kindly deeds, impartial and sincere." We could take each of those qualities and think of a multitude of ways in which our society rejects such a person. Those qualities would hardly represent "survival gear" for business, for politics, nor even, sadly, for Church leadership. The wise person is dressed for martyrdom, not success.

Who is the "good guy"? Jesus describes the good person in today's Gospel. He says it's the person who remains "the last one of all," "the servant of all."

Are we, then, the "good guys"? Perhaps we could answer that by examining how we treat the good person whom James describes. How do we act toward those who are peaceable? Toward those who are rich in sympathy? Toward those who are impartial and sincere in all their dealings?

Are we the "good guys"? Maybe we can answer that by searching our attitude toward those whom Jesus named "good." How do we treat those who are "the last one of all"? And, perhaps the most telling question of all: How do we treat those who are "the servant of all"? How do we act toward the waitresses and waiters in our favorite restaurant, or the janitors at work, or the clerks who wait on us? How do we speak to—and of—our police and fire persons? Or, of our priests?

Servants of God have a common bond, no matter whether they are garbage collectors or cardinals, entertainers or unemployed. The "good guys" feel that bond and treat each other with the respect that flows from a shared ministry and a common goal.

Goodness seeks and finds goodness in others. It is evil within us that is out to "get the good guy" and so to prove him more evil than ourselves.

The Gospel says that Jesus had been teaching his disciples about his death and resurrection. Instead of talking about that, and trying to understand Jesus' message, the disciples were arguing about which of them was most important. If we're too busy worrying about our own justification and our own importance, we might miss Jesus' message too. And we just might miss being one of the "good guys" who rises with him.

Carole M. Eipers

26th Sunday in Ordinary Time

Cycle B

Nm 11:25–29
Jas 5:1–6
Mk 9:38–43, 45, 47–48

What does the word "discernment" mean to you? Something tells me that, before we became so sophisticated, there were a few simple words that meant what this one word means today. "To perceive or recognize clearly . . . to have good judgment," Webster's dictionary definition, is certainly more understandable to most than this one word "discernment."

Moses desired discernment for all the people of the Lord. "Would that all the people of the Lord were prophets! Would that the Lord might bestow his spirit on them all!" Was this gift supposed to be restricted to an elite few—or did God desire then/now that all his people recognize clearly the Good News?

Our early Christian ancestors may have had a more intimate knowledge of Christ; they had access to recent stories of him. Today, we have more "head" knowledge—we have learned more, studied more, discussed more about Jesus. We've compared our faith experiences too often on what we *know about* Jesus. But I believe there must come a time for each one of us to let go of all the head knowledge, and allow the Spirit to come to rest on us. That posture of allowing/permitting the Spirit to come into our lives requires enormous openness and vulnerability.

But our God is a God of many surprises, and great power. He initiates change in our lives. We can choose to respond. Once we do, we are never the same again!

A personal example of the Spirit coming into my life occurred to me as I was walking down the street. My head was bent with concern over many loved ones struggling with many painful things. All I was doing on this walk was concentrating on their pain, and asking the Lord to be with them. All of a sudden, I heard the words: "I love *you*—I care for *you*. Give me all your loves, and then let me love *you*." I was floored! And more than that, I felt an enormous infilling of the Spirit—it was a physical sensation. It was so powerful I started to cry.

This experience was unique to me. But this experience is not exclusively mine. It is a pure gift, with no restrictions, no price tags. Today's reading in James talks about those price tags. If we substitute the word "security" for wealth, riches, perhaps we can see more clearly that this reading is for each one of us. For security can mean money, professional success, power. Security is anything that we're afraid to lose for fear that we will lose ourselves in the process.

There is a fairly decent definition of sin in liberation theology literature that speaks clearly to my life—and that is the sin of giving everything I am/have to God except my security. I can give my time in the form of social justice ministry, education, work, family life, neighbors, friends, parish involvement. But if I am unwilling to let go of the fear of physical disability, unemployment, homelessness, for example, then my security is still not in my God, but in myself, and whatever available resources I find *on my own*.

There is a popular psychological theory of self-actualization that has many merits to it. But it has one enormous failing. It infers that all this growth toward being able to think of others selflessly occurs only through the self. That is not only painful, but impossible.

We are communal by nature. In the Gospels, this communal nature is constantly being reinforced. Jesus lived in the midst of his people. He modeled for us both a vertical and a horizontal relationship essential for true Christian growth—the space and time he gave to be with the Father, and the life-giving energy of the Spirit (vertical), and the community of friends, disciples, those requiring healing that he walked with, ate/slept/prayed with (horizontal). We cannot heal ourselves, or anybody else. Only Jesus heals. But we can be with each other, support each other, pray for each other. Through discernment—that wonderful ability to recognize clearly the love Christ has for each one of us, and the direction he wants us to follow—we can learn to trust God as our wealthiest resource.

This discernment requires initial privacy, space, openness, where we can "stroke the face of Jesus" as we ask him for what we need. This parent/child image is a Hebrew interpretation of the words "to ask for."

But just as the child grows to include others in his/her life, so we too are encouraged to include others in our spiritual journey—others who will help us to discern, to discover what God wants for us.

"Would that all the people of the Lord were prophets!" Don't complicate that invitation!

Elizabeth Ann Walsh

27th Sunday in Ordinary Time

Cycle B

Gn 2:18–24
Heb 2:9–11
Mk 10:2–16 (shorter version: Mk 10:2–12)

Life in a modern, urban environment has often been characterized by a sense of "unconnectedness" with the world of nature. We have isolated and insulated ourselves from much of the harshness found in nature, as well as much of the naturalness there. We work in office buildings whose windows were designed never to be opened; the climate is cooled or heated according to the season. We can even drive home in an air conditioned automobile, wrapped in its stereophonic sound system that shuts out all noise, even the sound of the rushing wind. What can be even more disturbing in modern society is that we have learned to manipulate our environment, and yet it is quite possible to experience a loss of control of our very selves. There can be a sense of "unfinishedness" about us. We can't seem to bring ourselves to completeness. Perhaps our uncanny ability to detach ourselves from the surrounding environment only heightens our feeling of ennui about our lives.

The reading from Genesis speaks to this sense of incompleteness. The simple and touching story it tells reaches those very depths of "unfinishedness" that can be present in modern life. However, feelings of incompleteness may well be an ancient and deeply rooted experience as attested to in Genesis. The story comes from the second account of creation found in the Bible. It portrays a very tender and caring God who creates an environment for the newly formed creature, man. In having the man name all the other creatures in his world, the text suggests that he is to have control, or perhaps, sovereignty over his world. Yet, we are told, this is not sufficient nor satisfying. Somehow the man is still incomplete.

The story of the creation of woman as help-mate and partner seeks to cure the "unfinishedness" of God's creature. The story speaks to a very central issue in our lives: we will become whole and complete in our discovery of each other. People are made for relatedness and attachment. We will never satisfy our longing to be whole persons by isolating ourselves from the world and each other. The most significant aspect of our world is that it is populated primarily with persons, and wholeness shall be found in the discovery of the other; or, as the text says, " . . . they become one flesh."

The Gospel story of Jesus' teaching on divorce underlines the essential ingredient in any relationship: commitment. Jesus insists that living transitory lives in temporary relationships will never bring a sense of completeness and wholeness which God created for us in the beginning. Hence, Jesus harkens back to the Genesis story to remind us of God's original gift of a completed universe; and he emphasizes that we shall never be satisfied as persons without committing ourselves to each other.

In the Gospel, Jesus speaks specifically about marriage relationships. And it should be noted that Jesus stresses that both a man (v 11) and a woman (v 12) are called to live in committed relationship in order for both to realize fulfillment "in one flesh." However, we might widen out the horizon of this text beyond marriage relationships. The overall concern in this Gospel is that of commitment as the foundation of any relationship. No person, married or single, can ever come to wholeness living a detached and uncommitted life in a world filled with persons. No marriage, friendship, or family can long endure without the personal investment necessary for each member in these relationships to come to harmony and completeness in life. From the beginning of our creation, we were made to "become one flesh," and we will never be at home in our world and with ourselves until we seek out significant others to whom we must commit ourselves. Wholeness is found in the other, and so we will never really be complete in and of ourselves. Jesus stresses that full humanity is found in handing ourselves over to others in ongoing commitments. It certainly is a paradox, but nonetheless true that we have ourselves by giving ourselves away.

James Heimerl

28th Sunday in Ordinary Time

Cycle B

Wis 7:7–11
Heb 4:12–13
Mk 10:17–30

The scripture readings which we hear today provide us with an opportunity to reflect on those things which are of real importance in our lives.

The reading from the Book of Wisdom, though probably of first century B.C. origin, is often attributed to David's great son, King Solomon. The king is described as having more power and prestige than anyone else in Israel. He is also described as having great wealth at his disposal, yet he recognized the priceless value of the gift of wisdom.

Why is wisdom so precious? The answer is given earlier in the same chapter. Wisdom is "intelligent, holy, unique, manifold, subtle, agile, clear, unstained, certain, not baneful, loving the good, keen, unhampered, beneficent, kindly, firm, secure, tranquil, all-powerful, all-seeing, and pervading all spirits" (7:22–23). Further on, the author says: "For there is nought God loves, be it not one who dwells with Wisdom" (7:28).

Wisdom, a gift from God, enables us to seek the true, the eternal values of life. It enables us to cling to the one true God, not to the little gods of our own making. Wisdom is often seen as a virtue which the older members of society have acquired after many years of experiencing the successes and failures of life. The wise person knows where real treasure lies. But as described in the Book of Wisdom, and in the psalm response of the day, the grace of wisdom is one which all can receive, regardless of age, if we pray for the gift and keep our eyes fixed on God and the things of God.

The gospel passage for today tells the story of a man who apparently tried to keep his eyes fixed on God, but who could not open himself completely "because he had many possessions." By his own account, this person had kept the commandments from the time of his childhood. He was not a sinful man. Perhaps the reason he asked Jesus what was necessary to gain eternal life was that he wanted to be affirmed that he was, in fact, on the right path. But maybe he also had the deep sense that he could and should do more. Jesus, it appears, sensed this man's sincerity and earnestness because, as the Gospel says, "Jesus looked at him with love . . . "

And in fact, for this man, more WAS necessary. Jesus called him to let go of his possessions (those things that really possessed him) and give them away to the poor. Then, when he was free from those things that tied him down, Jesus invited him to join his special followers.

The scene is easy to picture. The man is earnest. He recognizes some special qualities in Jesus, senses that he is a true servant of God. He waits with eager anticipation for the teacher to give him the answers his heart desires. And Jesus does tell him very concretely what he is lacking in his quest for God. But Jesus' answer is more than this man can hear. We can picture him slowly turning away from Jesus, perhaps shaking his head, slowly walking away, "for he had many possessions."

Where are we in this scene? Can we use our possessions or achievements as means to live a holy life? Can we put these things at the service of others? Can we hold on to the things in our lives lightly? Is there anything in our lives which has become a stumbling block to our following Jesus? Knowing in our hearts that there are some things which hold us back, perhaps, with Jesus' disciples, we want to ask: "Then who can be saved?" Again, Jesus gives the answer: it is only the grace of God that can save us. It is only when we are empowered with the freedom and love which God shares with us that we can let go of the baggage which keeps us from the Kingdom.

During this Eucharist, let us pray for one another that we may see clearly that the only real treasure in life is union with God. Let us, with God's grace, put aside any baggage which keeps us from realizing that union. Then we will be truly wise.

Kathleen Flanagan, S.C.

29th Sunday in Ordinary Time

Cycle B

Is 53:10–11
Heb 4:14–16
Mk 10:35–45

The questions and answers heard in Jesus' dialogue with Zebedee's sons in today's Gospel reading provides us with a wonderful journey into faith and an opportunity to reflect on that same journey within our own lives.

The dialogue begins with James and John requesting glory. They want to sit on either side of Jesus in the Kingdom. So stage one of faith begins with ego, with a desire to be loved, with a yearning for more than we have. The faith journey begins with "I want."

Stage two in the conversation which Mark describes so dramatically involves a question from Jesus. "Can you drink the cup I shall drink or be baptized in the same bath of pain as I?" Jesus does not dismiss their desire. He challenges the ego's wants to lead James and John into a greater authenticity than they had wanted in the first place. They respond with youthful cockiness. "'We can,' they told him." Stage two in the faith journey, as it is told here, is a feeling that one can do everything necessary for salvation. I want glory and I know I can attain it.

Stage three brings about a reversal. First of all, the very opening request—the desire for glory—is drained of all its power. You can want glory with all your heart but I cannot give it to you: "Sitting at my right hand or left is not mine to give." But you can share in the suffering! It looks like James and John have been duped. They want glory and all they get is a share in the suffering. They are then asked to serve if they want to be great. Stage three seems to be a transformation of the person—one must leave the desire for greatness behind and become a person for others. The movement here involves:

(1) a desire to be loved;

(2) a false certainty that one can do something to achieve this goal;

(3) loving.

Jesus, with the logic of a man engulfed in the Spirit, moves the disciples out of themselves toward others. The faith journey begins with an inner need and ends with a life offered in humble service.

The homilist might want to offer some examples to help the congregation reflect on this movement in their own lives. I will offer two story possibilities here.

The first example is the life of Thomas Merton. Merton begins his journey with a desire for glory. He wants to be exceptional. The official biography by Michael Mott shows this clearly. The young Merton did not want to be like everyone else. Merton enjoyed the fame which came to him as a writer. He wanted holiness. He wanted glory. This would never be a monk who simply fit in. This would never be a person who was part of the crowd. A seat at the right or left looked pretty good to Father Louis.

Merton's early writings display a confidence in faith with answers. Reading *Seven Storey Mountain* or *Seeds of Contemplation* one gets the distinct feeling that Merton knows where he is going. "Can you drink the same cup I shall drink?" "I can."

Stage three occurs on a street corner in Louisville. Merton looks around at all the busy people going by and realizes "I'm like them and they are like me." In a moment he felt at one with them, with the world, with God. The desire for glory ends. Humble service begins. For the rest of his life we see a man who flees fame but continues to write the books which enflame a passion for the truth in his readers.

My second example is from the life of a friend. In our first years after college Mark desired fame as a journalist with all his soul. Life centered around getting the front page stories and the desperate need for a by-line. The most important aspect of life was moving from a small town newspaper to a big city daily. There was a need for glory within Mark and the confidence this could be achieved.

Mark's stage three began in his late twenties. The love of a woman resulting in marriage and a family brought about a change in emphasis. Mark no longer lived for himself. The most important thing in life was no longer a by-line but the needs of a wife and child. Being loved (in the form of recognition) became loving which continued in really being loved.

A last point to make in this homily could center around the reaction of the twelve to the dialogue between Jesus and Zebedee's sons. Mark tells us "they became indignant at James and John." The faith journey is best travelled not by the indignant but by the listeners. Confidence in the words and person of Christ can bring us to faith-trust in God's reality. Indignance at neighbor, fighting reality, leaves life a struggle which leads not to faith but to alienation. Invite your congregation to listen to their own lives, to trace a journey which leads out of self into loving.

Douglas Fisher

30th Sunday in Ordinary Time

Cycle B

Jer 31:7–9
Heb 5:1–6
Mk 10:46–52

com pas sion (kem pash en), n. a feeling of deep sympathy and sorrow for another's suffering or misfortune, accompanied by a desire to alleviate the pain or remove its cause.

The Good News is that our God is compassionate! In Jeremiah's "book of consolation," Yahweh gathers all of his people: in their imperfections, in their sufferings, in their expectations. In the readings from the Christian Scriptures, we are reminded that God's Son came to share our sufferings and our weaknesses, and to heal them. God is compassionate. He not only cares about the hurts in our lives, his feeling of sympathy is synonymous with his efforts to ease our pain.

God's compassion is Good News only if we have acknowledged our weakness and owned our imperfections. We need God's compassion and rejoice in it only when we have admitted our failures and wish to be healed. God's compassion is Good News to those who have claimed oneness with all humanity, and realized that it is our weakness which is the very foundation of our unity. It is in our weakness that we need each other and that we recognize our need for a compassionate God.

Jeremiah assures his people that God will gather "the blind and the lame, women with child, women in labor." This is indeed a consolation to those who are mentioned, but how did these words strike those who felt that they were better than the blind and the lame? Those who felt that women were inferior? If Jeremiah were writing today, whom would he have God gather as his people? Perhaps Jeremiah would write that God will gather "the mentally ill, the welfare recipients, the physically deformed, the women who have had abortions, the alcoholics and drug addicts." What feelings would this arouse in those of us who are certain that we are more faithful?

Jesus certainly had a list of those whom he wished to gather: the prostitutes, the adulterers, the tax collectors. And we know the feelings his list aroused—they killed him for his list.

The message seems to be either we recognize our unity with those who are listed, or we don't make the list. That unity is in weakness.

God cares. He cared enough to inspire Jeremiah to assure those who experienced disability that God would bring them home. He cared enough to send his Son to become one of us, to experience our human condition, to experience even our ultimate weakness: mortality. He cared enough to have that Son identify primarily with those who were considered the weakest of people. God cared enough to have his Son model a life of compassion for us, so that when he asked us to love each other as he loved us, we would understand what he meant.

"Love one another as I have loved you." Be compassionate towards each other as I have shown my compassion for you.

True compassion is a call to action. As the definition says, it is, "accompanied by the desire to alleviate the pain or remove its cause." If I am compassionate, I can't just feel sorry; that sorrow must lead me to do whatever I can to help.

God is compassionate. His compassion has led him to reach out and touch our pain. It led him to send us his Spirit who heals us, who strengthens us, who helps us in this difficult task of making real our compassionate God in today's world.

The Good News is that our God is a compassionate God. His list of friends includes the weak, and the more we identify with those who hurt most in our world, the more we are assured a place on his list.

If we can really believe all this, we, like Bartimaeus, will "follow him along the road," and we will BE the Good News of compassion to those we travel with.

Carole M. Eipers

31st Sunday in Ordinary Time

Cycle B

Dt 6:2–6
Heb 7:23–28
Mk 12:28–34

Today's Gospel offers two rich themes for preaching. One is the unity of loving God and neighbor. Terence Keegan has chosen to examine this theme in the exegesis section. The theme which will be treated here is that of courage and questioning. The final verse of today's Gospel, "And no one had the courage to ask him any more questions" is one of Scripture's most intriguing lines for reflection on growth in the spiritual life.

Mark clearly sees the courage required to ask questions of Jesus. His answers not only challenge: they can turn a world upside down. Examples in Scripture are numerous: the woman at the well, the feeding of the 5000, the question of the rich young man. To ask a question implies vulnerability to the answer. Look at the answer to the seemingly innocent "Which is the first of all the commandments?" The answer Jesus gives requires total commitment. What more could follow from another question if this one received the response "You are not far from the reign of God"? To get "into" the reign may involve even more. It takes tremendous courage to ask that question. Better to live in ignorance, and that was the choice this day.

Interestingly, Jesus constantly has the courage to ask questions. Sometimes he asks more than once. ("Simon Peter, do you love me?") Karl Rahner, the foremost theologian of our century, says the very definition of man is a question. Man is a question. It is his being to be open to reality in its fullness. Jesus, the fulfillment of humanity, has the courage to ask questions. He has the courage to be open to whatever reality a question brings about.

Let's go further with this notion of question. In John's Gospel Jesus is confronted with the ultimate question by Pilate. Pilate asks "Truth? What is that?" And Jesus does not answer. After the hundreds of questions he answered, whether with a quick response, a story, a quizzical statement or another question, Jesus is silent before the most important question of all. Why? Because the *person* has become

the *answer.* The very identity of reality lies not in words but in being. Jesus himself is the answer to "Truth? What is that?" The answer is not a word but a life. Jesus, all that he is for and with us, is the ultimate truth, reality in its fullness. The one we lack courage to question no longer provides answers. The one who does have the courage to ask questions is the truth. Questioning itself is the answer.

There is something within us which wants to stop asking questions. It takes too much vulnerability. Recently a popular disc jockey in New York admitted he switched the television channel every time a report from Ethiopia came on the news. He did not want to see the suffering because he knew it meant he had to ask the question. "What can I do?" And he did not have the courage to ask that question. (Eventually he did and raised half a million dollars for Catholic Relief Services.)

We stop asking questions because of the vulnerability required and because we never know where the questions can stop. Questions lead to questions which lead to questions. That is a frightening prospect because it means we are never complete as human beings. Life is process, a journey. We never "arrive." Questioning implies becoming more alive. Gaynell Cronin, a well-known religious educator, tells of the talent needed to ask questions of a class. It means asking a question you know they can handle, then one which is a little tougher and so on. If you ask the hardest question first, then the class stops. Perhaps our own lives need to be similar. We need to ask the "big" questions of meaning and truth. But perhaps that "stops the class"—it leaves us without an answer or an answer we cannot yet accept. Then it could be time to back up and ask reality an easier question. But stay on the road! Stay on the journey of questioning. Keep your courage, for that is the answer. Questioning itself is the answer. It is the vulnerability and trust to live a life we do not control. It means placing life in the hands of the ultimate questioner, the one who answers with his very life—Jesus.

Douglas Fisher

32nd Sunday in Ordinary Time

Cycle B

1 Kgs 17:10–16
Heb 9:24–28
Mk 12:38–44

We all have our ideas about what constitutes true and false religion. We have decided which people in our world, our neighborhood, or our church are holy and saved: the clean, the successful, priests and ministers, those who do not disturb the status quo, those who attend church services regularly or who work on church events. There are others we are quite certain stand outside the circle of true religion, and this often seems reason enough for us to reject or ignore them ourselves: persons of other faiths, homosexuals, the divorced, persons of other races or ethnic backgrounds, those who are dirty, poor, or hungry. The readings for today ask us to take another look at our neat categories of true and false religion. Our way of judging is not always the way God judges.

In the first reading the prophet Elijah visits a widow in Zarephath, a city in Phoenicia. The Israelites would not expect to find faith in God in a town outside their borders. But the widow of Zarephath not only believes the word of God which she hears through the prophet, she is willing to trust that word to the extent of sharing the last of her food with Elijah. She risks laying down her life for that word. In hearing this story we find our usual categories of true and false religion shaken up. For here, outside the borders of Israel, we find deep faith in the God of Israel. God's love and concern are universal. His word is heard and obeyed by those we may not consider visibly a part of our faith.

The story challenges our thinking in a second way. The Phoenician woman experiences God as one who has special care for the oppressed and the hungry. The Responsorial Psalm repeats this theme by listing what may be for us an unlikely group who enjoy God's special favor: the oppressed, the hungry, prisoners, the blind, the stranger, the widow, and the orphan. The story of Elijah and the widow calls us to enlarge our concern and acceptance.

These same points are emphasized in the reading from Mark's Gospel. We would expect to find the religious leaders of Israel, the Scribes or teachers,

practicing true religion. Surely they are the ones who belong to the inner circle of the saved. Yet we find that religion for them is mainly a matter of external show and observance. They like the honor and respect that comes from their position, but they have failed to live the justice and love which are the marks of true faith. Instead of caring for the widows and the poor, they devour the savings of widows. In contrast we find again that it is a poor woman, a widow, who is willing to give up her life for her faith. She represents all those who, without show or public display, quietly attempt to live out the deeper meaning of the Gospel. Once again, our standards for judging who is the true religious person are called into question. What counts is not external show, but the inner faith that attempts to carry out the gospel teachings.

The readings for today touch our lives in still another way. They remind us that God loves and accepts the gift we give of ourselves even when we feel it is given from poverty and need. Like the widow, we often feel that we have little to bring in terms of our own resources. It is that gift, however, that God praises. That is good news for all of us who are poor in various ways.

Kathleen R. Fischer
Thomas N. Hart

33rd Sunday in Ordinary Time

Cycle B

Dn 12:1–3
Heb 10:11–14, 18
Mk 13:24–32

As Rea McDonnell clearly points out, Mark's Gospel passage today is a sign of hope for believers. The Son of Man will gather his people on the judgment day. The persecuted will be vindicated and rejoice. We no longer need waste time speculating on the future. Neither should today's homilist. The "sure hope," as Paul calls it, should free us to concentrate on today. We do not need to just "get today over with," simply live through our time of misery. Instead, this people who knows not "the exact hour or day" (after all, not even the Son knows it) should live for today.

By assuring us of an end-time, Jesus makes now all the more important. A story told by Anthony DeMello brings this out. Once a popular Buddhist master was telling his students, "I was once visited by an angel who offered me anything I wanted."

"What did you request?" they asked anxiously.

"I asked for eighty years of life."

"But, master, why did you not ask to live forever? We love you. Think of all you could have done for us, your people! We could have had your leadership, your wisdom forever!"

"Oh, but children, if I had done that you would think the goal of life is longevity. It is not. It matters not how long you live—it only matters how."

When we want a vague forever, Jesus brings us back to an intense present. Yet there is something within us which refuses to accept responsibility for today. A Peanuts story drawn by Charles Shultz might help to image this. In the first cartoon frame we see Charlie Brown running after a fly ball in a baseball game. As he settles under the high fly, we hear him saying, "If I catch this ball, we'll win our first game of the season. Please let me catch it. Please! . . . On the other hand, do I think I deserve to be the hero? The kid who hit it doesn't want to be the goat . . . Is a baseball game really important? Lots of kids all over the world have never heard of baseball . . . Lots of kids don't get to play at all, or have a place to sleep, or . . ." And then we see the ball drop into his glove, and then out again, and onto the ground. Linus comes over and says, "Charlie Brown, how could you miss such an easy pop fly?" And Charlie Brown answers, "I prayed myself out of it."

Today's Gospel is not intended to make us otherworldly. Let's not pray ourselves out of this world. It is *this* world that God the Father loves so much that he sends his only Son. It is *this* world where the Son chooses to come in glory. Mark is beckoning us on to what we can be. This next story, told by Paul Wharton, helps shed some light on what this means.

> Hoping to find a few days work, a traveling portrait painter stopped at a small town. One of his clients there was the town drunk who, in spite of his dirty, unshaven face and bedraggled clothes, sat for his portrait with all the dignity he could display. After the artist had labored a little longer than usual, he lifted the painting from the easel and presented it to the man. "This isn't me," the astonished drunk slurred as he studied the smiling, well-dressed man in the painting. The artist, who had looked beneath the exterior and seen his inner beauty, thoughtfully replied, "But it's the man you could be."

Douglas Fisher

Feast of Christ the King

Cycle B

Dn 7:13–14
Rv 1:5–8
Jn 18:33–37

This feast of Christ the King can be a dangerous one to celebrate. The Kings we know of today no longer have absolute dominion, and many of them have become mere figureheads who often serve little purpose beyond being convenient anachronisms to lead parades on special occasions. The danger is that Christ will be King in name only, and the community will owe him no more than this yearly feast.

We are not asked to preserve the vestiges of a once-powerful ruler by conferring an honorary title. We are, rather, called to spread the dominion of one whom we have personally recognized as King. We are called to be radicals, revolutionaries, and dreamers.

The first two readings are apocalyptic. We have to begin by being dreamers, visionaries, by being able to imagine what it would be like if our entire world was, indeed, the Kingdom of God.

Our work begins with getting to know this Jesus whose kingship we dream about. It is interesting that Jesus never calls himself king. He never claimed titles for himself; rather, his words about himself defined his mission and purpose. Thus, we do not hear him say "I am King." He does not claim "I am the Ruler," but he tells us he came to serve. Likewise his followers were not declaring his "state of life" when they called him "Rabbi," "Messiah," and "Son of God." They were rather proclaiming their recognition of the way he lived and acted.

We can never make the Kingdom of God a reality in the world unless it is first a reality in our own lives. Jesus said, "The Kingdom of God is within you." The power to spread that Kingdom is within our grasp. That means we have read Jesus' Kingdom parables and we realize that the Kingdom is precious and that it must grow. We have to accept the fact that the spreading of the Kingdom will be done by love and forgiveness and not by violence. We have to realize that our enemies are called to be members of the Kingdom as well as we, and that drawing our swords to cut off an ear even "in the name of Jesus" excludes us from the very Kingdom which we purport to defend this way. And we have to be able to swallow the fact that the lost sheep will be sought after, prodigal sons and daughters will be welcomed with open arms, and workers who arrive at the eleventh hour will share our reward.

Jesus loved those who acknowledged their need for him: those who needed healing and forgiveness. He loved those who acknowledged that they were not kings of their own lives, those who had faith that he was in charge, those who recognized his dominion over them. You either have to let Jesus be your king, or be king yourself. You can either acknowledge that he can heal and forgive, or you can try to heal and forgive yourself. Or, you can despair of healing and forgiveness and turn over the kingship to money or power or sex and give those values the absolute dominion in your life. You can celebrate the Feast of Christ the King once a year and give the other 364 days to other pursuits. Or you can celebrate the Feast of Christ the King once a year and give the other 364 days to making that kingship more of a reality in the world today.

We start with faith in Jesus and in what he said and did. We give over to him the absolute power in our lives and make peace, love and justice our primary values. We work at spreading the Kingdom by loving and forgiving and doing good to our enemies. We set aside our desire to be served in favor of serving. We drink the cup of suffering and wash a few feet along the way.

Then we are ready to celebrate. We are ready to imagine that God reigns and his Kingdom is a reality. The Mass is our visionary experience, for there we are equals. We share one loaf and one cup. It is a reality for that hour, and if we are working for the Kingdom, the liturgy is both a comfort and a challenge.

Carole M. Eipers

1st Sunday of Lent

Cycle B

Gn 9:8–15
Pt 3:18–22
Mk 1:12–15

The gloom and doom of another season of Lent is upon us. It's time to break out the ashes, sack-cloth, and grim faces. We need to form a Puritan list of all the things we will give up. Perhaps if we are more modern and come of age, we have a list of all the positive things we will do. However, as we approach Lent one thing seems certain—we can't do business as usual. Even Jesus must venture into the desert and be tested or tempted by Satan. If we think our neighbors are bad, pity poor Jesus. He was surrounded by wild beasts! Only after being tempted is Jesus free to begin the public ministry with his central theme: "This is the time of fulfillment. The reign of God is at hand! Reform your lives and believe in the good news." The message of Jesus is certainly worth a closer examination.

"The time of fulfillment." We often think of time in terms of calendars and watches. Time is mathematical and easily quantified: 60 seconds equals one minute; 60 minutes equals one hour, and so on. This notion of time is referred to as *chronos* by the Greeks. *Chronos* time is uneventual and lacking in personal meaning. On the other hand, there is what the Greeks called *karios* time. This is the time that is beyond measurement because it is so deep with meaning. *Karios* time is the inbreaking of the sacred into the profane and ordinary things of this world. Jesus is speaking of *karios* time. God is doing a new thing in Jesus. Jesus not only announces the fullness of God's presence, but Jesus is the concrete particularization of God's love. What the prophets of the Old Testament longed to see, God's salvation, is here in Jesus.

"The reign of God is at hand!" Nowhere in scripture is the reign or kingdom of God defined. Jesus' audience knew well what it meant. God's active rule and presence in human history and in the history and life of Israel was reaching its zenith. The reign of God cannot be limited to a geographical area or equated with military power. The reign of God is the transforming presence of God in the hearts of men and women. This active presence of God is not for the end of the world or even the end of the week. God's rule is *now*. We can't delay or postpone God's rule. Burying the dead and looking back are no longer acceptable responses to God. In Jesus, the definitive rule of God is now and we must decide.

"Reform your lives." If we really hear the preaching of Jesus and respond to his message and person, this costs us something. We will need to *change*. However, this change is not a mere shallow rearrangement of our schedules, likes and dislikes, or the way we spend our leisure time. Rather, to reform and change is a fundamental reorientation of one's whole life and being. It is a process of having one's heart of stone transformed into a heart of flesh. In other words, the old ways of doing business in the market place of our daily existence no longer have "cash value." Jesus is the "New Being" of God who challenges us to help build the new creation. This will call for new values and a new way of being-in-the-world. The structure of history and our lives are radically changed by and through Jesus.

"Believe in the good news." Jesus challenges his audience and us to believe that in him God is *doing* salvation. Authentic belief requires that we live our personal and community lives in such a way so as to give evidence that Jesus is Lord. Authentic belief is more than mere correct doctrine; it also requires correct acting in our everyday lives. A first step in this direction is to believe that Jesus is the good news of God. Jesus is the news and announcement that God is a passionate, saving, loving Father who wants to share his life with us. We must resist the temptation to turn the good news of Jesus into mere information. We do this by learning *about* Jesus but never really being grasped by the Spirit of Jesus. During Lent it is easy for us to paint a rather gloomy picture of Jesus and the gospel. Good news becomes angry or bad news. The writer of Genesis in our first reading rejects this. Our God is a God of life who makes a covenant with all creation. The covenant of life and love between God and each of us reaches its apex in Jesus.

In the beginning of our discussion, we spoke about Lent and the temptation to join the "doom boom." There would be some plausibility for such a response if it were not for Jesus. If Jesus had come and announced a God who is indifferent, evil, or an occasional visitor, then fear might be legitimate. However, Jesus assures us that God is love and the Really Real is ultimately gracious. Life is not "a tale told by an idiot," but a gift from God who wants us to experience life to the full. During this opening Sunday of Lent it might be healthy, both physically and spiritually, to examine our ashes and grim faces. They have their place but eventually they must give way to celebration. I told you Lent wasn't easy!

William F. Maestri

2nd Sunday of Lent

Cycle B

Gn 22:1–2, 10–13, 15–18
Rom 8:31–34
Mk 9:2–10

"God's ways are not our ways," the familiar saying goes, and that is the point that today's readings drive home very emphatically.

First we are presented with the familiar story of Abraham's willing response to God's command. "Our way" would label Abraham's response an absurdity; God's way calls it fidelity. "Our way," which prides itself on its logic, would probably have Abraham answering God back in some way:

"What do you mean, sacrifice my only son? You said to me, 'Look up to heaven and count the stars if you can. Such will be my descendants.' How can that be, if at my age I begin by sacrificing my only son?"

Abraham, by contrast, presumes that God knows what he is doing, and though it might be tearing him apart inside, he steadfastly obeys God's command.

In the second reading, St. Paul reminds his audience that no matter what the adversity, they can be assured of God's providential care. "If God is for us, who can be against us?" Sometimes that seems equally paradoxical. A quick glance at the morning paper might cause one to question whether or not God is even awake, let alone on our side. In the midst of the AIDS epidemic, in days when terrorism rules the lives of millions, and political hostages are held for years on end, it seems as though there is much to prevail against us. That is another judgment of "our way" in contrast to "God's way."

In the selection from Mark's Gospel, Peter exemplifies "our way" typically when he wants to set up camp to commemorate the transfiguration. Would souvenir stands be far behind? "Our way" is to latch on to an experience and attempt to package it, rather than to savor it in the present and use its power to carry us into the rest of life.

What makes God's way so different from "our way"? God's ways are not our ways precisely because God is a master of dramatic irony, able to encompass the whole picture, while our vision is limited to one small corner of experience.

Abraham trusted God's way, because Abraham had experienced God's fidelity in other seemingly "absurd" circumstances. That didn't make God's request of him any less demanding, but Abraham was able to respond on the basis of his total experience of God, not isolating this command from any of the others. And Abraham's trust was rewarded.

The transfiguration derives its full meaning only after the death and resurrection of the Lord Jesus. To see it in isolation from the totality of the paschal event might make it appear to be a slick magical trick or a hallucination. Mark's Gospel has many such cautions for secrecy, but they are all motivated by this attempt to allow the entire experience unfold.

In facing the many trials that surround us in the world today we need to withhold the judgment of "our way" while working for the justice that characterizes God's way. Supported by our trust in God's providence, and fired by the message of the Gospel, we will be able to transform the face of the earth. We must strive to avoid the temptations to stray from "God's way" and veer off into "our way." Christianity, authentically lived, is counter-cultural, and the culture will continue to lure us in very subtle ways. When we feel the inevitable pull of "our way," let us remember the response we have to the first reading and carve it deeply in our hearts,

"I will walk in the presence of the Lord in the land of the living."

Julia Upton, R.S.M.

3rd Sunday of Lent

Cycle B

Ex 20:1–17
1 Cor 1:22–25
Jn 2:13–25

"If we knew how to look at life through God's eyes, we would see (life) as innumerable tokens of the love of the Creator seeking the love of his creatures. The Father has put us into the world, not to walk through it with lowered eyes but to search for him through things, events, people. Everything must reveal God to us. All of life would become a sign."

Signs—symbols which communicate an idea, effect a feeling or illustrate a reality—are a major part of every human person's life and daily living experience. Let us reflect for a moment upon the number of signs which have entered our experience of living just today.

How many signs affected our way of acting, our behavior? A clock informed us of the movement of the sun and we responded to whatever time it was. A red octagon informed us that we were not alone as travelers and therefore had to exercise caution. A sounding bell may have informed us that someone wanted to communicate with us and we responded by acknowledging a piece of technological equipment. A smile may have informed us of someone else's happiness, concern, or love and we responded accordingly.

Some of the signs to which we have responded today were signs which are known only to ourselves—signs which indicate our inner feelings or the inner feelings of someone very close to us.

Signs are what today's scripture readings are all about. In fact throughout this Lent, all the scriptures speak of signs which God employs to reveal himself to his people. All of these signs are part of the agreement—the covenant—which God has made with humankind.

The second readings each Sunday focus our attention upon the sign of God's fulfillment of his covenant—the cross on which hung the redeemer of the world. From this focal point—the cross—the other two readings inform us of the signs used by God in the Old Testament to lead us to the cross, and of the signs used by God in the gospels to identify the one who would be enthroned on that Cross.

The gospels this Lent offer us signs which identify Jesus as the fulfillment of that covenant and illustrate for each of us the way we must live in order to follow Jesus.

The question must be asked—does God continue to use signs as a means of revealing himself to his people, to humankind; as a means of providing his people with death-life opportunities which lead to the achievement of the kingdom?

Although at times difficult to recognize and often difficult to accept, the answer to that question is *Yes.* The following contemporary signs are offered for reflective meditation:

—Christ, unjustly treated in mock courtrooms throughout the world.

—Christ, suffering indignities simply because he is too poor to purchase legal assistance or to post bail.

—Christ, being oppressed not for what he did but for the color he is or the language he speaks.

—Christ, fallen into the gutter or slouched in the doorway of a cheap, skid-row hotel.

—Christ, working in the burning sun for wages that are below the minimum standard of living.

—Christ, falling victim to the self-righteous Christian who doesn't want to get involved.

—Christ, seen in the saddened eyes and the broken heart of a parent who is unable to purchase the necessary food for his family.

—Christ, being exploited by substandard housing, poor education or unemployment.

—Christ, fleeing oppression from his native land and seeking refuge in a democratic society.

—Christ, bearing the agony and suffering of physical or mental illness.

—Christ, experiencing the dependence, pain and loneliness of old age.

—Christ, identified for annihilation as the world builds more devastating nuclear weapons.

These are the signs of God, not very magnificent nor very powerful signs.

In the words of Paul "Christ is the power of God and the wisdom of God. For God's folly is wiser than men and his weakness more powerful than men." The folly of the Cross is the sign of God's revelation. "The Father has put us into the world, not to walk through it with lowered eyes, but to search for him through things, events, people." All of life is a sign—a sign of God's revelation!

James P. McGinnis

4th Sunday of Lent

Cycle B

2 Chr 36:14–17, 19–23
Eph 2:4–10
Jn 3:14–21

Jesus' statement to Nicodemus in today's Gospel from John goes right to the core of a living faith. The saving event has already happened. God, the one who is in love with the world, has sent his Son that we might have eternal life. The light is here. But does it make any difference? If we believe that reality, then we live differently. It is that straightforward. There is nothing subtle in this statement by Jesus.

What would happen if we truly believed that God has saved this world he loves? How different our lives would be than unbelievers' is expressed by the rabbi Baal Shem in the allegorical tale of "The Deaf Man": "Once a fiddler played so sweetly that all who heard him began to dance, and whoever came near enough to hear joined in the dance. Then a deaf man who knew nothing of music happened along, and to him all he saw seemed the action of madmen—senseless and in bad taste."

But the light is not the only reality. Jesus is clear that there are powerful forces of darkness and those forces are attractive. Again a story from a rabbi could illustrate this point.

Once some disciples of Rabbi Pinhas ceased talking in embarrassment when he entered the House of Study. When he asked them what they were talking about, they said: "Rabbi, we were saying how afraid we are that the Evil Urge will pursue us." "Don't worry," he replied. "You have not gotten high enough for it to pursue you. For the time being, you are still pursuing it."

Jesus' statement this Sunday is a challenging call to action. There is no getting away with non-committal reflection this week. Either act as a person of the light or as a person of darkness. The preacher could bring that call to action to the everyday level by asking the congregation to reflect on some questions of action. Do I live as someone who knows I am loved, or do I go about manipulating and trying to win approval? Do I treat others as the beloved of God or do I see them a threat to my comfort, my security? Do I take part in the political process, demanding that the government which represents me be a force of peace and justice in the world and not an oppressive war machine?

Ask these tough questions but also remind people that the internal struggle of light and darkness is always there. I found that struggle to be powerfully expressed by Philip Willis-Conger, a sanctuary worker on trial. In a recent issue of *Sojourners*, he said:

"It's a difficult position to maintain, trying to be faithful and being willing to confront the principalities and the powers—whoever it is that is standing in the way of a more just and peaceful world. It's hard to be faithful to one's vision and understanding of the kingdom and confront those whom we might usually call the enemy and, at the same time, also love and forgive these people we are confronting.

"I think many, if not most, Christians and churches in the United States end up avoiding conflict. We avoid confrontation, because we see that as bad. Yet at that point, we become less than faithful.

"The other side is to become completely confrontational—to refuse to forgive and love the enemy. We have that fear of being somehow politically naive. We know there's an enemy out there, namely the INS and the Border Patrol, and we believe that in order not to compromise our beliefs, not to betray the refugees, we have to continually fight that enemy and never give in until we attain our goal. And that leads to an avoidance of solutions to the problem, because we're afraid to negotiate, afraid to dialogue, afraid of becoming less than pure.

"We need to be willing to confront the evil in our society and yet still love the individuals who are carrying out an unjust system, who are creating misery among God's people. It means being able to hold on to one's faith and values while also looking for the openings in the other's position, because we're not living in an ideal world.

"We can't compromise our values, but at some point we must realize that we have to enter into negotiations and dialogue. There has to be some common ground, some meeting place."

As we go on this journey of living faith, of faith in action, let us know ourselves to be the people with whom God is in love.

Douglas Fisher

5th Sunday of Lent

Cycle B

Jer 31:31–34
Heb 5:7–9
Jn 12:20–33

This week's Gospel reading provides us with some insights into the invitation all of us have to on-going conversion. In this homily we will look at the unusual timing of engraced moments in life, the "trouble in the soul" which can be an opportunity for new life and the decision-provoking presence of Jesus as part of the conversion journey.

First, let's look at the strange timing of God breaking into our lives. Today's Gospel tells us that some Greeks went to the Passover to look for Jesus. When Jesus hears this from Philip and Andrew, he recognizes that his life must now change completely: "The hour has come for the Son of Man to be glorified." What makes this timing strange is that Jesus' life, with some notable exceptions, is spent in the Jewish world. It is his culture, his background. But now a critical moment occurs when Greeks enter the scene at a very Jewish moment—the Passover. God breaks in not at the times and places we set up for him but in the times of the unexpected.

Here is an example of such a moment in my life. I was at a workshop at a theology convention. The workshop was on Rahnerian ecclesiology. My background is in theology and I am very comfortable in that world. As the speaker gave his presentation I was thinking many things: How does this apply to books available on Rahner? Is what the speaker saying "book material"? Can he write such a book? In the midst of my musings, a person raised his hand to ask a question. The questioner seemed to have cancer of the throat, for he spoke through a device on his neck. His voice had an unpleasant rasp. I felt repulsed by his voice and hoped his question was a short one. It wasn't. But then I began to pray for him and what appears to be his battle with cancer. And I prayed for people like me who might make him feel uncomfortable socially with his affliction. The theology talk, part of my normal world, did not lead me to pray. The presence of the hurting person at an unexpected time did. We cannot control or predict the inbreaking power of God.

Next let's look at Jesus' answer to Philip and Andrew. He tells them several contradictory things which only hang together in our strange Christian logic. He tells them: (1) he is to be glorified, (2) a man who loves his life loses it, (3) his soul is troubled. For Jesus, the time of trouble, the time of personal anguish, represents an opportunity to give himself away in love, and that gift of self is glorification.

An example from a friend's life could illustrate this point. My friend sells bonds and recently the bond market has "dried up." Bond brokers do not have any good deals anywhere for their clients. For Barry, a married man with three children to support, this is truly a troubled time. What some of his co-workers have done to get some commission money for themselves is "roll over" the bonds of their present clients from one set of bonds to another. This does not help the clients as often they are going from one low yield bond to one even worse. But the broker makes money on the transaction. There is nothing illegal about this but it is certainly choosing selfish gain over the good of others. Barry, in his troubled hour, is faced with a choice. And he has chosen to do the moral thing and do what is best for the clients. The troubled hour has given Barry an opportunity to die to self and in the process to grow as a person. It is in the troubled time that conversion is possible.

Finally, Jesus says that the voice from the sky glorifying his name stands as a judgment upon this world. Because Jesus is who he is, everyone is forced to make a decision. The presence of Jesus as the glorified Son of God in our world demands that I stop my routine and make choices for or against him. When faced with troubled times, we can no longer just say: "What is best for me?" Now we must say: "What would Jesus do in this situation?" The action following an investigation into the answer has something important to do with salvation.

Douglas Fisher

Passion (Palm) Sunday

Cycle B

Is 50:4–7
Phil 2:6–11
Mk 14:1—15:47

Part of our conventional wisdom is the belief that love means you never have to say you are sorry. Related to this belief is the view that love is free and never makes demands. When examined, however, these two pieces of bedrock insight turn out to be built on sand. What at first blush seems so mature and liberated is in reality a rationalization of the fear of commitment. Those who do love and not merely talk about it know well the need to accept and experience forgiveness. We cannot escape the bumps and bruises of daily living which make it necessary to say "I'm sorry" and "That's ok; all is forgiven." In fact, part of the zest of living is the ability to transcend our feelings and reach out to others in love. Above all, love means *commitment* and *suffering*. Love does not come free; rather, love comes through freedom and maturity.

This notion of commitment, love and suffering is powerfully presented in our readings. In our first reading we see the vocation of the Lord's servant. This is not just any servant, but Isaiah's Suffering Servant. The Suffering Servant is one who is called to witness to God's justice in history. To be God's witness means to make a commitment to suffering, rejection and death. The audience of the prophet and the Suffering Servant often respond with anger, ridicule, violence and even death. To be a prophet or a servant of Yahweh is not the way to "win friends and influence people." The task of speaking God's word and experiencing the rejection and violence of the world calls for the gift of the Spirit. In the midst of such pain it is easy to turn from the Lord and chase after idols of popularity, status, money and group acceptance. The Spirit of the Lord is given to strengthen and confirm us in witnessing to the risen Lord. In our daily life it takes courage to seek the glory of God rather than the praise of others. The individual Christian witness is part of a larger whole (Mystical Body). We are to witness as a community and bear the burdens of each other.

The experience of commitment and suffering love reaches its culmination in the writings of Paul and Mark. Paul challenges the Christians of Philippi

to put on the spirit or attitude of Jesus. Jesus must become the center of individual and community life. Such a spirit is one of humility and service. Out of passionate love for humankind God became human in Jesus. Jesus reveals to us the way to the Father— servanthood and the cross in our daily lives. In imitation of Jesus we are to be obedient to the Father's love and word. Obedience is not denial of our freedom but its highest expression. Only those who are mature and free can hand themselves over to another in trust and hope.

The passion narrative of Mark makes one thing clear; Jesus is the Son of God and the death of Jesus is part of the divine reconciliation. Like the prophets, servants and Israel itself, Jesus must drink the cup of suffering, rejection and death. What makes this more profound is the realization that Jesus is supremely innocent and without sin. Those who come in the name of Jesus must experience the same baptism and drink the same cup. Jesus reminds all of us that to follow Jesus is to know the cross.

What can we make of all this in relation to our growth in Jesus? First, we must remember that our God is a God of passionate, suffering, enduring love. We don't worship an indifferent God but one who is so moved by our condition that he becomes one like us. Jesus is truly human, suffers, knows rejection, and dies. This human Jesus may offend some who want a Superstar Jesus. We know, however, that this human Jesus is the real cause of our hope. In the Spirit we too can hope, believe, and love knowing all the while our God cares.

If God's loving commitment to humankind is revealed in Jesus then we are to do the same for each other. In a time of playing it cool and aloof, the Christian is committed to Jesus, others and life in general. A passionate God requires a passionate people. Passion Sunday speaks to us of what it means to truly love and freely give ourselves to each other. The story of Yahweh and Jesus is our story as well. Passion Sunday speaks of suffering and death but also of love, commitment and above all, hope. These are the whispers of Passion Sunday and they can be heard by all who are grasped by the Spirit. Do you hear them?

William F. Maestri

Easter Sunday

Cycle B

Acts 10:34–43
Col 3:1–4
Jn 20:1–9

An enriching and insightful part of every culture are bits and pieces of wisdom that grow out of daily experience. In the Scripture we have the wisdom literature. In our own society we have *Poor Richard's Almanac*. A much used saying is "never put off until tomorrow what you can do today." Unfortunately, we do put off until tomorrow what we ought to do now. Tomorrow becomes the busiest day of our lives. One committed to the Christian life can fall victim to the same "tomorrow syndrome." Tomorrow we will give ourselves to Jesus and others. Tomorrow we will leave the nets of our daily concerns and follow Jesus. But today? Today is filled with the anxious and necessary tasks of keeping my world together. In a strange way, Easter can contribute to this wrong-headed approach to Christian existence and the future.

It is not uncommon to go through one's religious formation burdened by certain "Easter myths." One such myth is the "Jesus only" approach. This view holds that we celebrate the resurrection of Jesus *exclusively*. We are spectators to what God has done in Jesus. This view overlooks the fact that Jesus is the first-born of each human being. In Jesus we experience our hope of new life in God. Second, there is the "end of the world" approach. The resurrected life is for those who love God and neighbor. The experience of new life will take place at the end of time. Our immediate task is to suffer through this vale of tears. The unfortunate aspect of this view is that we can ignore the *present*. Also, we can become passive in the face of social injustice and oppression. The final myth around Easter is the rather gruesome "body out of the ground" belief. Resurrection is understood as the revivification of dead bodies out of the tombs.

Paul reminds us that the resurrection is a whole new order of existence. Resurrection is a *process* which begins *now* and comes to completion when Christ will be all in all.

As we celebrate Easter our readings offer some valuable insights into the process of daily Christian existence. St. Luke's account of Peter's sermon in Acts reminds us of the importance of a *living*

tradition. In our parish celebration of the Easter liturgy we are one with the early apostolic community. Jesus is the good news of the present and coming kingdom in which God's justice and peace are established. Jesus is the final liberation of humankind from the enemies of sin and death. The vocation of the Christian is the same as that of the early apostolic community: preach and witness to Jesus as the hope of the forgiveness of sins and reconciliation with God.

In some cases there are times when we must be willing to lay down our very lives. In our Eucharist and our "liturgy after the liturgy" we are to celebrate the Easter event. The Easter event is a whole process which culminates with the risen Lord ascending to the Father and sending the Spirit at Pentecost. By our daily lives of love and service we witness in hope until the Lord comes again.

The dignity of the Christian vocation to witness to the Easter event is powerfully expressed by St. Paul in Colossians. We have been raised up in company with Jesus and so we must live a God-centered life. The idols of this world do not offer life. The same Spirit which raised Jesus must raise us each day in saying "yes" to God and others. In living a God-centered life we must avoid the temptation to overly spiritualize Easter by rejecting the material world as evil. However, we are called to see through the creation to the goodness, beauty and truth of God. In effect, creation becomes a sacrament graced with God's presence. Not only does nature need our reverent care but we are dependent on nature as well. Second, we exercise the proper use of the goods of creation by seeing to it that our brothers and sisters have what they need to live truly human lives. We do not seek to possess more than we need in order to live with dignity and hope. As Christians we *actively* seek the well-being of the other in his or her attempt to live with dignity and hope.

We are often like the disciples on that first Easter as recorded in John's Gospel. They run to the tomb in expectation of seeing Jesus or some divine manifestation. What they find is an empty tomb. Easter faith, like Christian existence, is not the "buzz and boom" of big events but the whisper and rumor of the divine presence. Often we rush around looking for God in the great events of our daily lives. However, Jesus is still in our midst as the beggar, the prisoner, the hungry and thirsty. Granted, this is not very flashy, but such is our faith and that is our hope.

William F. Maestri

2nd Sunday of Easter

Cycle B

Acts 4:32–35
1 Jn 5:1–6
Jn 20:19–31

As I reflect on the words of today's first reading from the Acts of the Apostles, I can't help but laugh inside. Somehow, as I savor the image of this community of believers, with all possessions held in common, no one needy among them, bearing united witness to the risen Jesus, it always ends the same way in my mind. Television's famous Mr. Rourke, in his white suit and tie, lifts his glass toward me and says, "Welcome, my dear guest, to Fantasy Island!"

I can imagine some of those who might choose to live this fantasy of Christian community with me. There must be pastors facing parish debts who would love to see a time when "all who owned property or houses sold them and donated the proceeds"; there must be criticized parish staffs who would like at least to live one day when "great respect was paid to them all"; there must be D.R.E.s caught between parochial school and C.C.D. programs who would welcome being able to say "the community of believers were one heart and one mind" for at least one decision.

Perhaps, though, if there really were a Fantasy Island, I'd find my first wish in today's Gospel. It must have been wonderful to see the risen Jesus in person, to hear him say, "Peace be with you," to have him personally send me to spread the Good News of the Father's love. I can feel how enthused I would be—how deeply I'd be converted—if only Rourke could grant my dream.

"Blest are they who have not seen and have believed," Jesus says after offering to prove himself to the doubter. "Blest are they," I suppose he says to us, "who do not need their fantasy of the Christian community or of me fulfilled in order to believe." Dietrich Bonhoeffer perhaps says it for Jesus when he writes, "He who loves his dream of a community more than the Christian community itself becomes a destroyer of the latter, even though his personal intentions may be ever so honest and earnest and sacrificial."

There is another extreme though. Certainly counting our dream as greater than the reality of our community can be destructive; on the other hand, to simply accept the reality of our community and have no dream for it can be equally destructive. There are those whose only dream is the status quo for themselves and their community as well. Faced with the opportunity to meet Rourke and live out their fantasy, it would be only to have things never change.

Jesus certainly accepted the reality of who his followers were, yet he did not simply settle for that reality. He loved the shakeable Peter, yet dreamed him to be Rock; he loved the prostitute Magdalene, yet dreamed her to be holy; he loved the blind, yet dreamed that they could see; he loved the lame, yet dreamed that they could walk. Jesus dreamed that all would be one as he and the Father are one; he dreamed that people would recognize his followers by the love they had for one another. Neither of those dreams came true while Jesus was alive on earth, yet he never abandoned his community. In fact, despite disappointment and betrayal, misunderstanding and desertion, Jesus promised he would be with them always, even until the end of time.

Jesus never escaped to Fantasy Island and sought out Mr. Rourke to fulfill his dreams, but he did go off by himself and seek the Father's guidance in prayer. Jesus loved people just as they were, and never demanded that they become his dream as a condition for earning his love. He invited and gave example; he lived the dream of unity and love and united with others to share the dream by living it. And so, the dream became reality, and people said of the first Christians, "See how they love one another!" Jesus had one dream: the Father's dream, the Father's Kingdom, and he himself in life and by his death proved the worth of his dream, while never rejecting the reality of the people the Father had given him to build the Kingdom with.

So forget it, Mr. Rourke, and forgive us, Father. We look for fulfillment of personal fantasies rather than working to bring about the reality of your Kingdom. There is no need to travel to Fantasy Island, only to seek the Father's will and to center our community's actions and goals and organizations on his will. Then, perhaps, we shall no longer think of Mr. Rourke and his Fantasy Island—even wistfully—and when people say of us, "See how they love one another!" it will not be wishful thinking, but the Kingdom of God made real; Jesus' fantasy-come-true.

Carole M. Eipers

3rd Sunday of Easter

Cycle B

Acts 3:13–15, 17–19
1 Jn 2:1–5
Lk 24:35–48

There is no such thing as an unforgivable sin. This is hard for us to grasp. Because we have such a hard time forgiving those who hurt us, we imagine God is the same. But the Scriptures are full of stories of God's forgiveness. And, in a way, Jesus' death and resurrection is really a story of sin and forgiveness. It is the story of the greatest sin imaginable—the murder of Jesus, the Servant of God, the Holy and Just One, the Author of Life, the Messiah. But it is also the story of the greatest forgiveness imaginable, where those who were responsible for his death not only get off scot-free, but become his trusted witnesses.

Our first reading today is taken from Peter's preaching after he and John had cured the crippled man on the steps of the temple. It is a sermon about betrayal and forgiveness from someone who knew these first-hand. It was, after all, Peter who had three times denied Jesus as he stood in the courtyard watching Jesus' trial before the high priest. It was Peter whose eyes met the eyes of Jesus and who went off weeping. And it was Peter who three times had to answer the Risen Lord's question, "Do you love me?" Peter, who found forgiveness in the Lord's greeting "Peace to you," now speaks confidently because he knows that he is forgiven. "You put to death the Author of life. But God raised him from the dead, and we are his witnesses."

Jesus is forgiveness. As St. John says, "We have in the presence of the Father, Jesus Christ, an intercessor who is just." Jesus' greeting of peace to the disciples is a greeting of forgiveness to those who had run away, who had disowned him. Perhaps the disciples' panic and fright was not only due to the thought that it was a ghost they saw. Perhaps it was a feeling of embarrassment. What do you say to the friend you have betrayed? How do you ask forgiveness?

While we cannot know what was in the mind of the disciples, some Scripture scholars have speculated that at the heart of their encounter with the risen Lord was this experience of forgiveness. Certainly the Scriptures testify to this in Peter's case, and Peter makes this the heart of his message to the crowd. So it is safe to say that it was this experience of forgiveness that transformed Peter from despondency to strength and the command Jesus gives to his disciples in the Gospel today is to become witnesses of forgiveness. He says to them, "Penance for the remission of sins is to be preached to all nations."

Traditionally, we think of Lent as a time to focus on repentance and the Easter season as a time when we dwell on our mission. But these are really two sides of the same coin. Forgiveness is the vital link that transforms repentance into witness. And so Easter is a season when we should allow the presence of the risen Jesus to break through whatever blocks us from accepting God's forgiveness.

This resistance to forgiveness can have many forms. We may feel that what we have done is so bad that God won't forgive us. We may feel that it makes us unlovable or unworthy in God's eyes. We may even feel angry with God or blame him for the way we feel. If so, listen to Jesus's voice in the Gospel: "Peace to you. Why are you disturbed? Why do such thoughts cross your mind?" Jesus always takes the initiative. He who humbled himself to accept death on the cross invites you to turn to him, to trust that there is nothing he will not forgive. He who forgave Peter who denied him, who gave peace to his disciples who disowned him, and who loved the crowd that chose Barabbas over him, calls to us. He invites us to turn to him that our sins may be forgiven. He calls us to be his witnesses, to preach the good news of forgiveness.

Robert Hamma

4th Sunday of Easter

Cycle B

Acts 4:8–12
1 Jn 3:1–2
Jn 10:11–18

The beauty of a metaphor is that it can give new insight by means of juxtaposition or contrast. We are able to hold at one and the same time seemingly incompatible realities in order to create something entirely fresh. Ann Sexton in her book of poems, *The Awful Rowing Toward God,* induces new insights by means of this device. She writes about " . . . the pond wearing its mustache of frost," or she says, "Perhaps the moon is a frozen tear . . . " We are more sensitive to our everyday world by means of her metaphors. The parables of Jesus perform just such a function; they often involve stated or implied contrasts (for example, the Pharisee and the Publican or the mustard seed).

Today's gospel selection takes up one aspect of the parable found in the preceding verses of chapter 10. John selects two metaphors, sheepgate and shepherd, to speak of the mutual relationship between Jesus and ourselves. Then the characteristic "I am" passage at verse 11 begins to make the shepherd metaphor more explicit by means of contrast. The parabolic metaphor in vv. 2–4 is extended into a discussion of a true shepherd and a hireling.

In our highly urbanized society the shepherd metaphor may lose some of its impact, but the contrasting images presented in vv. 11–18 offer entry into the metaphor. The characteristic of "involvement" appears as the central contrast between shepherd and hireling. The hireling has no investment in the flock (v. 13) while the shepherd is not only known by the sheep but knows the sheep as personally as the Father knows the Son. This certainly suggests intimacy, interaction and involvement. As a result the sheep will instinctively follow because, as the parable tells us, they recognize the voice of the shepherd.

It is an easy temptation to allegorize the shepherd metaphor and think only in the pastoral images of Jesus as shepherd and Christians as docile sheep. It may be more productive to attend to the contrast between shepherd and hireling. Jesus, the good shepherd, sets the standard by investing his very life in the flock and, in contrast to the hireling, cannot flee, for his intimacy with the sheep has forged permanent bonds.

Christians are not only called to follow after the shepherd; they are also called to exercise a shepherding role modelled after the good shepherd. Following after also calls for imitation. There are many modern examples of shepherding by intimacy, interaction, and involvement. Dr. Martin Luther King could have been content to remain in his pulpit preaching against injustice and prejudice while his flock languished in the everyday experiences of those evils. Instead he chose to intimately know the sheep by identifying with them, marching in their streets, being insulted by the same hatred, and joining them in prison cells. We saw how many sheep instinctively knew the authenticity of his voice. Mohandas Gandhi shepherded by the power of his example and the identification with the aspirations of his people. His voice was heard by his involvement with the poorest of sheep. Mother Teresa of Calcutta shepherds by her intimacy with the diseased and dying. In contrast, none of these are hirelings who flee at the first sign of conflict or threat to personal safety.

The Gospel says that there still is much shepherding to be done (v. 16). If there are many more who need to hear the good shepherd and then follow, it would seem that we must give sound to his voice. We must interact with each other in intimacy and involvement for there finally to be one flock, one shepherd. Again, because we have been sensitive to the contrast in the metaphor, we know that a hireling could never help effect such unity. The hireling is too quick to abandon the flock. Where there is no intimacy and involvement there can be no unity. Because a metaphor gives fresh insight we now know that the sad refrain "I don't want to get involved" could only be spoken by hirelings!

The metaphor of the shepherd and the sheep seems to open up two realities. We are called to follow after the one who has so identified himself with us that we are instinctively drawn to him. His voice is not alien to us because it is a very human voice speaking care, involvement and identification. At the same time we are able to be shepherds identifying with the poor and disenfranchised so that our human call to them might evoke the sound of the Good Shepherd.

James Heimerl

5th Sunday of Easter

Cycle B

Acts 9:26–31
1 Jn 3:18–24
Jn 15:1–8

Let's do this week's readings in reverse. We begin with Jesus' familiar teaching of the vine which needs pruning to truly live. A fine example of a trimmed vine is the person of Paul we meet in Acts. The man who was such a fervent Pharisee has been knocked to the ground and has come up an apostle of Jesus Christ. A conversion has redirected a life.

But the converted man is in for some tough times. The people want to kill him. This is in sharp contrast to the very next paragraph which speaks of Christians living in peace. This contrast leads us to the theme of this homily—conversion produces confusion and community.

A legend about St. Francis of Assisi is an example of conversion leading to confusion and a rearrangement of relationships. Francis, a high-living playboy in Italy, frequently passed the begging lepers on the outskirts of his city. One day, however, something made him stop and look. He felt the usual disgust for the leper. But he also felt a stirring of compassion. He saw a bond between them and he got off his horse and kissed the leper. A never-go-back turning point had been reached. Francis knew in his heart his life must change. God is with the poor! But the conversion was not simply grand and glorious. His friends deserted him. Francis struggled for many years with how to live his new life and it caused him great anguish. The conversion brought him closer to the Lord and brought him confusion. Sean Caulfield tells us this is the stuff of transformation, of "pruning." "Chaos holds out the possibility that we may become people greater than anything others could have planned. We cannot be legislated into Christian and mature personhood. Chaos is the place where many decisions to love take place."

"Pruning" never affects only a single person. That is why we hear of Christians living in peace. "Pruning" leads one to ask more than "who am I?" The converted person asks "Whom am I for?" Conversion leads to community. Rosemary Haughton in *The Transformation of Man* tells a wonderful story of a family which is being forced to move. As they come to a point of decision as to where to move, each person must go through a conversion. The father must let go of his desire to make all the decisions. The mother must let go of her need to control her husband. The in-laws have to allow themselves to be loved by their son-in-law. The eldest daughter is required to grow up and speak up. As they each change, as they are each "pruned" through the confusion of their own feelings, they are drawn together. The family, which was always there, becomes a family which decides to be there for each other. "The creating of community . . . the point at which the accidental community becomes the on-purpose community, happens through conversion, mutual self-surrender and faith."

In a recent play about Thomas Merton, we hear a humbled Merton say "I have learned the extraordinary fact that none of us is very different. The truth unites, not separates." Merton's conversions, bred in self-doubt and conflict, led him to unity with those who suffer, with his enemies, with people of different religions. The pruning of Thomas Merton brought forth the skills which would put words onto the faith of millions.

Let us pray that in our search for truth we might have the stamina to survive the pruning and still believe within the resulting chaos. And let us draw others together into a community of peace.

Douglas Fisher

6th Sunday of Easter

Cycle B

Acts 10:25–26, 34–35, 44–48
1 Jn 4:7–10
Jn 15:9–17

It is quite obvious that the primary theme of today's readings is love. What is not obvious in today's society, however, is the meaning of love.

We tend to use, perhaps even over-use, the word "love" in our day-to-day living. We talk about loving peanut butter, or hot fudge sundaes, or London broil. We "love" to play tennis, to golf or swim.

Advertising bombards us with a whole host of images that juxtapose love with a wide range of actions that have nothing whatever to do with love. Television has introduced us to people who love to squeeze rolls of toilet paper, who love their dishwashing detergent, and who love their mouthwash.

"Love" has become an umbrella term to encompass enjoyment, fascination, infatuation, and lust, to name a few, all the while disguising the real meaning of love.

In order to appreciate what the Scriptures have to say to us today, we must first put aside all in our vocabulary that is not love, remembering that love is not a feeling, but a decision we make to bind ourselves in relationship to another.

God first loved us. We were created in his image and likeness, and no matter what sins we might later commit, we can never alter the reality or the reality of God's love.

God's love for us is unconditional. There is nothing we can do to earn it. God's love was poured out in us before we were able to respond to any stimuli, and his love will be there to sustain us no matter how we might try to deny its presence. We might abandon God, but God will never abandon us.

God's love for us was so intense that he took on our humanity, taking on all the joy and sadness that accompanies the human condition, to redeem us and to show us how we might live this convenant of love.

God's love for us is so perfect, that even though we are his creation, clearly less powerful than our Creator, and surely more deserving to be regarded as slaves, he calls us "friend."

We did not choose God. God chose us, and his purpose in choosing us was so that we would manifest his love to the world.

As mirrors of God's love, our embrace of the world's people must be unconditional, all-encompassing, and tireless. We must be willing to address each person, even the worst criminal imaginable, as friend, and if our imaging of God's love is to be perfect, we must be willing to lay down our life for our friend.

That is some tall order! The message proclaimed today is not just some sweet poetic verse composed for a greeting card; it is a challenge for each one of us to examine our quality of loving.

Alongside the love God has for us, how does our love for others measure up? If your love for your children, spouse, parents, friends, neighbors, or enemies is not unconditional, turn again for help to the one who first loved you and sustains you in love.

God knows that love requires commitment and perseverance each day of our lives, and he will be there with the grace we need, if we turn to him and not to empty phrases from advertising.

Julia Upton, RSM

7th Sunday of Easter

Cycle B

Acts 1:15–17, 20–26
1 Jn 4:11–16
Jn 17:11–19

Mike stood on the ledge of a rooftop of an old building on New York's Bowery. At 17, he had given up on life. He had been beaten by his father, abandoned by his mother, and bounced around from one foster home to another. He had run away and had drifted from one state to another, finally arriving in New York City and ultimately to this tenement ledge. Someone in the crowd below shouted for him to "jump." But a policeman from the city's emergency services squad talked to the boy for almost two hours, pleading with him to come off the ledge. "Someone does care for you," he told Mike. "I'd be proud to have a son like you."

At first the boy, hardened by many bitter experiences, ignored the pleas of the policeman. But as they continued to talk, the boy's despair began to melt away. "Could this really be true? Could this policeman just be giving me a line, or does he mean what he says?" Finally, Mike took the risk to believe the policeman, and came down off the roof.

Six weeks later, the policeman fulfilled his pledge to the boy, winning temporary legal custody of him, taking him into his home and helping him to get settled in a new school and life.

This true story makes concrete what St. John is saying in our second reading: "Beloved, if God has loved us so, we must have the same love for one another. No one has ever seen God. Yet if we love one another God dwells in us, and his love is brought to perfection in us."

The Christian message is not some theoretical, other-worldly call, but a challenge which demands concrete response. In the same chapter from which our passage from the first letter of John was taken, the author states: "If anyone says, 'My love is fixed on God', yet hates his brother (or sister), he is a liar. One who has no love for the brother (or sister) he has seen cannot love the God he has not seen."

This response of love is not easy. Each of us knows the many times that we fail in our response. The commitment to one another must be based on more than feeling (though feelings can be a help at times).

We are able to respond to the commandment of love through the power of the Spirit, given to us in baptism and confirmation, and nurtured throughout our Christian life. That life must be characterized by a deep faith in Jesus, and the power of Jesus to overcome the sources of sin and alienation.

Through the past several weeks we have heard again the preaching of the early church about Jesus and the new hope and life offered us if we respond in faith to Jesus. Over and over again we have been called to deepen our faith in Jesus, and to live that faith in a posture of love for one another.

In the gospel passage from John, which is part of the Last Supper discourse, Jesus is seen praying for his followers. He prays that they will be true to his word, live it and proclaim it in the world.

"The world," for John, is an alien environment. The world, which contains the elements of idolatry, hostility, and selfishness, has closed itself to the word of life proclaimed by Jesus. If the world has rejected Jesus, so too will it reject the followers of Jesus. Yet Jesus does not pray that the disciples flee from the world, but rather that they be protected from falling victim to the evil forces of the world.

The Christian proclamation that there is a God, a God whose name is love, rings true in our world only if people see that those who call themselves Christian really do love. That love must be more than words; it must be embodied in the deeds of love. That policeman literally gave life to Mike because he loved.

Have we fallen victim to those alien forces in the world? Have we decided to isolate ourselves from those brothers and sisters who need our love?

Do we really believe that all human persons receive their life from God and are children of God? Can we reject those children of God whom we see, and proclaim that we love God whom we don't see?

These are hard questions, demanding a prayerful examination of conscience. It would seem however, that the Word of God proclaimed to us today demands such a soul searching. Through the centuries, many people have rejected Christianity because the lives of Christians have not followed the message of Christ. On the other hand, many have embraced Christianity because they saw the message come alive in those who called themselves Christians.

In the case of the young boy spoken of in the opening story, the policeman's commitment to him, offered in love, was the means to a new life. With the help of God's grace, we too can show forth the love of God. Then we will really be one with God. For as St. John says: "God is love, and he who abides in love abides in God, and God in him."

Kathleen Flanagan, S.C.

Pentecost Sunday

Cycle B

Acts 2:1–11
1 Cor 12:3–7, 12–13
Jn 20:19–23

Breath is so integral to our life experience that we seldom reflect on its power or significance. On the other hand, there are moments when we are very aware of its reality. The newborn struggles for his or her first breath, and its cry brings relief, telling us that lungs have received air and life is announced. Athletes gasp for oxygen, breathing deeply to keep strength replenished. Rescuers struggling to restore pulse and heartbeat in CPR work frantically, watching for the first sign of breath to reappear. Parents bend over their young sleeping children to catch the warmth of breath signifying that all is well with them. The asthmatic's struggle for breath unnerves us, and breath blown on dying embers ignites flames, restoring warmth and light. Breath is taken for granted most of the time except when it is in short supply, and then suddenly we realize how precious it is—it is *life*.

In today's Gospel story, Jesus comes to disciples who have barred doors out of fear and bestows the breath of life—the Spirit—upon them. God's life-giving breath has been recognized as a gift to humanity from its dawning, as expressed in the second creation story of Genesis. Throughout its history Israel understood how crucial God's breath—*Ruah*—is, not only to individual existence, but also to the life of a people. "If you take away their breath," says today's responsorial psalm, "they perish and return to their dust. When you send forth the spirit, they are created, and you renew the face of the earth." This powerful breath is life, but more than that, it is salvation.

Today's readings announce that this life-giving breath—Spirit—is given not only to those who would stand in roles of prominent leadership or possess unusual gifts or charisms. It is given to each and to all of us, and it is given to share. The disciples are sent out to breathe the *same breath* of life upon others, to share his breath according to the needs of those who will receive it: forgiveness to the errant, healing to the wounded, consolation to the sorrowing, light to darkened hearts, strength to the weary or wavering, gentleness to the hardened, warmth to the frigid, peace to the fearful. Whatever is needed, gifts are given appropriate to meet the needs. As these gifts are shared, they become life-giving—the very "breath" needed to survive and to grow.

The Spirit's life-giving breath does not enliven apart from those of us who are the body (and we are increasingly challenged to expand our vision of the parameters of this body). The paradox is that the very Spirit who enables and equips us can be embodied only through our touch, our voices, our imagination, our actions, our gifts exercised. Unworthy though we may be, life does not seem to be given *despite* us. Forgiveness, compassion, peace, renewal cannot happen without forgiving, compassionate, peace-making, renewed people. Individuals, communities, nations can see and hear only what is announced and lived.

Pentecost is frequently described and celebrated as the "Birth of the Church." That is not inappropriate, provided we remember that birthing is a long process. Passing on life to a new creature involves the powerful mystery of symbiosis. Identity-sharing and nourishment happen slowly, and the new being generally does not appear until it is equipped to handle life on its own. When that moment arrives, it draws its first breath, but the breath is always the gift of another. And so it is with the Church. We who have been gifted with the breath of life remember the source of our being and that we have been created to continue that life-giving process until the face of the earth is renewed. "Come, Holy Spirit," we pray, "fill the hearts of your faithful . . . " Our plea is earnest. We are involved in a matter of life and breath!

Joan R. DeMerchant

Trinity Sunday

Cycle B

Dt 4:32–34, 39–40
Rom 8:14–17
Mt 28:16–20

When a child is born it is given gifts that as yet it certainly hasn't earned. A child is born into a family, cradled and loved because it is dependent and in need of nurturing. Born into a society, it is given rights and privileges of citizenship and consequently guarded by laws granting freedom and possibilities. For the most part a newborn enters into nurturing relationships with family and society so that eventually growth and maturity might happen. We recognize that at the outset of human life there must be an atmosphere of community in order for full human potential to be realized. It certainly is a truism to say that no person is an island, but our experience of the basic need for community and relationships makes such a statement seem so banal. Being taken up into a wider network of persons makes us realize that we come to wholeness only by interaction.

The Deuteronomy reading is the expression of our coming to wholeness by virtue of an even greater relationship. The text rehearses the mighty "signs and wonders" God has done for us. We are like a tiny child unable to earn any gift or privilege, and God has been active on our behalf. The beautiful expression found throughout the Hebrew Scriptures " . . . by a strong hand and an outstretched arm" (v. 34) and the events of Israel's history reveal the One God. The reading reminds us that we are in the same tradition as Israel: God is One and we have been called into a love relationship with the Lord (Dt 6:4). Jews and Christians are a people chosen for relationship which allows them to "prosper and have long life" (Dt 4:40). We have all been elected!

The Pauline reading reveals an even greater grace. Not only have we been elected, we have been adopted and been given a greater identity, we are rightfully to be called children of God (Rom 8:17). This new adoptive relationship gives us but a glimpse and perhaps even an experience of the mysterious inner life of God. Deuteronomy attests to the unity of God whose deeds are meant to be a testimony that God is One (Dt 4:35). The Christian Scriptures reveal that within this unity there is community. Somehow the oneness of God and the fullness of God nevertheless allows for interaction, reciprocity and relationship within the Godhead. Naturally, at this point words become like empty shells, they lose so much content before such a mystery. The oneness of God contains a relatedness.

Our adoption as children and fellow-heirs with Christ invites us into the mystery of God and thereby to know something about ourselves. We come to wholeness and fullness by means of a relatedness and interaction.

The Bible is not a text book revealing propositions about God. We are the "subject matter" as well. Scripture reveals and reflects the truth about ourselves, the truth of who we are as children of God. We are incomplete in ourselves; it is only in a network of relatedness that we find our wholeness. The awesome mystery of God as one yet as related is echoed in our own experience.

Jesus commissions us at the end of the Gospel of Matthew to create the atmosphere of community after the manner of the mystery of God (Mt 28:19). We have rightfully seen in this text the command to speak the Good News and to create a network of relationships which later was named the Church. The Church must be that warm place where together we can enter the very center of our being and discover the outer edge of God. We become one with ourselves when we discover each other, and in that discovery we begin to experience the mystery of God.

The Church should be the premier meeting ground where these two mysteries are found. The Church should provide that atmosphere of freedom in which we can become one with ourselves as we join in community together with other adopted children of God. The Church must be truly "catholic," that is, an open space that is wide enough to encompass all who seek the one God and their own wholeness.

James Heimerl

Corpus Christi

Cycle B

Ex 24:3–8
Heb 9:11–15
Mk 14:12–16, 22–26

Many of us are familiar with the slogan popularized by the American Red Cross, "Give the gift of life; give blood." Although there have been many technological advances in recent years, there is still no substitute for blood. We share with the ancient semitic people of today's first reading, and with all people, the recognition that blood is life. To give one's blood, either to another or for another, is to give the gift of life.

In each of today's readings, blood plays a central role. In Exodus Moses uses the blood of animals as a symbol of life. He pours half the blood on the altar and half he sprinkles over the people. The unity between God and the Israelites is expressed and ratified through the sacred sign of blood. Moses says to the people, "This is the blood of the covenant which the Lord has made with you." And the people respond, "All that the Lord has said, we will heed and do."

In the Gospel, Jesus takes a cup of wine, blesses it and gives it to his disciples who all drink from it. He says, "This is my blood, and the blood of the covenant, to be poured out on behalf of many." Jesus' words refer to his impending death. He recognizes that his fidelity to the Father's call will lead him to the cross. And this pouring out of his blood is done "on behalf of many." Jesus likewise sees his death in terms of the covenant. But no longer is it the blood of goats and bulls which unites God and humanity. It is Jesus' own blood, sacrificed on the altar of human blindness and cruelty, which overcomes sin and forges a bond between God and us that can never be broken.

In both of these Scripture passages we find two common elements—commitment and unity. In response to the sprinkling with blood the people acclaim, "All that the Lord has said, we will heed and do." Thus they are united, together as a people and with the Lord, in a new way. Jesus, in faithful obedience to the Father's call, shares the cup of wine with his disciples and expresses his commitment to obey that call, even unto death. He says, "I will never again drink of the fruit of the vine until the day when I drink it new in the reign of God." In sharing this cup, the cup of his blood, with his disciples, Jesus expresses his profound love and unity with them.

These two elements can also be found in our own experience of giving blood. Those of us who have had the experience will readily recognize that it is an action undertaken out of commitment to others. At the same time, we find a sense of unity with others, those who are engaged in giving blood with us or, more profoundly, the one who is to receive the blood we give.

On an even deeper level what we do in this Eucharist is an expression of commitment and unity. For once again, in memory of Jesus, we take a cup of wine and listen as the priest repeats his words, "This is the cup of my blood, the blood of the new and everlasting covenant." When we drink this cup we proclaim our commitment to remember Jesus, not just in our minds, but in our actions. To remember him is to do what he did—to pour out our lives for one another. When we drink this cup we proclaim our unity in him. He is the source of our fellowship; he is the reason why we do what we do.

Today's feast of Corpus Christi is a feast of the Eucharist. Although the words mean body of Christ, the Scriptures have led us to reflect on the blood of Christ. They are in reality two dimensions of the same mystery. They are inseparable. As we come to receive the body and blood of Christ, let us remember the meaning of what we do. Let us renew our commitment to remember Jesus in our actions. Let us wipe away all that keeps us from being one.

Robert Hamma

CYCLE C

1st Sunday of Advent

Cycle C

Jer 33:14–16
1 Thes 3:12—4:2
Lk 21:25–28, 34–36

Over thirty years ago, Dom Helder Camara wrote the following meditation:

How long, my God—
mankind and sea
are we to waver
between flood
and ebb?
(from *A Thousand Reasons for Living*)

This season and today's readings remind us of how long humanity has been asking the question "how long?" If there is a characterizing thread that has run through endless generations of people from past to present, it is that we are a people waiting. The patience of humanity has been tested over and over again as we have balanced on tiptoe watching, peering, wondering, hoping, fearing that what we await might never come.

Most of our waiting has been for something or someone outside ourselves. People have waited and hoped for powers or persons to bring them whatever they felt they could not give themselves. Someday there would be a new king or in a few years a better administration. Maybe a new coach could pull the team together or next year's teacher would motivate. Another general might bring victory, or the next war might end them all.

Today's readings from Jeremiah and Luke reflect the flip side of our waiting. They voice the promise of what will come to those who wait. We, of course, stand in the center of these promises. We have seen the fulfillment of the promise to Israel and Judah; we await still the coming of the Son of Man in glory. And yet we are uneasy, for even the ancient pledge seems somewhat empty. Where and when was the safety of Judah and the security of Jerusalem? Our knowledge of history defies a simple answer. And who has seen justice? There is good cause to ask, "Where, O Lord, are your promises kept?"

Paul's word to the Thessalonians—waiters of an earlier time—may be a clue to us in the center. We know, as we ponder the mystery of incarnation and await its celebration at Christmas, that God's promise has been kept in Jesus. The Just Shoot has come and continues to be present to us. The Sign is here among us, calling us forth. But the impact of that presence will be felt most completely when we mirror it for others and, like the Thessalonians, we "must learn to make still greater progress."

Looking outside ourselves is crucial in one sense: we seek empowerment for our own weakest places. But we know that ultimately good kings and better administrations, new coaches and effective teachers can only do so much. Kings and presidents cannot force the populace to act; coaches cannot play the game for team members, and students can refuse to learn with even the best of teachers. There is, after all, the old adage about leading a horse to water . . .

All of this points out to us what we already know: safety, security, justice—whatever we need to feel the Lord's active presence renewing the earth—will only happen in and through us. If we wait for justice to flourish, we will wait forever unless we realize that we have already been given all that we are likely to get: the Just Shoot in our midst. We need not wait for signs of promise. They are already here, enfleshed. And so waiting can become a preoccupation that diverts us from the work at hand.

There is validity in waiting, make no mistake about that. When and how the Son of Man will finally return is beyond our vision or understanding. The question intrigues but should not distract us. The Thessalonian temptation to wait it out is always alive. And our best efforts are limited. There is always that sense that no matter how hard we work at things, we are running to catch up. A sense of waiting, which is very much a part of our Advent stance, helps us to remember that ultimate power is out of our hands. No matter what we do—and do we must—there is more to come from the One who gives everything.

In our waiting, however, we are instructed to live in strength, holiness and love. We are urged to "try harder." We are given the words of the psalmist to make our own, asking the Lord to guide us, teach us, show us the paths. That response is hope-filled. It is the only thing we have to give meaning to the question we still ask: "How long, my God . . .?"

Joan R. DeMerchant

2nd Sunday of Advent

Cycle C

Bar 5:1–9
Phil 1:4–6, 8–11
Lk 3:1–6

There is a marvelous shop just around the corner from where I live. Hanging above its weathered wooden doorway is a hand-painted sign which reads, "APPRAISER." It is not, however, a pawn shop, nor the sort of place you bring your valuables to determine how much insurance you should get. This appraiser handles only decisions. You can bring in any choices you have to make in life—though they should be significant ones.

You can bring along all the options you face and have them weighed and measured. You can ask about the request you received to work on a parish fund raiser or the opportunity to make a lot of money, or a marriage proposal, and the appraiser will tell you exactly how many hours or weeks or years of your life the option is worth. You can easily decide, then, which are, as Paul says in today's reading, "the things that really matter."

In Antoine de Saint Exupery's book, *Wisdom of the Sands,* the King prays: "O Lord, I fain would safeguard the nobility of my warriors and the beauty of our temples, for which men barter their all, and which give meaning to their lives. But, walking tonight in the desert of my love, I came on a little girl in tears. Gently I drew her head back so as to see her eyes, and the grief I read in them abashed me. If, O Lord, I give no heed to this, I am excluding a part of life, and my task is incomplete. Not that I turn away from any of the lofty goals I set before me—but that little girl *must* be consoled. Thus alone will all go well with the world; for in her, too, the meaning of the world is manifest."

This, it seems to me, is the essence of Paul's desire that we "learn to value those things that really matter." It is a delicate balance—to see and act to alleviate the world's needs, yet be immediately compassionate too. The things that really matter are not things at all—but people. And, like Jesus, we are called to change the world, yet never to lose sight of those closest to us who need healing.

Often I find myself being either-or. Sometimes I am a world visionary hungering for global justice; sometimes I am a parochial caretaker drying the eyes of those at my side. Seldom do I find a comfortable blending, a bifocaled sight of needs which sees the entire human family, but can focus readily on individuals too. Sometimes I lose sight of people altogether and find my vision absorbed by the things that really don't matter.

We need prophets who call us to see all people as our brothers and sisters; we need people who call us to recognize that our real brothers and sisters, and parents and in-laws are our brothers and sisters as well. We need prophets who will proclaim that all humans are our neighbors, and we need those who will remind us that our real next-door neighbors are our neighbors too.

There are times when I feel I'm always listening to the wrong prophet. When I am befriending an estranged colleague, the prophets are crying "Reach out to Ethiopia!" When I am fasting to give money to Africa, the prophets are shouting, "Feed your own family!" And I chase the prophesies near and far and back again, wishing just once my deeds could match what they ask.

I think of Paul again and his words, "Learn to value those things which really matter" and I know he means people and I hope he means me too.

Perhaps that's why I listen to the prophets. They make me feel important. They convince me that if I act to help the world or the kid down the block, I can make a difference. The real prophets, those who not only convince us but convert us, are those who also proclaim forgiveness in the face of our failed efforts, unconditional love in the face of our uncertainties.

Jesus rejected the vision of those who saw him as a world conqueror with political goals; he also rejected the vision of those who would have him as savior only to his own people. Jesus bought the Father's vision of the reign of God which included all people; Jesus bought the Father's vision of the overwhelming importance of each individual, and so he forgave Mary Magdalene and spoke with the Samaritan woman and restored the blind man's sight.

This Advent we are invited to welcome Jesus more deeply into our lives. Had he not become one of us, perhaps we would never have known "the things that really matter." His life and his words teach us to value people and to keep the delicate balance which neither overlooks those near to us nor excuses us from looking beyond them as well.

There is not really an appraiser around the corner from where I live; I just wish there were sometimes. Yet, I know the only measure for my decisions is the Lord.

Carole M. Eipers

3rd Sunday of Advent

Cycle C

Zep 3:14–18
Phil 4:4–7
Lk 3:10–18

Today's Gospel is populated by many fascinating people—John the Baptist, Pharisees and Levites from Jerusalem, and by a person who is not there: "The one who is to come after me—the strap of whose sandal I am not worthy to unfasten." One way to approach preaching this Gospel is to point out how all three groupings of people are alive within the individual by using a Jungian method. Within the Self is someone doubting (the priests and Levites); someone crying out (John the Baptist); and Jesus.

Within me there is a voice crying out. There is within me a prophet who says this world can be better, this world can be saved. There is hope. There is someone within me who pleads with others to create the Kingdom, to live in love and truth. Sister Joan Chittister tells this story: "There was once a man who went about crying 'The sky is falling, the sky is falling.' In the midst of the chaos that went on around me as a reaction to this horrible prediction, I came across a sparrow lying on the ground with his spindly little legs straight up in the air. 'What are you doing?' I asked. 'I'm trying to keep the sky from falling,' he said. 'Do you really think you will keep the sky from falling with those little legs of yours?' 'One does what one can,' he said, 'one does what one can.'"

Within each of us there is the courage of that little sparrow. Ask your congregation to think how many times they have "bucked the odds." Ask them to reflect on how many times they have kept on trying when others have said their marriage is failing, their job is meaningless, their political cause will lose, their health is collapsing. Within each of us there is a John the Baptist saying convert, hope, act.

John the Baptist calls for change with hope but he has his sceptics. Who are you anyway? Are you someone who should be dead (Elijah, the prophets)? Do you have messianic aspirations? What gives you the right to go about baptizing? In short, why don't you crawl back to the hole from which you came? Why don't you just fit in? Become what the television ads say a man or woman should be and quit these esoteric, unreal rantings.

Each one of us has a doubter within. There is a little voice which never seems to leave us alone, a voice which says, "Who do you think you are?" An image which might serve to bring this out is from the movie "The Empire Strikes Back." Here is a wonderful scene in which Yoda, the little creature who has tremendous wisdom and serves as the guru to future "Jedis" (people with incredible powers), is teaching Luke Skywalker what he needs to know to be a Jedi. As Luke is doing one of the exercises he loses his concentration and fails to keep an object in levitation. Yoda says "Why did you stop?" "I tried," says Luke. "There is no 'I try' here," says Yoda. "There is either 'I will' or 'I won't,' but there is no 'I try.'" Within each of us there is a voice that says you might try but you really can't do it. You really can't will it. You really don't have that much power. You really can't proclaim any message other than that which you are programmed into.

The one who is alluded to but not seen in today's Gospel is Jesus. Taking the story as a journey of the self, we recognize that within all of us is a savior alluded to but not seen. The Kingdom is within. Within us is someone worth making a path straight for. Within us is a grace, a spirit which is worthy of more than anything we could ever allow ourselves to imagine. Paul Wharton, in a book soon to be published by Paulist Press, tells this story called "finding Grace at the Center".

Once upon a time there lived in Cracow, Poland, a rabbi named Eisek who dreamed three times that there was a treasure beneath a particular bridge in Prague. After the third dream, Eisek walked the long distance to Prague. When he found the bridge, the guard asked him why he had come. Eisek told him of his dreams.

The guard remarked that if he had faith in his dreams, he would have gone to Cracow long ago when he dreamed there was a buried treasure underneath the stove of a Jew named Eisek. The rabbi hurried home and, sure enough, dug up this treasure in his own house.

Douglas Fisher

4th Sunday of Advent

Cycle C

Mi 5:1–4
Heb 10:5–10
Lk 1:39–45

What are you waiting for? Really, as you read this article, can you list those events, people, situations, which you are anticipating, either with joy or dread? There are the "little waitings"—for a bus, or a phone call; we wait for friends, for appointments, and for opportunities. There are the "big waitings"—for marriage, for a job, for retirement, for the death of a loved one, and for our own death. There are positive waitings: for arrivals, for promotions, for celebrations. There are negative waitings: for departures, for surgery, for the bad news we know is on its way.

What we wait for, and how we wait, can color our attitude toward life. Dreadful anticipation can rob us of the joy of the moment; overwhelming expectation of something wonderful can prevent us from attending to present needs. Yet, those who wait for nothing are merely apathetic; no feeling now, no hope of future feeling.

We can wait by preparing for an event; we can wait by distracting ourselves with unrelated busyness; we can wait by doing nothing, or by doing so much that we forget we are waiting at all.

We spend a lot of our lives waiting, and it seems, therefore, that we might want to learn to do it well. Advent is a season of waiting, of anticipation, and today's readings say something to us about the power of positive waiting.

The prophets of the Hebrew Scriptures often had to remind the people that they were, in fact, waiting. They recalled for people God's covenant, they reminded them of God's promise that the Messiah would come, they pleaded with their people to wait—to be a people anxiously expecting their God. It was difficult for the Israelites. Their times of waiting were long and hard. They tired, as we do, of waiting, and were distracted by present needs and the promises of other gods. The prophets begged them to be patient, and to wait rightly for God's promises to be fulfilled.

Today's Gospel is a story of productive waiting, of outgoing expectation. Mary modeled for us how the person of faith waits. After the Annunciation, Mary began to wait. Yet, while her whole being waited, she shared the joy-to-come and the joy of her very waiting with Elizabeth. Faith waits actively, building anticipation, sharing hopes, growing in trust. Faith reaches out, and in meeting others' faith is affirmed and renewed and made courageous. Faith does not "hole up" and wait for God to come; faith finds God with others while we wait.

"Sacrifice and offering you did not desire" Paul quotes Jesus as saying, "but a body you have prepared for me." Our bodies measure the times of waiting. We gauge our longing by months, years, by degrees of loneliness and pain. Our bodies wait, finally for death, but ultimately for resurrection. It is this ultimate goal that can color our attitude toward life, toward other people, and toward all the intermediate waiting which we must face.

Advent is a season of waiting, a time for us to practice the kind of expectation which the prophets recall for us; a time to learn from Mary and to imitate her style of "shared waiting"; a time to remind our weary and aging and cumbersome bodies of the eternal life which we have been promised and so, await.

We recall Christ's coming in history at Bethlehem, we look forward to his final coming, but while we wait we can celebrate his presence in our faith community, in the Scriptures, and in the sacraments. Sharing these present experiences of the Lord heightens our anticipation of his coming in glory. We can wait with our faith nourished and strengthened.

Advent changes my opening question. It is no longer "What are you waiting for?" but rather, "Whom are you waiting for?" And if we wait rightly, we catch glimpses of him. This colors our attitude toward life, and impels us to share the joy of anticipation so that we can patiently await his final coming.

Carole M. Eipers

Christmas Day

Cycle C

Is 52:7–10
Heb 1:1–6
Jn 1:1–18

Everyone loves a story. Whenever someone begins with, "Once upon a time . . . " or, "Let me tell you a story . . . " immediately restless children begin to grow quiet, while listless adults perk up. Stories have a way of captivating us and engaging that distinctive human activity of imagination. It seems that at Christmas time storytelling is a regular feature of family gatherings; stories of past Christmases are traded around, reminiscences of old family members are retold, and as a result the whole family is drawn closer together.

Some of us might remember as children how we would sit in the glow of Christmas tree lights and hear stories about various members of the family. Being told the story of the family is a way of being initiated into the family. We become real members of the family when we hear and know its story.

Some people might remember their first Christmas spent as newlyweds with the in-laws. They may have come into a house filled mostly with strangers and were introduced all around. It seemed they'd never remember all those names; some individuals also may have seemed odd or perhaps strange. Sooner or later all kinds of stories were exchanged and the newlyweds began to feel a little less ill-at-ease; and, inevitably, all those characters no longer seemed so odd or strange. Hearing the family's stories helps us feel part of it all.

Soon a Christmas arrives when we hear the family begin to tell stories about us! Now we know that we've really arrived. All those stories have now become our story. So, it would appear that the charm and lure of storytelling is that eventually we begin to feel a part of the story. We begin to identify with the real or imagined characters, we make them our own.

Each year we hear the Christmas Story told again. Why is it that we're still moved by this tender tale? It is such a familiar story that we already know the outcome at the first mention of a star-filled night, shepherds in fields, and angels from on high. We have even surrounded the drama with all kinds of traditions, colored lights, holly and evergreen. What is it about the story that has held generation after generation in nostalgic awe? What is it that compels us to repeat the story over and over again each year?

The reason, perhaps, is that ultimately the story is about us, and everyone's longing to be part of a family. But the family we seek to belong to is much larger than one gathered around the tree; it is the family of humankind. The Christmas story is the tale of the family of God. The Christ child is the promise that God has drawn near to all of us, and so we are almost compelled to gather around the crib. The beauty of this child and his story is in its simplicity. It is easy to identify with this story, since we have all begun life in the same way: small, fragile, and helpless. And, in a way, we remain so, no matter how self-reliant we have become. What we need to hear again is that our God is not far removed from us, and that we are still God's children.

It is no wonder, then, that at Christmas time, truces are declared, neighbors seem more friendly, greetings among strangers are more readily exchanged, and wishes of peace are more sincerely granted. It's all because of that simple story. Stories have a power to transform us and transport us into worlds other than the everyday. We must repeat the Christmas story to release its power. It is only in telling the story that we can become who we were meant to be, a family under God.

Historians and theologians may investigate and even question all of the details of the story. Well they should, for that is their task and their duty. We shall always have an insatiable appetite to know exactly what happened. However, this story must also be entrusted to the poets, artists and musicians as well. For it is their task and duty to release the meaning of the story in all its visionary details. What we strain to hear are not simply the facts separated from the legends, but the story enshrined in the narrative. What we need to discover is our place in the story, so every detail, whether fact or fancy, is essential to the tale; thus our imaginations are free to roam until we settle into our place in the story.

Christmas is not merely an age-old story of long ago, it is ever new and always true in every detail we choose to make our own. For Christmas is our story, the story of everyone's family, the story of everyone's acceptance.

James Heimerl

Feast of the Holy Family

Cycle C

Sir 3:2–6, 12–14
Col 3:12–21
Lk 2:41–52

The American writer and humorist Mark Twain once greeted an audience by saying, "the rumors of my recent death have been greatly exaggerated." The same could be said for the rumored death of the American family. From pulpit and television the message is the same—the American family is suffering a terminal illness. What many are terming the death of the American family is in reality a profound change in its structure. We have witnessed what sociologists call the transition from the extended family to the nuclear-isolated family. Much of the present concern over the demise of the American family results from what might be termed our propensity for mythical-romantic thinking.

The mythical-romantic mode of thinking longs for the good ole' days when every family was just like the Waltons of television fame. In the not so long ago there was no divorce or domestic violence. The number of illegitimate children and the instances of pre- and extra-marital sex were quite small. Abortion was considered murder by the courts and society as a whole. Children were wanted and the notion of a "wrongful birth" was unknown. Marriage was forever and the possibility of spouse desertion was remote. However we all know that such days and arrangements existed only in the mind.

There have been many forces which have caused a change in the composition of the family. The process of urbanization has reduced the economic value of children. The mass media has presented a pluralism of values to the young which many parents find troublesome. The divorce rate is shocking. The number of teenage pregnancies, and children having children, must cause us to reevaluate our values and their transmission. Over one million abortions each year must trouble our collective conscience. The view of children as unwanted or as an economic burden makes the possibility of violence more likely. Marriage has lost, like so many other institutions, its permanence. Trial marriage and living arrangements speak loudly to the degree to which we feel that all commitments must be short-term. Perhaps the most disturbing aspect of the current discourse on the family concerns its inability to transmit values that enhance human growth and well-being. Many are concerned about the *moral* character of the family and its ability to teach a responsible sexual ethic. Therefore, we often witness moral silence in the family. In the long run it is the child who is left with only television models and peer pressure as guides for responsible moral action. Often it is the blind leading the blind.

The above mentioned analysis is sociological. However, the Scriptures remind us that the family is so much more. The family has a faith or religious dimension to it. It is a *gift* from God who called all things into existence out of love. The Second Vatican Council calls the family the "little church" and the tiniest seed of the present and future kingdom of God. Our readings speak to us of family life and its transcendental or faith dimensions.

The theme or insight that unites our three readings is the necessity of living a life focused in God. The wise man of the Old Testament, Ben Sirach, reminds us that in serving and respecting our parents we serve and respect the Lord. Family life is a blessing from the Lord and one that gives rise to joy. In our second reading the Colossians are reminded that in Christ they have been chosen to be the "new people of God." Their entire array of relationships must reflect Christ-like love. This began in the family. The truly Christ-like family is one that is filled with compassion, sincerity, gentleness, patience, kindness, and humility. What unites them together in perfection is love. The peace of Christ is a dynamic harmony which results from the various elements or members of an entity working and loving for the common good. In such a family experience we raise our voices and lives in thanksgiving. We begin to experience, however imperfectly, what God has in store for us when Christ will be all in all.

William F. Maestri

Epiphany

Cycle C

Is 60:1–6
Eph 3:2–3, 5–6
Mt 2:1–12

Epiphany is an intriguing feast for poets, dreamers, and lovers of the imaginative, for it carries us into the realm of the universe and play with wonderful stories and images. Even in a practical world, thoughts about journeys and shining cities and stars capture our attention. We love stories about warring space empires and follow with great curiosity scientists in search of the hypothetical tenth planet and the sun's proposed companion, the death star Nemesis. Thoughts about trillions of stars millions of light years away snatch us out of our preoccupation with the mundane and boggle our minds with the proportions of immensity and the contrasts that constitute life.

The readings for this festival provide their own study in contrasts and reversals. There are the vast contrasts between light and darkness, between the mysterious East and the tiny town of Bethlehem, between the mighty empire and the child, between vision and illusion. There are strange reversals: the besieged Jerusalem will shine and be radiant; the belief that salvation is only for the few is shattered; the plight of the warring, the poor, and the afflicted is resolved; homage is redirected from the mighty to the lowly, and new paths of pilgrimage are chosen. What a celebration!

One message among many that emerge here is that light is not visible to all. Rather, it comes to those who search for it. In a sky full of stars which dazzle the eye, only some can see the star that truly leads to the source of life and hope. And this clarity of vision seems to be related to the knowledge that light is not self-generated. The empire, therefore, or those of the mentality of the empire, cannot see it. For the star overshadows their own desire to be the light. The true Light is not within them; it emanates from another source and is frightening and threatening.

Ultimately, the true Light points away from the empire to the child. The place where the star points is unexpected. How often reason is defied when we look for light! We would expect to find it in the mighty nations, not the beleaguered Jerusalem; in the powerful, not the weak. But Herod does not know where it is to be found. Only the truly wise are willing to follow through in the search, though it may (and usually does) lead them to the most unanticipated places.

Of course, stars themselves can be illusionary; the light that appears to shine may no longer be there. Or, we may be dazzled by stars that distract us from less auspicious but more genuine radiance. Being described as having "stars in one's eyes" is not necessarily a compliment. Sometimes it means being led astray. Star-gazing or star-following can be pretty risky business.

These ruminations about light and stars and seeing lead us to some pertinent questions. Why is it so difficult to find this Light? Why, after all of these centuries, is it not readily visible not only to others, but to ourselves as well?

Perhaps we are blinded by the Light. Or, it may be somewhat like trying to star-gaze. Stars are invisible if you stand in bright light to look at them. The eye must peer into absolute darkness and focus carefully on the sky. Other light is not only distracting, but a barrier to what we seek.

Maybe we are afraid of the Light or are looking in the wrong places. What "empires" attract us, mislead us, promise to bow in homage with us while they capture our own allegiance? We may not want to search further. Why continue on, only to be led to a child and his mother, when there are more significant sources of bedazzlement? Who is foolish and who is wise? . . . more mind-boggling reversals.

There are clues to help us recognize Jerusalem among all the apparent splendors that compete for our attention: in this, the home of Light, all will be welcome, "members of the same body and sharers of the promise. . . . " There will be justice and "profound peace, till the moon be no more"—when all other sources of light shall cease to be. The poor and the afflicted will be rescued; there will be pity for the lowly. True Light is easy to find, for it illuminates true darkness.

The Gospel for today also tells us something about the relationship between the search for Light and its effect upon our pilgrimage. Those who follow where the Star leads them do not return to the empire. Perhaps in the illumination it is seen for what it is and loses its imagined brilliance. Herod is only Herod. Whatever it is that leads to this process of enlightenment, those with vision—the truly wise—thereafter travel by a different route.

Joan R. DeMerchant

Baptism of the Lord

Cycle C

Is 42:1–4, 6–7
Acts 10:34–38
Lk 3:15, 21–22

In commemorating Jesus' baptism we celebrate his willingness to hear the call of God and accept his vocation. That vocation to bring justice to the world is spelled out in the first reading from Isaiah 42, for Jesus is the servant who fulfills Israel's mission of justice. Each follower of Jesus is called to live out this same call in the particular circumstances of his or her life.

Sometimes when people talk about vocations and pray for vocations they are thinking of the priesthood or religious life. It is something for a special few. Actually, a loving God calls each of us to be someone and do something of significance. Each of us is asked to love, to care for the world, and to witness to the Christian faith in a particular way. Just as Jesus' baptism is the acceptance of his vocation, so our own baptism is the statement that we are willing to follow Jesus and live out the Christian vocation of service. We can see this more clearly in adult baptism. But if we were baptized as children, we can and must reaffirm our acceptance of this vocation as adults.

How can I recognize God's call to me? It is grounded in the gifts and inclinations I find in myself: my abilities and limits, my hopes, my deepest wanting. It comes through the challenges and the modeling of significant people in my life. And it is shaped in terms of the special circumstances of my life. For Dag Hammarskjold, the call meant working on an international level amid the complications of world politics. For Dorothy Day it was work among the poor, the hungry, and the homeless in the streets of America's cities. For some it is the invitation to be a parent, with all the courage and love this demands. The Christian vocation can take as many shapes as there are Christians living in the world. It need not be lived out in a public and dramatic way.

If Jesus' mission of justice is to come to fulfillment, each Christian must answer the call to work for the Kingdom in some way. Since Vatican II, it is clear that all Christians are called to a life of holiness, and everyone's gifts are needed in the Church: painters, laborers, students, teachers, lawyers, writers. This point is made in a child's story about a coal mouse who asks a dove the weight of a snowflake. "Nothing more than nothing," answers the dove. So the mouse tells the dove how he had rested on a fir branch, counting the snowflakes until their number was exactly 3,471,952, and then, with the settling of the next flake, the branch suddenly cracked and fell to the ground—such was the weight of nothing. Perhaps only one person's generous response is needed to bring about the just community which it is our vocation to help build.

When we weigh our gifts of love to the world and the talents we bring to God's work, they may appear small in comparison with those of others. That is why it is important to notice the emphasis on community in today's celebration. The servant stands for the whole nation of Israel; as Jesus begins his ministry of announcing the good news, he will call together a community to share that mission. Our baptism inserts us into this same community. In such a community all our small gifts can be brought together, and each vocation can be strengthened by the others in the common call to follow Jesus.

Kathleen R. Fischer
Thomas N. Hart

2nd Sunday in Ordinary Time

Cycle C

Is 62:1–5
1 Cor 12:4–11
Jn 2:1–12

Today's gospel reading from John offers the intriguing question of God's action in our lives and what role we play in influencing that action.

The first question to reflect on with your congregation is whether God acts in particular events at all. Remember the Deists, who numbered our founding fathers among them, believed in the "clock worker God"—the Being who creates the world, gets it going and then leaves it alone. As a people in incarnation, as a people who believe that God takes flesh, dwells among us, we believe that God is present to us.

A story which might help to illustrate the point of incarnation and God's action in human life is the following. One time I was driving to West Virginia and became lost somewhere in Pennsylvania. I stopped at a local store and asked for directions to Wheeling. The clerk said she did not know how to get there, but if I looked outside I would find a map on the wall. I thanked her and went outside assuming I could find the main road into Wheeling, a city which was only a few miles away. The clerk was right: there was a map on the wall outside—of the entire United States! Needless to say, this map was not going to help me determine whether to make a right or a left at the next light.

The story serves as a model for talking about God's action in our lives. Our God cannot simply be transcendent and the horizon of our existence. God must be more than "the big picture" if he is to mean anything.

If God does act in our lives, then why does he "refuse" to answer our prayers? Everyone has prayed for things which have not come true. Why is our God so capricious? It even looks for a moment that Jesus is going to turn Mary down in John's story today. A wonderful cartoon from Charles Schultz' Peanuts gang could serve to introduce this topic. In the first frame Lucy says to Charlie Brown, "Charlie Brown, if you had a choice of hitting a grand slam home run in the bottom of the ninth inning to win the game or the little red haired girl, what would you choose?" In the second frame we see Charlie Brown thinking and then saying, "Both. I would like both." "You can't have both, " says Lucy. "Why not?" says Charlie Brown. Lucy responds with great profundity, "Because it is the real world, Charlie Brown!"

In the real world, we cannot have everything. We are limited and an important sign of maturity is the ability to accept limitation, to accept our positions as creatures and not the Creator. The Deists were not entirely wrong. As a matter of fact, they stress a very important truth: God is transcendent and "totally other."

If God does act in our lives, which we believe as Christians, but is totally separate from us and acts according to his own plan, then why ask him for anything? He is going to act in our real, limited world without any input from us, so why talk to him in prayer? Who has influence with God? A story which illustrates this dilemma happened at Yankee Stadium 30 years ago. When one of the hitters from the visiting team stepped to the plate, he drew a cross in the dirt with his bat. Yogi Berra, the Yankee catcher, quickly rubbed it out and said, "Why don't you leave God out of this?"

Yes, why don't we leave God out of this? The answer to this question lies in Mary's action at Cana. Mary wants more wine for the celebration. She asks Jesus and gets a negative reaction. This does not stop Mary from instructing the waitress, "Do whatever he tells you." Mary is ready for God's action. She is open to possibilities. And she is open to those possibilities because she has a relationship with Jesus. She is part of his life and he a part of hers which means that anything can happen. There is someone to talk to and to wait for.

Mary is the one who addresses Jesus, addresses the divine and then allows herself to be open to what happens. How many times do we see ourselves as isolated, as separated from God and others? There is no "getting to" us. The separation is not on the side of the transcendent God but on the side of the fearful, angry, defensive human being. Mary does not seek to control God. She appreciates the holy, the totally other. She does not see herself as God and she is not a manipulator. But she is open to what God can do. She is "there," waiting for God.

Using Mary as a model, let's invite Jesus into our lives. Let's attempt an attitude of trust and openness. The "real world" might not be what we want. Our specific prayers may not be answered in the manner that we want. But let us continue to talk to the transcendent God who is very close and trust that he will do great, unexpected things with us.

Douglas Fisher

3rd Sunday in Ordinary Time

Cycle C

Neh 8:2–4, 5–6, 8–10
1 Cor 12:12–30
Lk 1:1–4; 4:14–21

Today's scripture readings tell us much about Scripture itself and our approach to it. In our reading from the book of Nehemiah, Ezra reads the Scriptures to people and they react with tears and sadness. Ezra and Nehemiah react with joy and celebration. In Luke's Gospel those who hear Jesus respond with anger and disbelief (you need to remind the congregation here of this reaction which occurs in Luke 4:22–30, the section immediately *after* today's Gospel). Jesus reads Scripture with confidence and trust—he allows it to mold his life. This Sunday is a good time to invite your congregation to reflect on their own feelings toward the Scriptures.

In the reading from Nehemiah, the people hear the Scriptures and cry. Why? Perhaps they saw "the Law of God" as just that—laws which are far too difficult to ever fulfill. The Scriptures are demands from God which far surpass our human capacities. Do we ever react that way? Did you ever tell someone about something Jesus did or said only to have the person respond with "Yeah, but that was Jesus. He's God. I can't do that"? One way to read Scripture is to see it as totally detached from our own lives. That is God and we are human and doomed to lives of futile striving to please him. It is an approach which is sad, but one all of us are tempted to take at times.

The Jews in Luke's account of Jesus the Lector are similar. These people loved and respected the Scriptures. They held a place of honor in the community. They were sacred . . . and safe and sterile. These Jews wanted to peacefully listen to the Scriptures, not to reflect on their day-to-day application. How many people do you know who hear these Scriptures every week, but when it comes time to give to the poor, to act compassionately, to act for social justice, will tell you the stories do not apply here? How many times do we say that to ourselves?

Jesus read the Scriptures and he allowed them to change his life. The words of Isaiah are not just poetically phrased, nice words to him. Jesus lets the words teach, challenge, and transform him. *He* is the one to bring good news, *he* is the one to give sight to the blind, to set captives free. The story is his story. Can we read the Scriptures that way?

Flannery O'Connor did. She was overwhelmed by a sense of sin and the inadequacy of the human response to the divine. But she saw the redemption story enacted here too. Many of her stories follow the pattern of sin and redemption—the pattern of the Scriptures. Redemption happens not just in the Bible but in the lives of people today.

Diarmuid McGann in his book, *The Journeying Self,* tells of a man who hears the Scriptures with his heart. "More than anything else Fr. P. J. Brophy seemed to love Scripture. The way he spoke of it, listened to it, prayed it and celebrated it said something to me of its position and presence in his life . . . his love for Scripture came across, and that love somehow reached down inside me."

Denise Priestly was pregnant with her second child and worried about bringing that child into a world constantly in peril of nuclear destruction. It was at this time that she heard the story of Revelation 12 (about the mother threatened by the dragon). Here is how she listened: "I discovered a passage from Scripture which engaged my mind, my imagination, a passage which spoke to me of the struggle going on within me between hopelessness and hope. Not surprisingly, it is a passage on giving birth, a symbol which is the most hopeful countersign to annihilation I can imagine"*(Bringing Forth in Hope).*

Henri Nouwen in *With Open Hands* describes a method of prayer which could be about listening to Scripture. In this quote, where he has "prayer," substitute "listening to Scripture": "Praying means being constantly ready to let go of your certainty and to move further on from where you are now. It demands you take to the road again and again . . . Praying demands poverty, that is, the readiness to live a life in which you have nothing to lose so that you may always begin afresh . . . But this demands courage. If you are to make real all the consequences of a prayerful life, you might well be frightened and wonder if you should dare. Then it is vital to remember that courage also is a gift from God."

Let's listen to and read the Bible in a new way. Let's not see Scripture as dealing with God and not us. Let's read it the way Jesus did—in a manner which changes our hearts, changes our lives and leaves us open to the great things the Lord will do with us.

Douglas Fisher

4th Sunday in Ordinary Time

Cycle C

Jer 1:4–5, 18–19
1 Cor 12:31—13:13
Lk 4:21–30

"Tell it like it is!" How many times have we heard that one? Perhaps we've even said it ourselves on occasion, when we thought we had something important enough to say no matter what the reaction would be. But, let's face it, it's a pretty facile slogan, especially when measured against today's readings. "Telling it like it is" is fine for people who like to "hit and run," for those who have tough skin, for some folks who have little regard for the feelings of others—and for prophets. "Telling it like it is" is not something highly recommended for the faint of heart, the insecure, or those who are unwilling to face the consequences of their words.

Today's readings tell us something about prophecy and the prophet's role. They give us an insight into what is likely to happen to those who assume that role. We learn about the struggle with the call to prophecy, the prophet's task of speaking to God, the response to words that people would rather not hear, and God's promise that though things may not go well, God will be there for ultimate deliverance.

In hearing about Jeremiah's and Jesus' introduction to prophetic ministry, we are equipped with some valuable insights into the call that is issued to us as well—as individuals and as community. For, like it or not, the summons to function as prophet is ours as members of Christ's Body. We have some awareness of individuals whose lives more obviously reflect prophetic ministry. We can name and discuss examples of such people, expressing our irritation or admiration at their words and actions. Most of us would probably prefer to leave it at that, assuming— if not hoping—that the call is directed to some other outstanding or unusual persons.

But, says Karl Rahner, " . . . the Church itself is the permanent presence of the word of the prophet, Jesus Christ." And so the Church is called to continue this ministry of speaking for God: announcing the inadequacy of what is, witnessing hopefully to what can be. But the task is not merely one of pronouncing words, though that in itself, as we know from Jeremiah's life and read in the Gospel, can be dangerous. The charism of prophecy carries its own particular pain, for the prophet feels deeply, is deeply human. Knowing that things are not as they could/ should be involves considerable inner conflict: the prophet feels compassion for others and their shortcomings, for he knows his own unworthiness.

Gifts are empty, says Paul, if they are not exercised in the greatest gift of love. When the Church exercises its prophetic role, therefore, it (we) know that what is witnessed to among others must be lived out among its own members. The prophet stands under judgment of the same powerful Word that is addressed to others. What separates the prophet from the strident critic is a deep love born out of the knowledge of oneself and of God's love.

The task of prophecy, then, is given to Christ's Body to continue. As members of this Body, we are called to lend our voices and actions to this communal task. And we are called to do this within our own individual lives, sometimes addressing ourselves to those outside the Body and at other times, perhaps, to the very Body itself. The task is difficult, not only because God's Word may be resisted no matter who utters it, but also because we know that we ourselves often resist the prophetic word.

But there *is* a welcome side to this business. God's word is always given ultimately for good, particularly for the good of the community. The word is always creative of something new, despite the pain attendant to the letting go of the familiar. The prophet is constantly the learner—searching for what God is doing or what God can do. The prophet is visionary, imaginative, proclaiming by word and action how limitless and abundant are God's ways and God's desires for us. In that there is enormous hope.

And so the sword is two-edged, and this paradoxical quality is clearly articulated in our readings for this day. We will be urged forward, resisting all the way. We will experience pain, lack of acceptance, indignation, but we must continue to speak, to witness and, above all, to love. We will be addressed by God's prophetic word, as well as summoned to utter it ourselves. That word will ultimately unite God's people if it is heeded; the telling of it may occasion our being disenfranchised from those very people. But somehow, in the telling and the doing there is hope and salvation for hearer and proclaimer alike.

Joan R. DeMerchant

5th Sunday in Ordinary Time

Cycle C

Is 6:1–2, 3–8
1 Cor 15:1–11
Lk 5:1–11

The movement from "reluctance" to "acceptance" in many areas of our lives is a common experience. Last July, at the conclusion of a retreat, 30 persons shared their experience of the weekend. Everyone seemed to say God had moved them from some area of fear, anxiety, stagnation, and inability to move forward, into a renewed trust, openness, and ability to say "yes" to God, life, and neighbor. Each felt able again to be used by God and to accept his call to them in their lives. The concluding hymn of our liturgy was: "Here I am Lord. . . . send me . . . I hear the cry of your people." That is exactly what Isaiah experienced in today's reading. He moved from "reluctance" to "acceptance" of God's way in his life.

The Isaiah (and other prophets') syndrome: "not-me . . . I-am-not-capable-or-worthy," plagues all of our lives. Reluctance in believing God wants and can use us blocks the spread of his kingdom. To hear the call is the first step. The guts to follow are needed.

Another woman on that same retreat, heavyset, gifted, caring and loving, was plagued by her poor self-image, and her desire to be part of the action. God relieved her anxiety, which had caused a dark, cold, and lonely feeling to pervade her heart, by speaking to her the words from the Song of Solomon: "You are my beloved." She heard the words that say the winter was over and a time for new blooming was ripe. Because her own life had been so "wintery" lately, it moved her deeply. She accepted his love again.

Isaiah's sense of his own sin, and of God's holiness, made him conclude: I am unable, and unworthy to be used. He wanted to be perfect first! God does not want that. He wants our "yes," and he takes care of the rest. Remember Mary's "yes"? Remember Moses who could not speak well? Remember David and Goliath? Remember St. Paul who told us: God chose us, we did not choose Him? Babbsie Bleasdell, a noted evangelist from Trinidad says: "When he calls, he enables." But, we are reluctant!

Reluctance is normal. All saints and sinners struggle with it. Before we "buy into" anything, we want a certain surety about it. We just bought a car, and what looking and examining we did! We touched, tested, examined more cars . . . and sized up more dealers! Or when grocery shopping, fondling those tomatoes and peaches to get the right one. Two engaged persons: the courting, questioning, talking, dream sharing, probing, trust-examination which takes place before the final commitment. We want signs and certainty before we venture into anything: job, purchases, housebuying, volunteer groups, etc. We want some certainty. So too with the Lord: we want to know something *before* we let go or commit ourselves.

I have a prayer card which reads: "nothing would be done at all if a man waited till he could do it so well that no one could find fault with it" (Cardinal Newman). Perfectionists suffer through that one! God seems more relaxed about those whom he chooses (just look around!).

God broke through Isaiah's reluctance and worry about his sinfulness. Jesus broke through Peter's in the Gospel today. After the great catch, Peter says: "Leave me Lord. I am a sinful man." Jesus does not deny that, but says: "Be not afraid . . ." In his love, God cuts through our worry and invites us to step forward in hope. Undue focus on our sinfulness (such as the scrupulous suffer), prevents us from seeing how God's holiness intends to pervade us and love us into life! "I am not worthy" becomes an excuse, and a denial of God's power.

Paul writes of his own unworthiness. But, he proclaims the "gospel": Christ died for our sins! "Because I persecuted the church of God, I do not deserve the name (Christian/apostle). But by God's favor I am what I am." God makes him worthy!

This is the nature of God's holiness: it is so powerful that it overcomes in love the unholiness in our minds, hearts, and bodies, squeezing it out of us! It squeezed Isaiah so he could say "Yet, my eyes have seen the king, the Lord of hosts."

Jeffrey Archambeault

6th Sunday in Ordinary Time

Cycle C

Jer 17:5–8
1 Cor 15:12, 16–20
Lk 6:17, 20–26

The term "delayed gratification" refers to a postponement of a reward for some action, or fulfillment of some want or need, until a later time. It happens to a person by accident, or by choice. It seems that some aspects of the Christian life include such a delay. The "ultimate" hope or reward of our faith is not fully seen or experienced until death. At that time, we are freed from this life's disappointments and variabilities and limitations, and we encounter the full truth and joy and reward.

The "son of man's" teaching in many ways counters the philosophy of "eat, drink, and be merry, for tomorrow we die." The Lord's way, though seemingly demanding that we delay and control many of our appetites here and now in anticipation of a future bliss, does have a present joy included. Yet, it often includes the cross and a rocky path.

In today's first reading, we hear a tone that likewise sounds unpleasant: "Cursed is the man who trusts in human beings, who seeks his strength in flesh, whose heart turns away from the Lord." It *seems* to negate the possibility of hoping and trusting in others. Who would be attracted to such a faith teaching this? A closer look, though, reveals a wisdom, a challenge to understand the limitations of human love, support, and power. After all, others die leaving us alone. Others sin and disappoint us. So what should our attitude be?

We are *not* to despair of others, but to know the proportion and limitation of human reality. Hoping in the Lord lasts forever, beyond the disappointments and death of others. It does not mean having nothing to do with them! Jesus teaches: to love God requires love of neighbor.

The Gospel assures us of reward for doing what is right and good. It also promises the cross. To do good and be good might mean little respect from some, and may not make us materially rich; yet, true wealth and affirmation come in the long run, in the ultimate moment.

Jesus say the prophets testified to this fact with their lives. It is part of the paradox of living with God: it turns everything upside down; for the poor, hungry, weeping, and hated will be winners. Those who understand and perceive this, smile. Those initiated into this mystery, dwell in its truth.

The ultimate issue of today's readings is the "Resurrection." Do we, or do we not really believe in it? If we do, it changes how we live. It means to live *now* in hope, in the expectation of something good. This expectation is powerful. It gives meaning *through* things which at the present might otherwise not: hunger, poverty, grief, persecution, and death.

People amaze me by their resiliency! We all know heroic people whose lives have endured immense suffering with hope and positive outlooks. Rosalind Russell was exuberant in life through cancer. Viktor Frankl endured the concentration camp horrors of Auschwitz in World War II and wrote *Will to Meaning*. Helen Keller, Anne Frank, Hubert Humphrey, and so many others, tell us of the power of a hope-filled human spirit! It can endure anything. Psychologists tell us the same.

In 1974, I met Kaye, confined to a bed with multiple sclerosis, neglected by family who could not accept this, unvisited, alone and depressed. Through our sharing, and contact with a prayer group, she came to know the Lord in a powerful new way. Upon our leaving the area, people said her spirit would wane. I contended: if God started this, he will sustain it. He did, through friends, and the stability of a nursing home. Eight years later, her spirit remains high, her prayer life central to all, and her family more united. Her physical condition deteriorates, yet she is indomitable! Her love and confidence flow directly from her trusting in the Lord. Rejoicing is her strength. She knows her destiny and her reward, and runs the race, living in daily hope of it.

Following God, believing in Him, is an exciting adventure! It is a "blessed" way to live, here and now! It is a present-living which is future-oriented. It is life hungering for what is to come! Living now, knowing that "the reign of God is yours," and ultimately "your reward shall be great" is powerful.

Jeffrey Archambeault

10th Sunday in Ordinary Time

Cycle C

1 Kgs 17:17–24
Gal 1:11–19
Lk 7:11–17

One approach to this week's homily is to look at Luke's gospel story from a Jungian perspective. The entire story is a story of the journey of the Self. Within me I have something which is dead and a feeling of mourning. Within me is a healing, challenging, comforting dimension—Jesus Christ who lives within all our hearts. And within me is someone who looks at reality and feels a need to praise the God who "has visited his people."

The gospel story begins with a dead man being carried out of town. Ask your congregation: has anything died within, something that you feel is no longer a part of you? Help your listeners to reflect with an example. The example I would use comes from the lives of many of my friends. Ten years ago, right out of college, we set off to change the world. Our politics were liberal, although by no means radical. Our activities centered around helping needy people and our social lives were "community oriented." Now, with commitments to marriage and family, talk centers around mortgage rates, how to get the best deal on a station wagon, and job moves which are upwardly mobile. Some even back conservative political candidates because they believe these people will reduce taxes. Our idealism has died. Our sense of community has given way to family isolationism. And our need to help the poor is not nearly as important as discovering a good tax shelter. We let ourselves get caught in this spiral, but in our more reflective moments, like the widowed mother, we mourn.

What has died within you? Love? The ability to forgive? A healthy dose of ambition? Selfless involvement in church, community, politics? Do you mourn this death?

Like the sorrowful mother who meets Jesus on the road, there is more within us than death and sorrow. As believers in the Risen Lord, in the living Kingdom within, there is a dimension to us like Jesus. Is there anything within you which is healing, forgiving, energetic, loving? Ask your congregation to get in touch with this dimension of themselves. Ask

them to find the Jesus who lives within and ask them to bring him over to the dead person within. What happens if we allow these two sides of ourselves to meet? An example of such a meeting comes from the book *Letting Go of Fear* by Gerald Jambloysky. Jambloysky was at a low point in his life. His marriage had failed. He was devoid of meaning in his life. Something had died within. As part of his search for meaning, he went on a retreat with Mother Teresa. Her words moved him tremendously. When the retreat ended, he wanted to hear more and so asked Mother Teresa if he could go with her on her trip to Mexico City. Mother said to him, "What I think you should do is find out how much an airplane ticket to Mexico City costs. Then take that amount of money and give it to the poor. That will do much more for you than listening further to me." Jambloysky did just that and began his life anew. He allowed his "Jesus" to meet his "dead man" and the result was a new life.

There is more to this story than dead sons, mourning mothers, and Jesus. Luke describes a crowd of people who are afraid at first and then praise God. They see reality and respond to it by deepening their relationship with God. Reflection, of course, is critical to living a whole human life. Invite your congregation to get in touch with their own ability to reflect. The following story might bring out its importance.

In the movie "The Razor's Edge," Bill Murray (in a serious role) is distraught over the death of his friends in World War I. He does not know if life has meaning and goes on a world-wide search to find it. Eventually he comes to live on a mountain with Tibetan monks. One day he arrives at his greatest insight and we see him burn his copy of the holy book. He comes down from the mountain and tells his spiritual advisor, "I have discovered anyone can be holy on a mountain. I need to discover holiness in the world." The monk replies, "This is true. But to find salvation in the world is like walking on the razor's edge."

And this is what you and I, like the people in the crowd 2000 years ago, are called to do. We must walk the earth, not in a dream world, but with ourselves, with people who have death within, mourning within, and Jesus within. We are called on to confront the terrible and the beautiful in our lives and praise what God has done. God has visited us, not just on mountaintops, but as we walk the razor's edge of everyday living where death and grace meet.

Douglas Fisher

11th Sunday in Ordinary Time

Cycle C

2 Sm 12:7–10, 13
Gal 2:16, 19–21
Lk 7:36—8:3

Sinfulness is not a very favorable topic these days. Its discussion is not likely to stir up a lot of interest, and people would probably back off if it were brought up in conversation. Renowned psychiatrists such as Karl Meninger and M. Scott Peck have observed that unpleasantries like sin and evil are generally covered over with more socially acceptable euphemisms which mask the harsh realities involved.

Despite the social parlance, however, people's lives do not always reflect this same freedom from the dark side of human action. We don't need old-fashioned fire and brimstone sermons or missions to point out to us that we spend plenty of time thinking about and talking around the obvious. Keep an ear tuned to how often we defend ourselves, protest our innocence, point out the faults of others or try to deal with guilt feelings, and a more accurate measure of how we really feel begins to emerge. How many books, for example, are written on how not to feel guilty or how successfully to overcome feelings of guilt? " . . . Thou protesteth too much!"

Maybe a good part of the problem is our reluctance to name the reality (Meninger and Peck talk about that). Naming is important because it dispossesses what is named of excessive mystery and gives us power over it. When we have named who we are or identified our qualities, for better or for worse, we can stop dancing around them and begin being ourselves. There is freedom in that, and today's readings gives us an insight into that kind of living.

Not that calling things as they really are takes away all of the pain. As we know from the example of David's life which is recounted in later chapters of Samuel, actions do have consequences. The ramifications of bad choices and selfish moves may have to be lived out over a long period of time—perhaps a lifetime. The formerly sinful woman in Luke's story cannot easily escape being labeled. Her actions, whatever they were, may long be remembered by unforgiving observers who have not yet named their own ills.

But the readings announce a happier name which we are invited to accept as our own: forgiven. That, in the final analysis, may be harder for us to accept than any other name.

In the first reading Nathan tells David: "The Lord on his part has forgiven your sin. . . . " The implication here is that there is something more involved; David, too, has a role to play. In the gospel reading Jesus simply names the reality in the woman's life: "Your sins are forgiven. . . . " He does not tell her to sin no more. There are no injunctions attached to the announcement of her forgiveness. But we suspect that we see the ramifications already present in her gestures of love and generosity. She is already living out her identity as a forgiven sinner.

Claiming God's forgiveness—or anyone's, for that matter—is a humbling thing. We acknowledge that we can't fool anyone, least of all ourselves, about who and what we are. Forgiveness is related to fault. One does not exist apart from the other. Accepting that we are forgiven is accepting that we have sinned.

But "God's gracious gift" of justification or forgiveness, when truly accepted, is not merely an internal reality. The forgiven life is a life renewed, a life which clearly speaks conversion to others. We all know people who have done stupid things, made horrendous choices or glaring mistakes, but whose lives are radiant in their own way. Their new choices and moving forward are a sign of hope to us that newness is possible. The person who has accepted forgiveness in particular areas of life will probably never live those areas in quite the same way again. Here, in this corner of life at least, something is deepened and changed, touched in a new way.

And so, forgiveness is not just for oneself; it is for others, too. Others can grow because one has grown. The generous woman can share her ointment and tears, and presumably, the peace which Jesus announced in her life will not be hidden from others' eyes.

Living in forgiveness may be fragile because our lives tend to be fragmented. Healing in one area may not mean healing of the whole, just as one member's healing does not automatically heal the entire community. But another choice is made, another beginning has been made, and life moves forward.

"Be glad . . . you just," says the psalmist; "exult . . . you upright of heart." We realize that these words are not addressed to the sinless, but to us who are forgiven. The truly upright and just are not better than we: indeed, they know best of all that God has made them new.

Joan R. DeMerchant

12th Sunday in Ordinary Time

Cycle C

Zec 12:10–11
Gal 3:26–29
Lk 9:18–24

Yesterday I spotted a sad sight. There in front of me, lying on the hot asphalt of a neighbor's driveway, was a bouquet of flowers. It looked more purchased than hand-picked, for it was neatly bound and wrapped in cellophane. There were daisies of different colors, some species I could appreciate but not identify, and some greens which, in the heat, had begun to wither and pale.

It was a gift, I presumed, this abandoned bouquet, and I found myself wondering about the incident or circumstances which led to its lying there.

Flowers are a unique kind of gift. They celebrate significant occasions—both happy and sad. They have the flexibility to adorn a prom dress or to soften a funeral chapel. Flowers, it seems, are seldom purchased for one's self; part of their identity seems to be "gift." They have a reputation for mending marital troubles, for healing hospitalized friends, for beautifying birthday buffets. Why, then, was this gift-bouquet lying on the ground? What potential it had!

I envisioned three scenarios that might have led to the bouquet's landing on the driveway. First, I imagined an anxious giver running down the driveway to catch she-whom-the-flowers-were-for, and, with loving abandon, reaching the bouquet out to the receiver. The receiver, alas, was expecting a better gift and pushes the giver's hand away until the gift drops. The receiver drives away in a Porsche, running over the stems.

In my second fantasy, the giver arrives at the receiver's door, nervous and uncertain. "Will my gift be good enough? Is it what my receiver wants?" Having debated internally, the giver decides that the bouquet is perfect, just what the receiver needs. But, to add to the mystery of why one gives a gift at all, the giver decides to give it in a rather unique way. Setting the flowers near the frequently-used driveway, in plain sight, the giver leaves and returns home, anticipating the receiver's joy upon finding this unexpected gift. The receiver, however, is out shopping for flowers and upon returning finds only dead flowers.

The third scene in my mind is of a giver who has this bouquet all ready to bring to a friend who is ill. But, wanting to give yet more, the giver also buys candy, a stuffed animal, and a crossword puzzle book. The receiver, overloaded with gifts, accidentally drops the flowers. When the receiver meets the giver again, the giver says, "How did you like the flowers?" "What flowers?"

Today's readings remind me of those flowers I saw. And in many ways, the readings are as sad a sight as the orphaned flowers. Each of the readings speaks of gifts, gifts more beautiful and more lasting than flowers. Do God's gifts to us sometimes end up lying on the asphalt too?

Zechariah speaks prophetically about the Messiah. "They shall look on him whom they have thrust through." God's gift of his own son was rejected. Like the receiver in my first bouquet scenario, they were expecting a different kind of gift, a "better" Messiah. Jesus, like the flowers, was rejected because he wasn't good enough for the receivers.

The letter to the Galatians speaks of the gifts of faith, of freedom, of equality, of a share in all "that was promised." God, like the giver in my second flower-fantasy, sets these gifts in our lives unexpectedly sometimes. We are too busy trying to earn them or to purchase them elsewhere to notice that God has placed them "right in our own backyard."

Luke's Gospel speaks of the gift of our own life, and the purpose for which that life is given. God gives us many other blessings for our use, but our lives are meant to be spent—to be, as it were, lost in service to others. Like the recipient in the third scenario I envisioned, sometimes we get so caught up in life's other good things, that we forget about life itself. Instead of caring for our life and using it for others, we drop it, like the flowers, accidentally.

One final fantasy I had for the flowers: they were reclaimed! Perhaps the receiver re-thought their value and ran to pick them up; perhaps, arriving back from the frustration of looking elsewhere, the receiver spotted the half-dead flowers and nursed them back to life and beauty; perhaps, having tired of the other gifts, the receiver returned to the flowers and carefully pressed them and made them into gifts for others. Or, perhaps the original receiver never did appreciate the flowers, but a little boy spotted them and took them to his mother who did not even notice that they were wilted, but only saw that they were a special gift to be treasured.

Seen any abandoned bouquets lately?

Carole M. Eipers

Peter and Paul
(13th Sunday)

Cycle C

Acts 12:1–11
2 Tm 4:6–8, 17–18
Mt 15:13–19

Her name is Anna—she is an apostle. I came to know her in my position as director of Adult Ministry in our parish. She joined the weekly bible study group which I facilitated. It didn't take long to see that this was a person sensitive to life and the Word of God; the two were interwoven. God was a part of her marriage, her family, her job, her parish, and her community. After thirty years of marriage and raising three children with her husband George she had, in the words of Paul, " . . . fought the good fight (and is still fighting) and kept the faith."

When it came time for our parish to choose a coordinator of Family Ministry, Anna's gifts for the position were already evident. She accepted the call even though she, like Peter, was "chained" to other commitments. But through the power of the Spirit, she found the freedom to carry on the challenging work of enabling our parish to better care for its families.

After one year in this ministry, she summarized the results in an article she wrote for a newsletter:

"1. Ministry to engaged working successfully for thirteen months. Nine couples experienced at administering PMI (Pre-Marriage Inventory). Several more couples being trained in September.

2. Family Ministry team in existence. Special training planned for fall months.

3. New Widowed Group meeting for several months in response to specifically expressed need.

4. Family Cluster Group formed to share socially and spiritually.

5. SMART Team (St. Mary's Alcoholism Recovery Team) formed to help people with alcohol-related problems.

6. Dale Olen series on Parenting and Marriage presented.

7. Aging Parents series presented.

8. 'You Can Help With Your Healing' support group meeting weekly."

This was a great beginning, but it was no surprise. Anna's faith, like Peter's, is rooted in the firm foundation of faith in the Son of the Living God. Those she touches come to know him better, and she herself is enriched. She suggests this in her own words taken from her article:

"Reflecting over the past year, I am aware that it takes many ingredients to make an idea work. For me there was the support and cooperation I received from associates, participants in the various ministries, and our parishioners, which stimulated my creativity and energized me. There were the generous expressions of belief in and appreciation for this ministry. Who would not be encouraged by such warmth of spirit? Another very essential ingredient to my ministry has been my participation in a weekly scripture study. Sharing the scriptures with this group of our parishioners has helped to develop in me a better sense of who I am and has enabled me to make connections with stories of faith that form the foundation of my Catholic tradition.

"Finally, two ingredients which I found crucial to my survival in ministry are a healthy self perspective and a sense of humor."

Anna has since moved to another state but has continued in her ministry. She, like many other modern apostles, shares the Good News wherever she journeys.

John R. Schmitz

14th Sunday in Ordinary Time

Cycle C

Is 66:10–14
Gal 6:14–18
Lk 10:1–12, 17–20

Jesus' traveling instructions to the disciples in Luke's Gospel could be seen as guidance for us as we travel through life. What he says to these seventy-two ministers applies to more than ministry. Jesus presents insights which can be helpful to all on the human journey.

It is interesting that Jesus sends the seventy-two out in pairs. The human "task" is secondary to human "bonding." Jesus does not give his disciples a list of jobs and goals and hope they meet a friendly face along the way. He unites people and then asks them to travel out from there. The starting point, the center of living, is not an issue or a goal, but another person. In today's Gospel Jesus establishes friendship and community as primary. We reach out to the world only *after* coming to know intimacy with another.

This insight might seem fairly obvious until we look at how often we stray from it. As an example from ministry I offer the summers I spent with college volunteers working in poor areas of the country. All of us were "issue oriented." We wanted to help the poor, to give of ourselves. But as a volunteer and later as a director I recognized that all our work, all our passionate good will, was empty without a community life which was nurtured with the same energy. The volunteer who spent all of his or her time "giving to the poor" became impoverished later on through burnt-out cynicism. The volunteer who was committed to life with the other volunteers could minister out of a fund of love. Those are the same volunteers who get together years later and still give out of the energy and attitudes those friendships engendered.

Ask your congregation to consider examples from their own lives when friendship empowered them and when the lack of it damaged the "work" of life. How often is the "job" meaningless when life at home is strained? How often does the work of your company falter when the people within the company do not relate well? Look at those examples and then ask yourself where you place most of your time and energy. Is your day "people oriented" or "task oriented"? Jesus gave us a model for living when he sent his workers out two by two.

And how should these pairs travel? Jesus asks us to travel lightly—without walking staff, traveling bag or sandals. Perhaps he also asks us to travel without the baggage of security and ego protection. How often do I approach people "loaded down" with defenses, with impression-creating lines which keep another from getting close to me? An example from a recent lunch with a prospective video author might illustrate this. I was meeting with this person about a play he was writing. I was seeking to find out how he saw this play developing, which meant getting to know him and the truth he wished to convey. Instead I heard story after story of his conversations with big Broadway stars, of high praise he received from important people for his most recent book. I am sure that underneath it all lies a very warm and interesting person. But he is carrying so much, I might never find out.

How lightly do we travel? How much do we carry around to impress people? The temptation to take plenty on this trip is always there for me. But Jesus asks for something far different. He asks for vulnerability with confidence.

Notice too the power Jesus gives us for the journey. We can do great things. We have "power to tread on snakes and scorpions and all the forces of the enemy." Jesus does not call for us to be a timid, powerless people. We should travel through life confident that we are a gifted people. The whining, "victim" approach we all give in to at times is not part of the Christian way.

A story which can serve as an analogy for this point is a conversation Dustin Hoffman and Laurence Olivier supposedly had. They were in a movie together when one day Hoffman showed up looking haggard and exhausted with bloodshot eyes. Olivier said "What is the matter with you?" Hoffman replied, "I have to play a scene today where I am having a nervous breakdown. I have kept myself awake the last two nights so I could look this way." Olivier said, "Son, have you ever tried *acting*?"

Hoffman did not trust his abundant gifts. Do we ever do the same? Do we think other people "control things" and we are mere tired victims? Jesus calls us to recognize our power, appreciate the many gifts the Father has given us, and use them.

To sum up, Jesus asks us to travel with others in intimacy, and to live out that shared journey with honesty, vulnerability and confidence.

Douglas Fisher

15th Sunday in Ordinary Time

Cycle C

Dt 30:10–14
Col 1:15–20
Lk 10:25–37

Pleading ignorance seems to be an ancient device. That's not strange, considering what an easy device it is for distancing ourselves from truth we may prefer to avoid. Once a question is asked, however, and the answer given, we are faced with having to act—or not act—on what we know.

Today's readings suggest that the answers to some key questions that believers might ask are really quite close at hand. If we were to ask what we have to *do* to live in God, the answer, it seems, is not hard to find. It is not written in dusty books or catechisms that we no longer use, nor is it couched in language from another age. God's "voice" and "commandments" are not spoken or written in expressions from the past. That would make it too easy to dismiss them as irrelevant.

No, the answer to what we must do if we really want to live is found in the ordinary experience of our lives and in the word we have heard often enough: love your neighbor as yourself. The answer was close to the hearts and mouths of the Jews, for the Levitical command to love one's neighbor was an ancient injunction that every Jew not only heard but spoke often. The words were literally "in their mouths." They are just as familiar to us, though our tradition may not encourage us to speak them as often. Certainly what is required of us is "in our hearts"; we instinctively *know* what is asked of us. The trouble seems to be in acting on what we know.

Maybe we are in the same place as the lawyer in today's Gospel. The words are safe for us because we have not probed beneath them to discover what they name. When the lawyer asks the question, "Who is my neighbor" he can no longer hide behind the Levitical formula. For Jesus concretizes those words: the *enemy* is my neighbor.

We don't know what the lawyer did with that answer. He may have managed to keep it at the intellectual level, that age-old trick which still works well for us. To make the command operative, he would have had to take it one small step further and name his enemies. That would have been the risky part for him, as it is for us.

Speaking in the enemy's name places the whole thing in the realm of the absurd, because most of us have drawn invisible lines beyond which we will not go. Or maybe we're afraid that we cannot succeed. The "enemy" can be pretty formidable if we have no idea about how to approach them. Perhaps Pogo was right about the enemy being us!

Paul tells us in the second reading, however, that reconciliation is possible (and reconciliation is what this is ultimately about) because Jesus has already reconciled everything in himself. Jesus is even now "making peace." Turning to him in hope and in trust empowers us to do likewise. "Turn to the Lord in your need, and you will live," we pray. Dare we to hope that this might include the possibility of loving one's enemy?

In any case, the ancient message is that we live out of what is closest to our hearts and spoken from our lips. The daring is in the speaking and naming with conviction, so that we can truly act out of what we say. If we choose not to do that, the question will remain. We will continue to ask "What must I do?" when deep inside we know that a portion of the answer lies in us.

Joan R. DeMerchant

16th Sunday in Ordinary Time

Cycle C

Gn 18:1–10
Col 1:24–28
Lk 10:38–42

The theme of this Sunday's readings is *hospitality*. The scriptures suggest that we cannot truly be present to God unless we are present to one another. As we make room in our lives for one another, we also make room for God. John Pilch points this out in the exegetical section above: "He is as close as one's welcomed guest whether stranger (Genesis) or friend (Luke)."

How is the *hospitality* accomplished? The readings suggest that it is both through activity and through silence. Abraham was very much present to his three guests even as he moved about to serve their needs. Mary was equally present to Jesus even though she only sat quietly at his feet. At every Eucharist we need to practice both types of *presence,* shared activity and shared silence. Our Church should always be a place and a people of welcome. Maureen Gallagher points out the importance of this in her guidebook to the filmstrip "The Ministry of Hospitality":

> The need for the ministry of hospitality is further accentuated in today's society which has been described by some as a "world of strangers" where loneliness and alienation prevail. While there is an increased understanding of the need for the value of interpersonal relationships, there are enormous voids in the lives of many because of a lack of hospitality and acceptance. (page 5)

If there is any place where such needs should be met, it is at our Sunday Eucharist. Yet, far too often, it is precisely at Sunday Eucharist that we frequently feel most unwelcomed: the indifferent or even hostile glances that we receive as we try to find a place in the pew; the lack of greeting by the ushers or anyone else as we enter the church. These are only a few of the ways that we make each other feel unwelcomed at our Eucharist.

There is a Hungarian folktale which illustrates the "second theme" that John Pilch points out in the exegetical section: "The reward or satisfaction of hospitality nearly always surpasses its cost."

One day Jesus was making his way about the Hungarian prairie to see how the herdsmen were getting on. It was a hot summer day, and Jesus became thirsty from walking in the heat. Suddenly he caught sight of a well and bent his steps toward it. Near the well he saw a herdsman, stretched comfortably on the grass under a big and leafy tree. All his cattle were lying scattered around him, chewing their cuds contentedly.

Jesus asked him for a drink of water. The herdsman, however, was too lazy and too comfortable, so he only lifted one leg and pointed to the well. So Jesus had to help himself to a drink. When Jesus had quenched his thirst, he proceeded on his way; but to punish the cowherd he sent a swarm of gadflies to him.

After traveling a great distance, Jesus again became thirsty from walking in the great heat. When he saw another well not too far off, he headed toward it. Near the well he found a shepherd in great trouble with his flock, since the sheep were badly plagued by flies and were running madly about in all directions.

Jesus asked him for a drink of water. In no way could this shepherd have guessed who had asked him for some water, and yet he answered Jesus with good grace. He told Jesus he would be glad to get him a drink but he didn't know how to quiet his flock.

"Just bring me a drink of water and do not worry about the sheep," said Jesus. "I'll be looking after them until you get back."

The shepherd took pity on the stranger and went with his jug to the well. He filled the jug with fresh water and brought it back to offer a drink to the stranger. When he came back he found his flock bunched together, not a single one of them missing or running about.

Jesus quenched his thirst and thanked the shepherd for his kindness. Then he proceeded on his way in good humor.

From that very day, when the summer sun is blazing down with its hottest rays, the sheep will flock together for a midday rest. This enables the shepherd to cook his meal, or have a rest, or take a short nap.

But it is different with the cowherd. When the weather turns too hot, he must always be on the run after his cattle. For it is then that the gadflies appear, and the cattle run in all directions; so the herdsmen have to do quite a bid of riding before they can round up their cattle.

Michael Kurz

17th Sunday in Ordinary Time

Cycle C

Gn 18:20–32
Col 2:12–14
Lk 11:1–13

Mark Twain's character Huckleberry Finn prayed for a fishing pole and hooks. When he got only the pole, he gave up on prayer. Perhaps you have had an experience like Huck Finn's, and so have abandoned prayers of petition. Or maybe you continue to ask God for things, but wonder whether such petitions are not out of place in an adult spirituality. Today's readings stress persistence in prayer, and the importance of believing that if we ask, we will receive. The Our Father, with its several petitions, is presented as a pattern for Christian prayer. The readings revive our questions about prayers of petition: Should we ask God for things? What are we to ask for? Can we expect God to answer our prayers?

Should we ask God for things? Prayer of petition is deeply rooted in the human spirit. Prayer is being ourselves with God, bringing our life before God. Part of life is a deep experience of personal limitation and the need for divine help. Martin Luther King's book, *Stride Toward Freedom*, reveals the crucial role prayer played in King's leadership in the momentous Montgomery bus struggle of 1955–1957. Faced with preparing a speech which he called "the most decisive speech of my life," King prayed. He also prayed while besieged by telephone threats, and as he stood before the people. His dialogue with God came out of his awareness that his ultimate resource was not himself, but God.

Jesus prayed in the face of his approaching death in the garden. And he told us many times to bring our concerns before God. We turn to God for help because we believe our expressions of concern really make a difference to God. We lift up our friends, our loved ones, and the whole world because we are convinced there is a caring Creator whose power and love are larger than our own. Our love and our need are received by that creative love, and transformed.

What are we to ask for? A married woman in her fifties who has raised a family of ten children recently remarked that she has come to realize there are only two things to pray for, the wisdom to know what to do, and the strength to do it. In the Our Father we are told to pray not only for our own needs, but also for the coming of God's kingdom of justice, peace, and love. We ask for protection from evil, for the capacity to forgive others, and for the fulfillment of God's purpose in the world.

Our prayer often begins with the needs most immediately apparent to us: success in a task, release from loneliness, help in a difficult situation. A prayer from *Children's Letters to God* reads: "Why don't you keep it from raining on Saturday all the time?" But persistence in prayer means more than showing up periodically in desperation. Prayer is an on-going relationship which changes us, and as we change our prayer changes too. We learn not only how to ask, but how to receive the gifts of God already offered to us. As we continue to pray, we become more God-centered, and God's interests become ours.

Can we expect God to answer our prayers? Jesus' prayer is the model for ours. In his prayer in the garden, he asks for what he wants: "Father, if you are willing, take this cup away from me." But he leaves it to God: "Nevertheless, let your will be done, not mine." Prayer is not magic. It leaves God free. The reading from Luke today assures us that God knows how to give good things to those who ask. Our answer may come as an expansion of the self, an enlarged capacity for suffering, a new sense of our interconnectedness with all people, renewed courage to face a situation, or insight into a path of action. Since prayer is exposure to God, it prepares us to hear God's message in the many ways it comes to us: Scripture, nature, other people, or the events of our lives. Luke says that God's response to our prayer is a generous and mysterious one—the gift of the Holy Spirit. The Spirit is indeed the fullness of wisdom and strength.

Kathleen R. Fischer
Thomas N. Hart

18th Sunday in Ordinary Time

Cycle C

Eccl 1:2; 2:21–23
Col 3:1–5, 9–11
Lk 12:13–21

Many of us find a recurring question tugging at our hearts: How can I be happy and satisfied? When will I know some lasting peace and joy? In pursuit of an answer we follow the leads of commercials: "K-Mart Is Your Saving Place," "Datsun Saves," "GE: We bring good things to life." Happiness seems as close as our next purchase of something to eat, a new house, new clothes, a car, or a vacation. Yet somehow it is never enough. These consumer goods do not quiet the questions and the longing.

Our readings today provide another response to our questions about happiness and satisfaction, an answer that turns our accustomed values upside down. Life, they say, is not found in an abundance of possessions. True life is the life which has Christ as its measure. Both parts of this message are important. The Gospel not only tells us to "Go, sell what you have and give to the poor"; it adds, "Come, follow me."

The author of Ecclesiastes states a truth we know from experience: Life is transitory. We cannot hang onto what we acquire. The gospel story of the fool and his full barn tells the same tale. Yet we do try desperately to hang on. Somehow we identify *being* with *having*. I see my self-worth as dependent on success, grades, degrees, positions, promotions, rewards, and possessions. The ultimate significance of life seems somehow dependent on what I can do, make, or accomplish. Yet these things often leave me with an inner emptiness and boredom.

My obsession with things has an even more serious consequence. It means that countless people throughout the world must live in oppression and poverty. This question of the use of wealth plays a larger role in Luke than in any other Gospel; one out of seven verses in his Gospel is about the rich and the poor. But the oppression of the poor which results from the hardness of heart of the rich and comfortable is a central concern of the entire Bible. Our global economic system has marginalized millions of people in the underdeveloped countries of the world, in Central and South America, in Africa, in Asia. Even in the United States, the richest nation on earth, there are those who go hungry and die for lack of life's basic necessities.

We are tempted to blame this situation on the failure of governments to take action, on patterns of foreign trade and land control, or even on the poor themselves for their lack of initiative and dependability. The Bible would have us find the sources of such injustice rather within our own hearts, in a greed for possessions which leads to the consumption of the earth's resources far out of proportion to our numbers.

The solution to these problems begins with our own conversion to a new life in Christ. As Paul tells the Colossians, true life means being formed anew in the image of the Creator, setting aside those attitudes that are contrary to God. Find happiness, the Gospels tell us, in a new kind of security that comes from trust in God. Experience the joy that comes from knowing that you are really loved. Discover those possessions which last—the Spirit's gifts of love, peace, forgiveness, gentleness, and kindness, and the blessings of a human community which really shares life. No moth can destroy these possessions; nor can a thief creep in and steal them.

When we have allowed our hearts to be converted in this manner, we will find ways to touch the larger problems of wealth and poverty. When Dorothy Day began her work for the poor in the 1930s there were thirteen million unemployed. Her efforts to help seemed small by comparison. She writes of that experience in *The Long Loneliness:* "We were just sitting there talking when lines of people began to form, saying, 'We need bread.' We could not say, 'Go, be thou filled.' If there were six small loaves and a few fishes, we had to divide them. There was always bread." And she also writes of the joy that came to those whose community grew out of this sharing: "We know him in the breaking of the bread, and we know each other in the breaking of bread, and we are not alone any more. Heaven is a banquet and life is a banquet, too, even with a crust, where there is companionship" (285).

Kathleen R. Fischer
Thomas N. Hart

19th Sunday in Ordinary Time

Cycle C

Wis 18:6–9
Heb 11:1–2, 8–19
Lk 12:32–48

Life is such a delicate balance. We live always on the edge with one toe dangling somewhat half-heartedly into the future and the greater part of ourselves clinging as if magnetized to our present place. That in itself is a bit ironic, for the spot to which we cling was only yesterday on the fore side of the edge. But no matter how recently acquired, "home" is usually deemed familiar and safe.

Try as we might to anchor ourselves in a secure place, the human experience is always transitory. We are called out, pushed, cajoled or enticed from one space to another. The thing that inches our toe forward might be some intriguing new knowledge, boredom with our present place, a sense of danger about where we are or a nagging sense that something or Someone is urging us on. A desire for sheer survival might encourage us to hitch up our tunics and take off at night across the marshes, or the hope of new horizons might encourage us to leave our family home and sojourn into unknown territory. In a way, the reasons for going—for moving on—don't really matter, because often we have no control over them. The process of aging or the inevitability of death come to us all.

Being on the move, while exhilarating in its own way, is also scary. The biblical images support our experience of this. The Hebrews moved out from Egypt into the night. We can imagine that Abraham's journey, too, was a journey into darkness; God, after all, asked him to count the stars in the sky. And the master who will come may likely appear at night as well, for we are warned to keep our lamps burning and ourselves wide awake in readiness. Futures, we know, are always somewhat obscure.

While our readings today acknowledge that the experience of not knowing exactly where we are going is the story of every person, they also point out to us that we do have some control over *how* we will go. We can hardly imagine the Hebrews hesitating once they made their decision to go for the escape. And Abraham likely did not inch his way into a new

territory. Sarah, too, while doubtful about her procreative possibilities, doesn't strike us as particularly cautious. Once the decision is made to be open to the future, the quality of the leap is unconditional. The step may be tentative, but it is sure.

How can this be? What inspires the conviction that stepping over the edge will not carry us into a bottomless hole? Our readings tell us that we can dare to push into the next unknown space because of our hopefulness and trust in the One who has prepared the space for us. "Faith," we read in the letter to the Hebrews, "is confident assurance concerning what we hope for, and conviction about things we do not see." Abraham did not know where or if he would find it, but "he was looking forward to the city with foundations." Sarah believed "that the One who had made the promise was worthy of the trust." Those awaiting the master did not know the hour of his return, but they were ready, for they believed that he would come.

Not knowing the exact outcome should not deter us from setting out. For one thing, outcomes of our larger steps will never be completely clear except in faith. To wait for demonstrated certainty could guarantee our waiting forever. The Hebrews would have died in slavery. Furthermore, creativity vanishes without our inclination to try new things. The human community will survive in relationship to its willingness to risk new solutions and dream new dreams. And if we go only kicking and screaming into the future, we may very well miss seeing what is there.

The final secure spot for the dangling toe will never be bound in this life. Abraham lived in tents and so shall we. The disciples waited for the master's return and the wait goes on. Life is one transition after another, and we live it with the constant hope of "some day," . . . "one day." But for Christians the quality of the hoping and the surety of the One in whom we hope is everything.

Joan R. DeMerchant

20th Sunday in Ordinary Time

Cycle C

Jer 38:4–6, 8–10
Heb 12:1–4
Lk 12:49–53

Anyone who thinks that the Christian life is meant to be easy should read the Scriptures we have heard today. In them we find Jeremiah tossed into a pit because of his preaching; we are reminded how Jesus endured the opposition of sinners to the point of shedding his blood; and we are told that Jesus came not to establish peace, but division, and that we can expect households and families to be divided because of him. The images are far from sanguine. If anything, they should make us pause in order to consider whether or not we really want to get involved in such a thing as Christianity. Do we really want to commit ourselves to a way of life that causes division, misunderstanding, suspicion, maybe even suffering and death? Most of us don't even like the ordinary patterns of our lives to be disrupted by minor inconveniences, much less by more radical demands. Yet Christianity is a radical demand, for to heed God's call, to open oneself to God in prayer, and to follow the path of Christ is to say, "My life is not simply my own; I belong to another." This means relinquishing final control over one's life and finding security not in oneself, but in God. And it involves a struggle not for power and possession, but for a vulnerability to the cries of the suffering, the poor, and the afflicted, of whoever is in need.

This of course is not the way the world works. Power, prestige, possession, control are the values of our secular, Western society. To be vulnerable, to risk one's security, to be different is to be foolish. But, are true happiness and security found any other way than by laying down our defenses, our striving for "making it" in this world, our concern only for ourselves?

In the film *Beckett*, Thomas Beckett, chancellor of England, confidant of the King, second most powerful man in the kingdom, remarks that despite his success, his power, his position, there remains a void in life. "Always the void," he says. It is only after he becomes Archbishop of Canterbury (albeit for other than sacred motives) that the void is filled. He then realizes that his call to serve God's kingdom is far more important than his service to the king of England. His refusal to defy God and laws of the Church in order to obey King Henry ultimately costs him his life. Nevertheless, he is able to meet his fate with courage and confidence that now at last his life truly has meaning.

And how about us? Though most of us will not be faced with the prospect of martyrdom because of our convictions, can we still say there is something about us and our lives that is worth dying for? Is there something or someone about which each one of us would be willing to sacrifice prestige, position, self image, security, or do we seek always to protect ourselves from any challenge to our own self interest and preservation? If the answer is no, there is nothing in my life worth dying for, then I think we need to look seriously at the direction of our lives: to our choices, our values, the things to which we direct most of our attention. And we then need to ask ourselves: Are these things worth the price of my immortal soul?

If the answer is yes, there are things about my life that are worth dying for, I think we then need to ask a further question: How do I deal with these things or these persons? Do I take them for granted, or do I treat them as if they are the things I value most? In other words, does my behavior demonstrate clearly that above all else these things matter to me?

Today's reading from the Letter to the Hebrews uses the metaphor of a race to illustrate how we should live for the sake of what most matters in our lives. Just as a racer must focus exclusively on the finish line in order to win a race, we Christians must keep our eyes fixed on Jesus as the goal to which we aspire. Jesus, the definitive revelation of God, has shown in his life how we should live for others and for the sake of the truth. The Spirit of Jesus will guide us in the daily choices of our lives if we seek her wisdom.

Jesus, Jeremiah, all the great prophets and saints maintained a single focus throughout their lives; all else about them conformed to this. If they are great in our eyes it is not because they strove to become great. They are great because their vision mattered more than anything else to them and because fidelity to their vision made possible the working of God's grace.

If any of us has a vision worth giving our lives for, let us not lose sight of it. Our lives and the lives of those we love depend upon it. "So strengthen your drooping hands and your weak knees" (Heb 12:12). Above all else, know that God wills for us a share in God's own holiness. The price we pay for this is nothing in comparison to the joy that lies ahead.

Helene A. Lutz

21st Sunday in Ordinary Time

Cycle C

Is 66:18–21
Heb 12:5–7, 11–13
Lk 13:22–30

The gospel story from Luke lends itself to that Jungian method, used frequently by this contributor, whereby we reflect on the story as the inner journey of each hearer of the Word. What happens in the story happens within each one of us and when reflected on leads to a discovery of the Christ within.

In telling the story of the closed door, Jesus reveals two dimensions within us. Within me is someone who closes doors—who locks out feelings, emotions and other people. I am at once secure and closed to any opportunities a God of surprises might provide for me. I do not know where need and fear come from because I refuse to acknowledge them in my past or present. And yet within me is another dimension—a person in need who futilely knocks on doors which do not open.

In the story Jesus tells, the people on either side of the door never meet. What would happen if they did? What would happen if the closed, cold dimension within myself dialogued with the dimension within which is hurting and in need of compassion? I had the opportunity to witness such an encounter recently in the imagination of a little child.

I was sitting with my 3½-year-old nephew on a bench at the beach. An important prelude to this story is my nephew's disdain of showers—he hates them. There is something about the water hitting his head which makes him give his mother a very, very tough time when she does not have a bathtub available and must bring him into a shower. As we were sitting on the bench, we heard blood-curdling screams coming from the direction of the showers. Matthew took a big-eyed glance in that direction and I asked him, "Matt, what is that?"

"Some baby, he doesn't want to take a shower."

"Oh . . . Matt, if you were that baby's mommy, what would you do?"

"I'd say, 'Enough of this. Be quiet. End of discussion.'"

"And what would the baby say, Matt?"

"No shower. No shower. No shower," he squealed.

"What would the mommy do then?"

"She would say, 'Be quiet. Don't be a baby. *This is life.*'"

The master of the house and the person pleading outside have met. The needy, powerless, baby dimension of Matthew talks with strong, all powerful, uncompassionate Mommy.

(Of course, his mother is responding as any mother would when faced with getting a dirty boy clean. The negative connotations from this story are simply useful for a reflection on our inner selves and having nothing to do with a statement about child rearing.)

As Matthew acted out the two parts, perhaps he came to a greater understanding of his own need to grow up and of his mother's frustration. Perhaps not—he is only 3½. But what could happen if we take the time to get in touch with the angry, bitter side of ourselves which says "I have earned what I have. I have power. I will use that power to keep people, especially people who want to take from me, away. I will not let myself be hurt. I will remain steady and unchangeable." Think about times you might be that way.

Now get in touch with the needy times—the times you feel rejected, weak, dumped on. What did it feel like?

Within is a healing Jesus who introduces these two dimensions of ourselves to each other in order to create new life. What happens when the "door locker" you meets the rejected you? Now reflect on the unwanted, needy people in your life. Can you find within a source of compassion?

Here is one example of what can happen when such a meeting takes place. A friend of mine, very successful and very "macho," recently had a heart attack. Although I know many wonderful aspects of John, I also know he can be harsh and cold at work, believing many employees to be "lazy bums" for whom he has no respect. John had the door firmly locked to them. In the three months he could not work due to the heart attack, John met a needy, unachieving person—himself. At first he fought this person. And then he rediscovered a wife who loved him through it. John returned to work as a man who could open doors to people less successful then he.

Matthew, this is life. Some who are last will be first and some who are first will be last.

Douglas Fisher

139

22nd Sunday in Ordinary Time

Cycle C

Sir 3:17–18, 20, 28–29
Heb 12:18–19, 22–24
Lk 14:1, 7–14

Humility is not exactly a virtue in vogue. Mention it among typical contemporary folks and you're likely to conjure up images of the shy and retiring "Milquetoast" with not too much backbone and less gumption. Our twentieth-century values lean toward "making it" in this world—living up to someone's expectations, if not one's own. Today's successful man or woman knows where to live, how to dress, what to drink, how to perform and what to drive. Readings about humbling oneself or sitting at the lowest place at table seem quaint, or worse—appropriate only to another time and place.

Stories about pushing oneself to the top, however, are not limited to the manifestations of a first-century Mediterranean culture. Our customs may be different, but we have our own systems for "knowing our place" in various settings and relationships. Social position is not even necessarily the issue, for even in various social strata people compete with one another, struggle to be well-regarded, or work hard at "keeping up with the Joneses." Listening to conversations at the typical cocktail party, backyard barbecue or family holiday get-together can give us clues as to what we regard as our own "high places." We undergo our own struggles to avoid being shamed or diminished in the eyes of family, friends, neighbors, or acquaintances.

Part of the struggle involves what we are willing to do to move ourselves up or whether we are willing to displace others in our effort to move forward. Our own counterpart to honor might be reputation or prestige or self-esteem. It could be our need to be "the best" or "#1", but needing merely to be better than others can be the same struggle written in small letters. In one sense, the scope does not matter. Families and nations play out the scenario in strikingly similar fashion. Broken relationships and wars bear witness to this.

There is an understandable tension in trying to maintain or build up our self-esteem, or in wanting to respond to the challenge to do or be all that we're capable of and yet resisting the urge to "move to a higher place." The actions seem mutually exclusive. People express their frustration at this kind of tension, for example, when they struggle with the Church's social teachings such as the recent Bishops' Pastoral Letter on Economics. Some maintain that they were encouraged in another era to provide for themselves and their families and yet they now feel that they are being challenged for what they have achieved. The tension is real and sometimes confusing.

But the key to resolving the issue lies not in demeaning ourselves; rather, it has to do with knowing who we really are. Today's readings remind us that we, like those who have gone before us, can approach God's presence not through our own efforts, but because of Jesus who has acted on our behalf. It is God who makes us worthy. It is God who cares for us in our defenseless moments and offers us whatever we need. Whatever we have is given as gift. If we find our way to the table at all, it is only because we have been invited there. If we come to the wedding party, it is as guests that we take our place at table. Knowing who we are is a humbling experience. And it is also probably one of the most important tasks of our human growth.

The challenge to live out of this self-knowledge touches our lives on many levels. Among family, friends, colleagues, neighbors, fellow-Christians or simply other human beings, knowing who we really are frees us to be with one another in equality. It enables us to sit down at table together, whether that table is the simple table of our family meal, the table of human fellowship, or the Eucharistic table which is above all the great "leveler" of all who partake there. This self-knowledge beckons us to invite those who do not yet know the dignity that has been bestowed upon them. It raises for us the discomforting question of who we are willing to admit to our own tables or our eucharistic tables. Our sense of hospitality is challenged as well as our need to humble ourselves.

Finally, knowing who we really are and acting out of that reality prepares us for our ultimate place that is described in the vision of the heavenly banquet. There, as Corita Kent once described it, " . . . the whole human running race could finally sit down in a big circle and eat together. . . . " Those who are seeking always to move higher would not likely be comfortable in such a gathering where all are gathered as one.

Joan R. DeMerchant

23rd Sunday in Ordinary Time

Cycle C

Wis 9:13–18
Phlm 9–10, 12–17
Lk 14:25–33

I imagine Jesus chuckling at us as he asks, "If one of you decides to build a tower, will he not first sit down and calculate the outlay to see if he has enough money to complete the project?" "Oh, yes," we reply. "We are intelligent and foresighted, and we check our resources carefully before we begin to build." Jesus knows better; he is aware of the reality which his listeners don't see—or at least won't acknowledge as something that could happen to them. There are, Jesus knows, a lot of unfinished buildings around!

If you have ever put an addition on your house or been involved in a church renovation, you know that no matter how well you calculate, the project always seems to cost more than you anticipate. There are unexpected delays, the cost of materials rises, there are unforeseen electrical or plumbing complications, and either you or the builder ends up declaring bankruptcy. Your unfinished project becomes another monument to the futility of our best laid plans.

I wonder if it wasn't this reality of inestimable outlay which Jesus was comparing to the cost of discipleship, rather than the surface message of "plan ahead." On several occasions Jesus speaks about the price of being his follower. Today he talks about turning one's back on family and shouldering the cross. On other occasions he asks that a disciple sell all his possessions, and finally, he asks his followers to be willing to give their lives. The cost of discipleship seems pretty clear: relationships, possessions, life. The price of following Jesus is high; in a word, he asks everything.

We have all known moments when our "yes" to Jesus was joyous and jubilant, when everything was precisely what we were willing to give, and even at that, it seemed a small price to pay to be named his disciple. That sort of yes is the enthusiastic plunge of youth, the pristine affirmation of conversion. We are ready to give everything, for we have not yet begun to realize in our hearts the significance of "everything." How the Lord must treasure those spontaneous yeses of our youth! Like the homeowner who wants to add a room, we have fallen in love with the blueprint but have not considered the sacrifices which will be necessary to meet the payments.

As we grow older, and we are building our discipleship through the seasons, we find that the cost of the materials goes up. The same "everything" we were willing to pay unquestioningly as twenty-year-olds becomes more dear as we reach forty. Our family has become closer, and it is harder to turn our back on those whose values do not reflect Gospel values and who tempt us to seek wealth or power; our friendships become more precious and it is more difficult to sacrifice a friend in favor of a right moral decision; we have accumulated more possessions and they represent security which, as we age, becomes more necessary; the life which seemed endless and indestructible at 20 now seems more precious as we feel it slip away. The cross which we bore easily in our youth now stoops our shoulders and tears our skin. The "everything" which we were anxious to pay for discipleship in our 20's is somehow MORE everything. Who can really calculate the cost of discipleship through the years?

I wonder if Philemon foresaw the price he would have to pay. How could he have guessed what his conversion would cost? Did he dream it would entail challenging the economic structure? Did he figure in the cost of friends who would not agree with his moral decision? Did he expect to be asked to befriend his own slave?

There is a popular song about loss which says, "I can count the tears but I can't count the cost." We can recall the times of pain which our discipleship has demanded. We can perhaps count relationships which had to be ended as we followed the Lord, and possessions which had to be sacrificed. But who can total the value of the isolation caused by an unpopular moral stand? Who can put a dollar amount on the farewells to family or calculate the cost of dreams abandoned in favor of ministering to reality?

How can we be certain that we have enough to not only lay the foundation of our discipleship, but to complete the work? Perhaps we can't. Perhaps we shall be judged as Jesus was when he died. Perhaps those who do not understand will say of us as they did of Jesus, "That person began to build what he could not finish!"

Only God will know that we have indeed finished, and we have built—yes, at great personal cost—our part of his eternal kingdom.

Jesus' message to us today is not to plan ahead—but to trust him. In his wisdom he says, "Let's build! I know exactly how much—together—we can afford."

Carole M. Eipers

24th Sunday in Ordinary Time

Cycle C

Ex 32:7–11, 13–14
1 Tm 1:2–17
Lk 15:1–32

Today's gospel reading brings us three of Jesus' most moving stories of God's forgiveness. Paul chooses the same theme in his letter to Timothy. He says he himself has experienced God's mercy; no one should doubt that Jesus came into the world to save sinners. The first reading's story of the golden calf in the wilderness also ends on this note of a forgiving God. These readings invite us to ponder the meaning of sin and forgiveness in our lives. Can we believe in the amazing mercy God offers us? Can we forgive ourselves? Are we able to forgive others, to rejoice when they experience God's love and mercy?

The gospel message on forgiveness will make a difference in our lives only if we recognize ourselves in the characters of Jesus' parables. Jesus' stories are not about other people whom we can sit back and observe at a safe distance. His stories are always about us. They challenge us to particpate in the parable itself.

I am the prodigal son. I frequently turn my back on love and run after other gods. I search for happiness in security, pleasure, power, and popularity, only to find myself empty and wasted when they fail to deliver their false promises. I squander and waste my gifts. I feel afraid, lost, and dead inside as I face my sins and weaknesses. I find it hard to forgive myself my failures and limitations, my wrong judgments and actions. Like the prodigal son I am imperfect and in process, growing by trial and error.

And like the prodigal son I struggle to believe in a love that embraces my far-from-perfect self; a mercy that welcomes me back with no questions asked, offering me gifts beyond any I deserve or have earned; a love that creates life out of the death I so often produce.

As the prodigal son I am like the lost sheep of Jesus' other parable. A sheep cut off from the herd becomes disoriented, and is so paralyzed by fear that it cannot walk. Its only hope is the fidelity of the good shepherd who must seek it out if it is to be saved. As that lost sheep, I have also known isolation, fear, or depression, the need to be called out to by another in order to be saved. Jesus' message of forgiveness is then truly good news.

I am also the forgiving father in Jesus' parable. I am often asked to forgive others, and to welcome them back into my love. I must not meet these persons with a reminder of their faults and failures. I cannot withhold forgiveness, weighing the full measure of my hurt. If I am going to be the father in the parable, I must run to embrace them and offer a forgiveness that is full and free.

As the father in the parable I learn that God's forgiveness is the model and stimulus for my forgiveness of myself and others. Not only is it my model, but in forgiving others, I mediate God's forgiveness to them. They then know the difference between simply being told that God behaves like the father of the prodigal son, and actually experiencing such forgiveness in their lives.

Finally, I am the parable's elder brother. I find it difficult to be as merciful to others as God is. I may resent seeing a reformed alcoholic welcomed into the community, a divorced person treated with love and respect, a brother or sister forgiven by my parents, a former prisoner offered a job in my firm. It is easy for me to forget that I, too, am greatly in God's debt and in need of forgiveness. The Gospel asks me to recognize the link between my forgiveness of others and God's forgiveness of me. Jesus asks us to find joy in reconciliation and forgiveness, to rejoice, even as he does, more over the return of one sinner than over the ninety-nine just.

Kathleen R. Fischer
Thomas N. Hart

25th Sunday in Ordinary Time

Cycle C

Am 8:4–7
1 Tm 2:1–8
Lk 16:1–13

In Luke's Gospel today, Jesus challenges us to live creatively. He tells the story of a manager in trouble. The manager is in a bind which might bring about his complete demise. Using his imagination, the manager finds a workable solution. Someone who appeared to be powerless "took the initiative," found an inner source of power and used it. We are called to do the same. We are not victims of life's problems. Within us is a spirit which wants release—which propels us to live lovingly, and responsibly, and creatively. We have but to get in touch with that dimension—a frequent subject of articles the past three years.

There is an interesting statement by Jesus which seems to be "tacked on" at the end of this particular lectionary passage. "No servant can serve two masters." Why does this belong with a story of "being trustworthy with someone else's money"? It seems out of place. But it is just this combination which I will reflect on here.

Jesus tells us to live creatively. Be enterprising. Take the initiative. Rise up and use the many gifts you have been given. But wait! Before you demand we make you king, consider what a Christian does with power—he or she uses it to serve the Father and that means serving his people.

This insight seems simple, but how difficult it is to live! Here are a few examples.

I have worked long and hard to acquire skills as a video producer. I attribute much of that ability to my faith—when projects were on the brink of creative or financial disaster, the Christ within, who calms storms and fears, kept me going, helped me to "be enterprising." Now that I know so much, should I continue working in religious education and humanities education video? Offers to produce some mindless, need-creating ads for cable TV are much more lucrative. I have discovered my power. Now comes a decision between two masters—values and money.

There are people who go to counseling and find power within through therapy. And then, with little effort to revitalize their marriage, they leave with a new, powerful self-image.

Have you ever discovered the charming depths of your personality? People often find that dimension of themselves which makes them a good friend, a good conversationalist, funny, witty. Using those gifts can make the world a better place. Or one can use those characteristics to be manipulative and controlling.

Television mini-series are filled with stories of poor immigrants who are resourceful enough to rise up and create financial empires. Then comes a time of decision—do I help the poor and downtrodden from whence I came or do I oppress them to my own gain, just as the powerful attempted to do to me?

We can see the combination in today's Gospel reading of "Take the initiative; be enterprising; live creatively" and "No servant can serve two masters" applies very practically to the hopes, dreams and passions of real people.

One person who knew his inner power and used his gifts to the fullest was Pope John XXIII. Anthony Padovano recently wrote a one-actor play about him. It begins thus:

"One of my earliest memories—my father hoisted me on his shoulders to see a parade. It was one of my best memories of him.

"He must have cared more than I realized. Would a father hold his son on his shoulders if he did not care?

"Sometimes I feel that as Pope I would like to hold the world on my shoulders. But then that would make me too important.

"Perhaps, a child on my shoulders. Or someone too small and frightened in a world that bewilders us all.

"How many people in my life held me on their shoulders? But then I grew too heavy and they found it easier to put an arm on my shoulders."

No one can serve two masters. Let's spend some time today appreciating our gifts, our power which comes from grace within. Then use that power to put someone above you, on your shoulders, in order to look around and see more easily the world of the Master.

Douglas Fisher

26th Sunday in Ordinary Time

Cycle C

Am 6:1, 4–7
1 Tm 6:11–16
Lk 16:19–31

There is a story told of a poor but pious peasant who died and arrived before the gate of Heaven. At the same time a very rich nobleman came knocking at Heaven's Gate. St. Peter came with his key and opened the door to let the rich man in, but apparently did not see the peasant, and shut the door again. The peasant, left outside, heard how the rich man was received in Heaven with all kinds of rejoicing, and how they were making music and singing within. At last all became quiet again, and St. Peter heard the peasant knocking, so he came and let the peasant in.

Now the peasant fully expected that they would make music and sing when he went in also, but all remained perfectly quiet. He was received with great affection, it is true, and the angels came to greet him, but no one sang. So the peasant asked St. Peter how it was that they did not sing for him as they had done when the rich man went in, for he was sure that, at least in Heaven, there would be no partiality.

St. Peter replied. "You are right; you are just as dear to us as anyone else and will enjoy every Heavenly delight that the rich man enjoys. It's just that poor fellows like you come to Heaven every day, while a rich man like this does not come more than once in a hundred years."

This and similar stories illustrate one of the major themes of St. Luke's Gospel: "How hard it will be for the rich to go into the kingdom of God" (Lk 18:25). It is not that Jesus condemns wealth. What he condemns is the lack of compassion and blindness to the genuine needs of others that wealth often brings. This condemnation is in the prophetic tradition of men like Amos. Amos warned the rich of impending disaster "because the good life was reserved for a few wealthy at the expense of the poor and the oppressed. The sin of the privileged class was their disregard for the pain and suffering of the poor and the fact that they keep adding to the plight of the poor by further inflicting indignities upon them."

Yet few, if any of us, are "super-rich." How then does the warning of today's Scriptures apply to us? It applies because all of us are affected by money. No matter how much we have or how much we lack, money seems to worm itself into our attitudes about life, about ourselves, and about others. Although we are a New Testament people, we continue to cling to the belief that wealth and possessions are signs of God's special love. Are we so different from the "latter-day Pharisees" described in the following passage? "These latter day Pharisees seemed to claim that their possessions were a sign of God's favor. The poor were in God's disfavor. Therefore, the rich felt they had God's blessings and felt no compunction to share with the unfortunate."

Above all else, the Jesus of St. Luke's Gospel is *compassionate,* he is willing to *suffer with* those in need. The Scriptures today invite us to use what we have now to express our care for those in need. However little or much we may possess, each of us has the potential to be compassionate. We know what Jesus expects of us. We know in our hearts that he never makes demands of us without showing us the way to fulfill those demands. What we need to do is to "fight the good fight of faith," to stop isolating ourselves from the pain of life, to make our possessions not a barrier that shuts others out but a bridge that unites us.

Michael Kurz

27th Sunday in Ordinary Time

Cycle C

Hb 1:2–3; 2:2–4
2 Tm 1:6–8, 13–14
Lk 17:5–10

Today's readings set before us the seeming contradictions of faith in God, and hint at the delicate but powerful balance that is required of the believer. Faith is both a total gift, freely given to us by God, and a task for which we are fully responsible.

The prophet Habakkuk questions God and mourns over the violence and ruin which he sees. God answers with a vision which "presses on" and "will not disappoint" but which "might delay" though it "will not be late." Habakkuk believes in God though he can't understand God's action—or lack of it. God allows him to envision an answer, yet the vision itself demands faith for it is promise, not reality. Though the fulfillment of the vision may seem to "delay," in God's view "it will not be late." Belief leads to questioning, and the questioning brings an answer which only asks for greater faith.

We don't know what prompted Paul's letter to Timothy, but it too seems an answer for the questions to which faith gives rise. Paul puts the responsibility for the growth of faith squarely on the believer's shoulders. You, he tells Timothy, you "stir into the flame the gift of God!" To paraphrase a popular saying, "Faith is God's gift to us, what we do with that faith is our gift to God." Or, rather, as Jesus points out in today's Gospel, what we do with that gift of faith is our debt to God.

"Increase our faith!" the apostles pleaded, or perhaps demanded, and Jesus responds, "Do it yourself!" Faith is not, he implies, like riches to be stockpiled, but rather, faith is a skill to be practiced and so perfected.

The example Jesus uses for the power of faith seems bizarre. "You could say to this sycamore 'Be uprooted and transplanted into the sea' and it would obey you." I always wondered, of all the marvelous deeds faith might accomplish, why would anyone send a tree into the sea? Yesterday I heard a naturalist on the radio who advised that discarded Christmas trees should be sunk in a lake or pond. Such sunken trees, he explained, provide lodging and refuge for small marine life, as well as a potential food source. Jesus' example, as outrageous as it sounds, makes sense. I finally came to understand a purpose for what seemed unreasonable. So, too, the decisions based on faith may appear inexplicable at the outset, and only later do we begin to fathom why the decision was for the best.

Unquestionably, faith is a gift. How often good people have studied and prayed and struggled, only to find that they could not believe. Faith is unearned and often eludes those whom we would deem most deserving. For those who have been gifted with faith, it is also unquestionably a task, something to be used, worked on, "stirred up" as Paul reminds us.

What does "I have lost my faith" mean? It could, indeed, mean that one's faith has been "misplaced"— put in money or power rather than in God. Could it mean that the flame of faith which Paul images has died out? How does one "stir into flame" a fire? One can rekindle the flame by fanning the dying embers, by adding new fuel to the fire, or by rearranging the materials. I've seen the dying ember of faith fanned into flame by processes such as RENEW and Christ Renews His Parish. I've seen new flames of faith burst forth from the materials provided by a retreat experience or a course in Scripture. How does one "lose faith"? Perhaps by not taking advantage of opportunities to "stir the flames." It might be more correct to say, "My faith has died." The natural response would be, "How sad! Was it sick for very long?"

You, yes you, "stir into flame the gift of God." It cannot be blown out by others, but left untended, it can, like any fire, die.

Hopefully the community helps its members to tend the fires of faith. Hopefully local parishes provide opportunities for fanning the flames of faith and offer experiences of liturgy and prayer and camaraderie which spark relationships and ignite the fuel of parishioners' lives so that their villages and marketplaces glow with faith-fire. Hopefully there is ample room in our communities for those whose faith is kindled by meditating on the rosary and those whose faith is enflamed by marching for social justice. And, hopefully, there is love and acceptance in our communities which allow the many expressions of people's faith to add new materials for each one's own faith-flames.

As the chill of fall fills the air, it's a good time to stoke the fires of faith, to "stir up the flame," to be on the lookout for chances to fan the flames and to add new fuel. Then we can welcome those whose faith has grown cold to come and warm themselves by our hearth. And you know how fire spreads!

Carole M. Eipers

28th Sunday in Ordinary Time

Cycle C

2 Kgs 5:14–17
2 Tm 2:8–13
Lk 17:11–19

Today's readings are concerned with proclaiming the message of God's salvation. In the first reading, Naaman, a foreigner, is healed by the Israelite prophet, Elisha, and then proclaims that the God of Israel alone is the one true God. The author of the second letter to Timothy says that despite his suffering for the sake of the Gospel, he will continue to preach so that all might be saved. And in the Gospel, we see one of the ten healed lepers, a Samaritan, return to thank Jesus and to praise God for his cure.

Two things stand out: first, the witness to faith in God is made by a foreigner, not by one to whom the message of salvation was first given; and second, proclamation of the Gospel involves suffering. Two questions immediately come to mind: What is this Gospel, and why should it cause some to risk even suffering in order to proclaim it?

The author of 2 Timothy puts it simply: "Remember that Jesus Christ . . . was raised from the dead." This is surely a hopeful message. Why then should it give such offense as to cause suffering to those who proclaim it? That someone should be raised from the dead, and furthermore that we too are to share in the resurrection, seems to be a cause for joy, not persecution. There must be something more to it all, and indeed there is.

What is more to the message of Christian salvation is not just that we must die in order to live, but that we must live at all. Despite claims to the contrary, we live in a world that has not, historically, valued life over death. It is a world that has fought wars for the sake of property or wealth rather than respected the rights of other peoples to be free or different. The Church has not been much better, as the Crusades and Inquisition have demonstrated. Nor have things changed much.

It is much easier to build up one's defenses and to harass one's enemies than it is to admit "I have failed as much as you; maybe we should stop fighting and start talking and understanding one another." It is easier to condemn sanctuary workers and the aliens they shelter than it is to understand the motives behind the movement and the sufferings of many Latin American people. It is easier to abort a fetus than to jeopardize one's career or reputation. It is easier to make a child conform to an adult's will than to understand the child's point of view, and to admit that maybe I, the adult, have been wrong.

To be for life, to be for the Gospel, is to be willing to forego oneself and to be for others; it is to give up one's ideologies and to look for the truth. To do both these things one must look at and value the other person, listen to and value the other point of view. To be for life is to be willing to change because truth is more than any one person can possess. Life calls us beyond ourselves, and it's not easy to get beyond ourselves. We are selfish and protective by nature.

There are times when we do see a need for change in ourselves and know we cannot make that change on our own. Today's Gospel story is a perfect example of this. Ten lepers, upon seeing Jesus, beg for his mercy upon them. Jesus immediately heals them all. Only one, however, thinks any further about God. The rest disappear from view, never to be heard from again. Only to this one, grateful man is salvation assured, for he alone of the ten had the faith to know that his cure came from God. He alone was thankful enough to praise God for the miraculous healing. How often do we forget the people who have helped us get where we are, as if everything we have accomplished has been solely our own doing? How often do we forget the God who has given us everything in the first place?

If we are to live fully, we must remember and believe that our life and all its accomplishments are God's gift to us. And if we are to witness to this faith we must share the gift with others by helping them reach the fullness of life. And, as the Jews at the time of Jesus had to learn that salvation is meant for everyone, not just them (the meaning behind the Samaritan's being the only one saved), we each have to realize that salvation lies not only in "my" way of doing things, but possibly in the ways of others that are very different from our own.

If this should cause us to suffer or experience resentment from others, so be it. Today's reading from 2 Timothy assures that if we hold out to the end, we will reign with God.

Helene A. Lutz

29th Sunday in Ordinary Time

Cycle C

Ex 17:8–13
2 Tm 3:14—4:2
Lk 18:1–8

One possible approach to preaching on today's Gospel is to take the persistence of the widow as a starting point for looking at endurance in living the Christian life. Jesus appears to admire the widow. He likes people to be persistent.

Let's reflect on this parable for our lives today. Are we persistent in our growth as Christians? Conversion is a lifetime journey. Ideally, we strive to become more and more Christ-like, more and more human. But are you ever tempted to stop where you are? Do you ever feel like saying "Enough. I am who I am—either accept me or reject me but I'm not changing (growing) anymore. I have done enough 'personal development.' Now it's time for everyone else to adjust to me."

The temptation to "freeze" my development as a person can occur personally, interpersonally, and socially. Let's examine each in turn through story.

A wise, old Middle-Eastern mystic said this about himself. "I was a revolutionary when I was young and all my prayer to God was: 'Lord, give me the energy to change the world.' As I approached middle age and realized that my life was half-gone without my changing a single soul, I changed my prayer to: 'Lord, give me the grace to change all those who come into contact with me. Just my family and friends and I shall be satisfied.' Now that I am an old man and my days are numbered, I have begun to see how foolish I have been. My one prayer now is: 'Lord, give me the grace to change myself.' If I had prayed for this right from the start, I should not have wasted my life" (*Stories for Preachers & Teachers,* by Paul Wharton, Paulist Press, 1986).

How easy it is to let down in personal development! "When the Son of Man comes, will he find any faith in me?" Or, will he find me set in stone, satisfied with myself and therefore having no need of faith?

Now go to the interpersonal level. Married couples could provide many examples of conflicts where one of the inner voices says "I will give in here,

I see her point there and will compromise but no more! I won't take another step further in her direction until she gives something." Every conflict needs to be reflected on differently, but how many times do I "shut down" in my relationships? How many times do I fail to be persistent in loving? A story to tell here could be "Fiddler on the Roof." Remember how Tevye watches each of his daughters marry men who do not meet his expectations, men who conflict with the "tradition"? Each time Tevya struggles within himself over giving his blessing or not. Each time he chooses to bless his children's weddings. When the youngest comes to him and announces her engagement to a Russian Christian, Tevye goes through the struggle between his fatherly love and tradition. But this time he says, "No! No more bending. If I bend any more I will break." He does not bless the marriage.

"When the Son of Man comes, will he find any faith in me?" Or will he find me unyielding to others, locked into my own needs, lacking faith in the good will of others, lacking the ability to let others grow at their own pace?

Now take this parable to the social, community level. Am I persistent, am I consistent in my political activity? Do I choose to support the poor, the oppressed, the marginal when it is convenient to me, but not at other times? The teaching of Cardinal Bernardin on "the seamless garment" approach is a challenge to be consistent with the teaching of the Gospel. Am I persistent in choosing the side of life on all issues, or do I pick and choose? Do I support nuclear disarmament but express no outrage at the killing of the unborn? Do I commit myself to the rights of the unborn but want our nation to have the capacity to destroy the world many times over?

An example which might apply here is to ask people to reflect on their own political convictions. Do you, consistent with Gospel values, desire all sorts of government programs to help the poor, the disabled, the elderly? If the answer is "yes," then ask yourself the question: "Am I willing to pay more taxes for this purpose? If that answer is no, then we fall short of the persistence of the widow Jesus praised.

Where is it that I "let down"? Where am I not persistent in my desire to grow as a Christian? Wherever, whatever that area of life is, that is the time and place for faith. "When the Son of Man comes, will he find any faith in me?"

Douglas Fisher

30th Sunday in Ordinary Time

Cycle C

Sir 35:12–14, 16–18
2 Tm 4:6–8, 16–18
Lk 18:9–14

"The Lord hears the cries of the poor" . . . "the orphan" . . . "the widow"; God is "close to the brokenhearted" . . . the "crushed in spirit." Today's readings are certainly good news for those of us whose luck has run out, who feel oppressed or overwhelmed. Some of us may indeed be in circumstances similar to those described today. Or perhaps we have been there in the past. If so, our readings may lift our spirits sufficiently to keep us going until things get better.

But what about those of us whose lives seem rather ordinary—who have moments of discouragement but who are certainly not "crushed?" Or what about those of us for whom things are going rather well? Are we doomed to identify with the self-righteous Pharisee, or must we force ourselves into a mold of humble submission that we suspect does not "fit" us? Does God "hear" our prayers, too?

Today's readings raise some interesting questions, not the least of which is whether or how God actually "hears" prayers at all. Such language conjures up images of "cosmic ears" strained under the weight of listening to every whisper or plaintive cry raised by humans everywhere. And, having heard, we imagine a God "thinking about" and "deciding whether to respond to" each and every request and need, spoken or unspoken.

These and related questions have been raised repeatedly and are too complex to answer, if indeed they can be answered at all. What we do know is what we don't know, and that is sometimes considerable. But we have been given some clues to lead us out of the maze. We do know—partly from today's readings—and partly from other words that we have heard that 1) we are called to rely on God, 2) we are loved and cared for, and 3) God generally provides for our needs through one another.

The question then shifts, it seems, from the openness of "God's ears" to the openness of *our* hearts and *our* ears. Like the Pharisee, we can be so filled with ourselves that we have little room for either God's word to us or the words of one another. Those who are focused totally inward may have difficulty looking beyond themselves. Dwelling consistently on the good works that we think we accomplish may direct us away from all that yet needs to be done through us. The sounds of our own voices may drown out the cries of others. Who can hear the feeble voices of the weak or the hurting in a cacophony of self-generated noises?

Needs are not met by magic, but by concerned people who can identify those needs and decide how to act upon them. The poor and oppressed will be served by those moved to compassion and action. The open ears and hearts of the just can be "filled" by God with the desire for and knowledge of how to perform that kind of service. Prayers can indeed be "answered."

Paul himself provides an example of this bountiful self-giving. An openness to God's word and the needs of others is bought at the price of pouring out everything one has. It may also mean abandonment by those who judge such generosity as foolish. But we gather from what we read in Timothy that what is "poured out" is filled again by God's own presence and strength. This kind of space, however, does not exist in the self-righteous Pharisee, who is already filled with self.

And so we are called this day to present ourselves in prayer and openness, to be filled to overflowing. In the abundance that is given us, we may be used by God to fill up one anothers' needs. In that process we are all redeemed.

Joan R. DeMerchant

31st Sunday in Ordinary Time

Cycle C

Wis 11:22–12:1
2 Thes 1:11–2:2
Lk 19:1–10

God's job is larger than any multi-national corporation head's: He has the whole cosmos to manage! The immensity of this care is hard to comprehend. He loves his creation. He is its source.

Do you love the things you have created? Relationships? Jobs? Hobbies? Skills? Profession? Artwork? Savings account? Household? Family? Do you feel tired sometimes keeping it all going? Have you even gotten angry because of fatigue, disappointment, imperfection, disillusionment in any of these things? Did you ever have to curb the "urge to kill/destroy" something you actually love? Did you ever threaten to pull out, give up, go on strike? Did your love and self-control win out over the anger?

Does the Lord ever get angry at *his* creation? Does he ever feel like giving up on the whole thing? We know the answer to this. In the words of the psalmist: "The Lord is gracious and merciful, slow to anger and of great kindness . . . good to all and compassionate to all his works."

The perception that God is "good" and cares for his "creation," not abandoning it, but perceiving it as "good" is first given to us in the Book of Genesis. No other primitive peoples perceived their gods as so loving and so committed to creation. The God of Abraham, of Isaac, and of Jacob was not capricious. He continually chose to love creation. He remains related to his creation, and chooses to sustain and redeem it over and over.

Genesis proclaims God as good, and creation too. The psalms reaffirm this truth. St. Paul later said "all creation groans as it awaits . . . " But it is a "groaning" with hope and destiny. God is in charge of the cosmos. Jesus' resurrection proves he is Lord of suffering, death, and life.

God chooses to check his anger. He chooses to love. His compassion outweighs his anger. Remember the Sons of Zebedee asking Jesus to call down destruction on Jerusalem for its disbelief? Jesus refuses. He had compassion. Jonah fretted when the Ninevites were not punished, but God's mercy was accepted and healed them. God's compassion contains his anger.

God knows our battles. He formed and created us. He is with us in them (Psalm 139). Paul also knew victory in the battle: good will overcome evil, ultimately. It comes step by step, choice by choice, decision by decision.

In Thessalonians, Paul calls us to keep working out our salvation. It is not once and for all, but a daily struggle and effort. God is with us. Rumors of the world's end will come. Do not let them unsettle or distract you from the fact of daily struggle. Keep walking firmly and strongly.

Zacchaeus's encounter with Jesus led him to let go of fear of condemnation, and move to repentance in Jesus. He came to know mercy and redemption in Jesus. His world perception changed. He felt no judgment, but hope and mercy. He moved from being lost to being found.

This is the business the Lord of the cosmos is all about! Ultimately, victory is his. Let us all enter into this reality and be empowered by it.

Jeffrey Archambeault

32nd Sunday in Ordinary Time

Cycle C

2 Mc 7:1–2, 9–14
2 Thes 2:16—3:5
Lk 20:27–38

One day God asked the first human couple who then lived in heaven what kind of death they wanted, that of the moon or that of the banana. Because the couple wondered in dismay about the implications of the two modes of death, God explained to them: the banana puts forth shoots which take its place and the moon itself comes back to life. The couple considered for a long time before they made their choice. If they elected to be childless they would avoid death, but they would also be very lonely, would themselves be forced to carry out all the work, and would not have anybody to work and strive for. Therefore they prayed to God for children, well aware of the consequences of their choice. And their prayer was granted. Since that time man's sojourn is short on this earth.

This African tale conveys the belief of many of the Old Testament writings that the way a man survived death was through his children. It was this belief that led to the "levirate law of Deuteronomy 25," whose purpose, as the exegetical section above notes, was "to ensure the continuity of a deceased brother's line by having his surviving brother produce children in his name." This tale also seems to indicate that man, in choosing children, gave up the possibility of personal survival after death.

By contrast, the scripture readings from 2 Maccabees and Luke speak of personal survival after death. As the exegetical section points out: "What is notable in these expressions of faith by the soon-to-be martyrs (and what links this passage with today's gospel reading) is their assertion of confidence in their personal resurrection from death by God's power."

What is our attitude toward death? Although we look on ourselves as "believers," many of us share the different attitudes toward death that are held by non-believers. Some of us are "fatalists"; we speak of an hour "when our time has come," or a "ticket" that has our name written on it. Others of us are "stoics": we think we are called to face death with self-discipline and good manners, because death is a natural part of life. We have been invited to the banquet and now it is time to leave. The proper guest does so quietly and gracefully.

If these are "Christian" ways to meet death, then how do we account for this description of Jesus in Hebrews 5:7: "He offered prayers and supplications with loud cries and tears to God, who was able to save him from death"? In Gethsemane, confronted with the end—the apparent end of all his efforts and the looming horror of the cross—Jesus begs for the cup to pass. Jesus saw death as "the great enemy," not as "a welcome friend."

It is this same Jesus we speak of, however, in these words of the Second Eucharistic Prayer: "Before he was given up to death, a death he *freely* accepted." What enabled him to pass from the dread of the Garden to the "free acceptance" of Calvary? His trust that "the Lord . . . keeps faith." The God that Jesus proclaimed by his words and actions was not a "puppet-master that cuts our strings when he is tired of playing with us." He is a loving Father who respects our freedom, and yet he has "the very hairs on our head counted." "Our very names," as the prophet Isaiah says, "are written on the palms of his hands." He is the kind of God, therefore, who will not allow even death to separate him from his friends. For "God is not the God of the dead but of the living. All are alive for him" (Lk 20:38).

Michael Kurz

33rd Sunday in Ordinary Time

Cycle C

Mal 3:19–20
2 Thes 3:7–12
Lk 21:5–19

Destroying fire, surging waters, shouting mountains, omens and signs in the skies, wars and insurrections—images of frightening devastation and surrealistic splendor assault our ears in today's readings. The only thing that may dull the images for us is our over-exposure to the inter-galactic wars of science fiction movies and novels and the obscene fantasies of nuclear conflicts played out among the stars. Special-effects technicians, scientists and statesmen have snatched the amazing and bizarre from our imaginations and thrust them before our very eyes. Our reactions to such images can range from paralyzing fear to a bored "ho-hum." To protect our psyches and allow us to continue living, our more usual response is, "What does this really have to do with me?"

In a sense, we opt to live as the Thessalonians in Paul's letter, though we may be a bit less reflective about it and our reasons might be somewhat different. Not sure about what lies ahead and feeling powerless about how to affect it, we live in the "wide crack between the present and the future" by doing nothing. The Thessalonians were considerably more crass about it; they refused to lift a finger and chose to wait it out, relying for their sustenance on others. The images of the future deluded them into doing nothing but waiting in the present. Even the drudgery of daily work was ignored in the anticipation of an imminent end to things as they were. Misreading the images robbed the Thessalonians of an accurate sense of what they needed to be about.

Our images of the future, on the other hand, tend to create a sense of powerlessness that buries us in the business of daily life. We go on doing the little things that have to be done because we doubt that we have any control over what ultimately matters. That, we believe, is in the hands of others "bigger" than ourselves. We may doubt the hands of the earthly decision-makers to do well with the future; we hope that things may fare better in "God's hands." And so

the images are debilitating for us, too. Like the Thessalonians we will wait it out.

Both Paul and Jesus have some words about living in the present moment. Paul addresses the inactive and Jesus the persecuted. Paul makes it clear that there is little time to sit idle. Citing himself as an example, he urges working "day and night . . . to the point of exhaustion." Jesus offers words of encouragement in the midst of persecution: Things will not be easy, but perseverance will be rewarded. To all of this, we might answer that indeed we know about working non-stop, and, thank you, we appreciate the encouragement but we are not living in persecution.

However, we know something that forestalls such easy dismissal of these words. Unlike the Thessalonians, we know that the "day of the Lord" is not yet here in its fullness. We know that the Lord's coming to rule the earth in justice and equity will not occur by some magic outside ourselves, but will somehow involve our untiring effort. And we know, too, that there will be persecution. Those who work to bring about justice and equity can well expect to be besieged by parents and siblings, friends and relatives.

What, then motivates us to lay aside our apathy and fears and take up the task of strengthening God's reign of justice in our own historical moment? What can move us beyond our daily preoccupations to take on a task that is risky at best and possibly life-threatening? The impulse, I think comes from the vision of the future—that same vision that has stimulated hope and energy for generations and that echoes in some of today's readings. The same vision that inspires fear, disbelief and paralysis in some stirs others to heroic action. Those who hope, dream and believe allow their imaginations to be stirred by images of seas that sing, rivers that clap their hands and mountains that shout for joy in praise of the Lord. Those who live in hope trust that the same fire that destroys can also give life. They are moved by the dream of the healing fire of the sun of justice.

The great anthropologist/philosopher/theologian Teilhard de Chardin spoke of God as the Fire which has penetrated the earth and empowered all reality to move forward, transfiguring, remolding, recasting everything into newness. The image empowered him to think and act creatively and boldly. Such images can empower us too. We can dismiss them as meaningless, discount them as figments of artists' imaginations or embrace them as glimpses of what can be. And contemplating such visions, we can move to make them happen.

Joan R. DeMerchant

151

Feast of Christ the King

Cycle C

2 Sm 5:1–3
Col 1:12–20
Lk 23:35–43

The letter of Paul to Colossae is a high point in the expression of early Christian faith. It matches the second chapter of Paul's letter to the Philippians and the first chapter of John's Gospel. We are used to having its meaning expressed in our creed when we call Jesus "the only begotten Son of God, God from God, true God from true God." But in hearing all that wonderful language of our devotion to Jesus we should not forget the mystery behind it: How could the crucified criminal have been Lord and Christ? We must experience this mystery, this most peculiar fact of human history, in something of the fashion in which the first Christians did.

Note how Paul puts the mystery: We already share the light, we are already numbered among the holy ones, we are already in the Kingdom of God. But remember two things. Remember where we had been or would have been, and remember who brought us to the light. We were in darkness; we felt its dominion. We did not know the ways of God; we did not do the works of God; we did not know God at all. How is it that we have come to the light, to the knowledge of God and God's ways?

In a series of metaphors and poetic images, Paul tells us just who is responsible for our safety, our clarity on life's important issues, our confidence in a final resolution of life's difficulties. Jesus has brought us out. He has been able to show us God to whom we once were blind. He does it because he is the image of God, the first born of God, the residence of God in the world, the bridge between us and God. And, as Paul goes on to explain, though once we were far away from God, we are now brought close to God, for "Christ has achieved reconciliation for you in his mortal body by dying . . . "

Is it not a curious thing that we read the story of the crucifixion on the feast of Christ the King? After all, if there was a low tide in the kingship of Christ, it was when he died, his life and work mocked, his hope crushed. Surely at that moment he was least a king. "If you are a king save yourself!" they said. But of course he wasn't a king in the only fashion in which they could understand the term, a king by exercise of power.

David was king in the sense in which the soldiers and the people understood the term. If we look beneath the carefully edited picture of David that the book of Samuel gives us, we find a revolutionary, a bandit, a man of the sword, a hardnosed ruler, and a sometimes lustful, proud, and deceitful man. He was, in other words, a "good king" in the world's terms, for he led his people to their few moments of glory on the mobile stage of Near Eastern history.

Is Jesus a king in this fashion? Hardly. By dying he displays the kind of king he is—one who suffers in trust of God and punishes no one—no sword in his hand, no lie on his lips, no spark of lust in his heart. And does he have a kingdom? In Paul's view, yes! It is a kingdom established by showing people what God is like, by exposing the fragility of our every human achievement and the permanence of the love of God by contrast, by building bridges between us and our lost innocence in God's embrace. Jesus' "Kingdom"—and we must use quotation marks around the term lest we be tempted in any way to take the term literally—is the hearts of men and women who know from whom they have come, to whom they go, and how to carry on in between.

If you would like to share in the Kingdom, do as the king does. Live in peace, die in trust, and cut through all the trappings of worldly power and desire to the serious questions of life and its values, and do it on a daily basis. STOP PROTECTING YOURSELF, TAKE A RISK, LOVE AN ENEMY.

Helene A. Lutz

1st Sunday of Lent

Cycle C

Dt 26:4–10
Rom 10:8–13
Lk 4:1–13

One day, so the account goes, Jesus and his disciples were walking along a stony road. Jesus asked each of them to choose a stone to carry for him. John, it is said, chose a large one while Peter chose the smallest. Jesus led them then to the top of a mountain and commanded that the stones be made bread. Each disciple, by this time tired and hungry, was allowed to eat the bread he held in his hands. Peter's of course, was not sufficient to satisfy his hunger. John gave him some of his.

Some time later Jesus again asked the disciples to pick up a stone to carry. This time Peter chose the largest of all. Taking them to a river, Jesus told them to cast the stones into the water. They did so, but looked at one another in bewilderment.

"For whom," asked Jesus, "did you carry the stone?"

"For whom did you carry the stone?" In the desert experience of Lent, we once more have to answer this most basic of questions: "Whom do our actions serve: God or ourselves?" *In whom* do we place our ultimate faith? Three times Jesus was tempted to make himself the equal of God. Three times he rejected the temptation and chose God's pattern of sonship, God's will for him. And what of us? These are the same three temptations that face each of us in one form or another.

In the first temptation Jesus was urged to exercise his leadership ability to work at bettering the living conditions of the poor and hungry. This is not evil, and therein lies the power of this temptation. For, whenever we are urged to choose a lesser rather than a greater good, we are ultimately choosing ourselves rather than God. By his response to this temptation—"Not on bread alone shall man live," we see that Jesus was tempted to limit his attention to the material needs of life. This same temptation faces us in countless ways through subtle pressures from multi-media advertising. How easily we are led to believe that "more is always better," and that luxuries are really "necessities." "God" or "ourselves"—which are we choosing?

In the second temptation Jesus was offered the lure of power. "Power" is also an apparent good. If we have the power and resources we can accomplish much more, or so we are led to believe. "If you used your unparalleled personal power to stir up the fighting spirit of Israel and all the other oppressed peoples of the Roman Empire, you could be emperor. Think of what you could accomplish for God as ruler of the world!" Jesus refused the bait. He was not willing to pay the price of holding that God does not intend us to be too scrupulous about how we get what we want so long as we can claim that we have a good purpose in the getting. "God" or "ourselves"—which are we choosing?

The final temptation is the hardest to recognize since, in giving in to it, we seem to be choosing "God" rather than "ourselves." The tempter implies that Jesus can do anything he wants, for God will surely care for his own son. Isn't that precisely the way we reason? We create impossible situations, we deprive others of the basics of life by rampant consumerism, we tolerate an escalating nuclear arms build-up, we condone all sorts of violence. Then when we see the suffering that results and begin to feel its impact in our own lives, we begin to pray for peace and for the unfortunate, counting on "Divine Providence" to set everything straight.

"You shall not put the Lord your God to the test."

Jesus refused to lay down conditions for God. He chose God by choosing to accept personal responsibility for whatever the Father planned for him. It was a choice he had to make again and again. For St. Luke reminds us that these temptations are ones that reappear in our lives. They leave us "to await another opportunity."

"God" or "ourselves"—which are we continuing to choose?

Michael Kurz

2nd Sunday of Lent

Cycle C

Gn 15:5–12, 17–18
Phil 3:17—4:1
Lk 9:28–36

For several years I have carried a small crucifix that once belonged to my godfather and uncle. It was part of a rosary—long since disappeared—and is heavily worn. The figure of Christ is nearly smooth, and part of one arm is missing. The crucifix for me is a relic of the faith of a simple man who died in his eighties. I frequently look at it, imagining the years of faithful prayer that honed it to its present condition and I wonder: what enabled Uncle Martin to "hang in over the long haul"?

Today's readings are about that very question, about "keeping the faith." Given the ups and downs of life and the ordinary struggles that consume human energy, how do any of us manage to live in faith? What nurtures our faith and moves it forward? How is it that others can look at our lives years after we are gone and find signs that, despite everything, we lived faithfully?

These readings touch upon several elements that seem to me at the heart of it all. Living in faith, I believe, is related to our memories and our dreams and visions. As we see in the readings and indeed in our lives and the lives of those who have preceded us, memories of the past empower our visions of what can be and enable us to continue in faith. Our faith-keeping in the present is rooted in the past and pointed toward the future.

We have here remembered stories of promise, pieces of our people's memories telling us that others have heard the "voice of God" in assurance of what is to come. There is the pledge of posterity to those whose only future was perceived in lineage, of land to those who were migrants, of bodily transformation to those awaiting death, of ultimate glorification to one who faced Jerusalem and the cross. These stories of promises which empowered others become empowerment for us, too. In the remembering of their dreams, our dreams take shape.

"Keeping faith" is probably easier because it is not a solitary thing. The stories and visions are gathered from our people, whether our ancient patriarchal ancestors, the early disciples, our Philippian brothers and sisters, or our aunts and uncles. And there is strength to be gained from the others, from their waiting and hoping and dreaming.

In an era focused on hard data and sensory phenomena, we may forget the power of knowing that generations ago Abram, too—or someone like him—struggled to hang on, on the strength of what he believed and hoped God would do for him.

Out of these memories, then, we search for signs of God's continuing love and action in the present. The Law—Torah—and the prophets were at the heart of Israel's faith, revealing God's very being to people, proclaiming what God wants for humanity, lovingly calling the people back when they had strayed. Voices, spoken and written, kept proclaiming the reality, telling the story, recounting the concrete expressions of love, pointing out how one was to follow.

We still hear these voices, spoken in the retelling of the ancient stories and the proclamation of the Law. Prophetic voices old and new continue to warn and cajole us. And of course the voices are summed up and spoken most clearly in the flesh and blood of Jesus, who stands as the ultimate promise of what awaits us.

But always there is the searching within our lives for echoes of the promises. We ask: Where have we heard God's voice? What are the life events which are clues that the promises are indeed being kept? When have we sensed the call to "Look up . . . and count the stars"? When have we heard the voice saying, "Listen . . . "? How do we let others know that we have had these, our own "visions," so that their faith can grow?

Somehow, our voices must be added to all the others, so that the memories can be kept alive. Somehow, my Uncle Martin must have heard the stories and had his own dreams. And he must have been urged by whatever he heard to "wait for the Lord." I can't be sure of what it was that enabled him to stay faithful, but I do have the old crucifix. I am grateful for simple signs.

Joan R. DeMerchant

3rd Sunday of Lent

Cycle C

Ex 3:1–8, 13–15
1 Cor 10:1–6, 10–12
Lk 13:1–9

God really knew how to get the people's attention during the time of Moses. Today's first reading is a wonderful example. The shepherd Moses spots a burning bush which is not consumed. Naturally, he is curious, and in approaching the bush to investigate, Moses gets more than he probably bargained for. The God of the Israelites was a showman: sending plagues, parting the Red Sea, feeding the folks with manna and quail. "I am" stood in sharp contrast to the other deities which abounded. God knew he had to get people's attention in order for his unique message to be understood.

Jesus knew how to get people's attention too. Certainly his miracles drew those who were curious. If they stuck around long enough, they learned his message and it changed their lives. But, beyond his miracles, Jesus, like his Father before him, stood in sharp contrast to the religious institutions of his day. In today's Gospel, Jesus again overturns a popular belief: that God punishes sinners and that we can determine people's guilt by their suffering. His stories, like today's parable of the unproductive fig tree, captured people's attention as well. His listeners perhaps became accustomed to Jesus' way of teaching, but there was always the element of the unexpected ending to keep them listening.

Paul must have been a real attention getter. The fact that he was able to begin Christian communities in so many different places and in spite of persecution is testimony to his charism and oratorical skills. The potency of Paul's written word was enough to sustain the communities when he had gone. His letters still capture our attention, convert people, sustain communities and challenge us, as today's second reading does, to "watch lest we fall."

Yahweh, Jesus, Paul: they knew that you've got to get the people's attention before they will listen. And they've got to be listening in order to ever understand the message and act on it and live by it. Yahweh recognized his competition: the multitude of other gods, the fertility cults, the superstitions. He had to speak more loudly than they did if the people were to listen. Jesus recognized the competition in his day: a firmly entrenched religion. The customs and beliefs were so much a part of people's lives that to challenge them was considered a personal attack, as well as an attack on God himself. Jesus had to speak more powerfully than the allure of the known, the established, the comfortable religion. He got the attention of both the sinners who longed to hear what he preached, and the self-righteous whom he outraged.

The obstacles Paul faced were powerful adversaries as well. To believe what Paul said meant not only a change of heart, but a willingness to undergo rejection and persecution. It was so much easier for them not to listen at all! Once Paul had moved on, it would have been easy to leave his letters unopened, unread, unheard.

The Good News cannot take root in the hearts of today's world unless people listen—but how can we get their attention so they will really hear?

We face the same obstacle which Yahweh faced: the voices of other gods vie for people's attention, and for their lives. Gods of power, of success, of wealth lure our would-be listeners away. The whispers of alcohol, of cheap sex, of selfishness tempt their listeners to settle for instant gratification rather than listen to the words of eternal life.

We encounter the competition Jesus met when the Gospel challenges established religions, beliefs, and institutions. Our contemporaries are as fearful of change as were the people of Jesus' time. When renewal challenges our traditions or reforms, rewrites our laws, we too can consider it a personal affront. When the message of peace seems to make us vulnerable to violence and the words of justice strike at our economic structures and threaten our comfortable way of life, we, too, are afraid.

We, like Paul's converts, can be tempted not to listen to a Gospel which asks us to forgive our enemies and treat all people equally. We can be tempted, too, to leave his letters unread instead of allowing his words to remind us of our failures and the need to strive for faithfulness.

How do we get people's attention so that they might hear the Good News? How, we might ask ourselves this Lent, might God get our attention so that we really hear what he asks?

Carole M. Eipers

4th Sunday of Lent

Cycle C

Jos 5:9–12
2 Cor 5:17–21
Lk 15:1–3, 11–32

The Prodigal Son story might be the most well-known of all the stories Jesus told about forgiveness. Forgiveness is certainly the main theme, even to the point where many commentators say it is misnamed, because the father is really the main character. While acknowledging the centrality of forgiveness, I would like to develop a secondary theme in this homily. I see three characters (the father and two sons) as expressing three different approaches to life.

The elder son sees life as contained, controlled and clear. The goal of life is to fulfill one's duty. He lives for his job. And he wants to please—desperately. He needs the approval of others. Yet, even though he needs the affection of others, he does not seem capable of being affectionate. He leads a life which lacks passion—at least on the surface. From his reaction to his father's decision to throw a party, it is evident he cares fervently about what happens to him, or at least to his standing in the family. Ask your congregation if they know people like this or if they ever feel this way themselves.

Perhaps the worst characteristic of the elder son is that he sees himself above it all. He would never make the mistakes of his brother. He would never get caught up in frivolity or greed or lust. He is not like the rest of men, and he despises them for being so common. The elder son has an elitist attitude toward life. He stands apart from greedy, lusty, irresponsible human beings. He is not a common man and he is no lover of common people.

The younger son takes a frantic, searching approach to life. Did you ever notice that the younger son is never happy where he is? When he is with his family he wants to roam. When he is on his own, he wants to come back. He is constantly restless. He wants whatever life is not his at the moment. A wonderful and very funny example of this is a movie which received little attention back in the spring of 1985 called "Lost in America." In this movie, a young couple become reasonably successful financially. But then they decide (when the husband does not get a promotion he was aiming for) to throw it all away and tour the country in a van, living like "Easy Rider." But they don't like that life either and the closing scene portrays them driving at 80 mph through city after city to get to New York where he has a job offer and they can go back to living a middle-class secure life. Something leads me to think they won't like that life either.

The life approach of the prodigal son is a common one. It is the theme of the restless heart and mind and body and soul. It is probably a necessary stage in life. But it is sad when that stage never ends.

The third approach is that of the father. This is a man who enjoys the present, unlike his younger son. He appreciates what he has. He has an irresponsible, immature son and he loves him. He has a stuck-up stodgy, selfish son and he loves him. He loves them, not because of what they do or don't do, but rather because he is a lover. Unlike his older son who lacks spontaneity and passion, the father has both in abundance. He drops all he is doing at the sight of his son and throws a party. He hugs and kisses his son. He loves music and dancing. We get the sense that the father is a man of this world; he loves life. At the same time he reflects on life—he sees life and death played out in the journey of his younger son.

The image the father invokes in me is that of the famous baseball player, Lou Gehrig. Gehrig was a tremendous athlete who was inflicted with a terrible, debilitating disease. While still in his baseball prime, Gehrig was forced to retire. The New York Yankees had a day in his honor and Gehrig stood at home plate to address his fans. This man, whom life dealt such a cruel blow, said "Today, I consider myself the luckiest man on the face of the earth."

The "Lou Gehrig" attitude is the approach to life of the father. Everything is a gift. In the words of the young priest who lies dying in *The Diary of a Country Priest*, "all is grace." The father walks in a world which he appreciates and loves with a passion. He celebrates being human, being alive. Which of the three characters do you most identify with? Which one would you like to be? Jesus will welcome you and celebrate with you no matter which one you are. The only question is: Do you want to go to the celebration?

Douglas Fisher

5th Sunday of Lent

Cycle C

Is 43:16–21
Phil 3:8–14
Jn 8:1–11

In today's first reading Isaiah says, "Remember not the events of the past." A strange admonition for a penitential season, and yet it is the theme of all three readings.

The reading from Isaiah goes on to say, "the things of long ago consider not. See, I am doing something new!" God asks us to let go of our preconceived notions of him. He asks us to let him be unpredictable, to resist forming him in our own image. God sounds almost like a child, "look at what I can do!" God, of course, can do anything, but he asks, almost pleads, for us to recognize his work in the world. Like a child, He asks us to have confidence in him, to give him the chance to do something new for us.

"Remember not the events of the past." Saint Paul certainly didn't. He could not have compared himself to a runner if he had been paralyzed with guilt over his previous persecution of the Christians. There is a "just guilt" which we feel when we sin. It is a feeling somewhere between the moroseness of prolonged guilt, and the premature, "O happy fault!" We regret what we have done, we make amends, and then we move on. Any runner who has lost confidence in himself because of past defeats isn't worth the price of his or her shoes. But a runner, or a sinner, who has learned from past mistakes, who has trained to strengthen weakness, can be a real winner. Paul realizes his shortcomings, and yet has confidence that he will attain the prize. His confidence is sure because it is based not on his own ability but on the faith that he has been "grasped by Christ." It is God who calls him to the finish line. We, like Paul, have to learn to forgive ourselves.

"Remember not the events of the past." The Gospel tells us about the woman caught in adultery; not the woman who had been an adultress, but a woman caught in the very act of adultery. The scribes and Pharisees were always tempting Jesus to fit their self-styled notions of God. "What do you have to say about the case?" they asked, hoping that he would agree with the proposed stoning. After all, if I believe in a vengeful diety, then, by God, he'd better punish all these other sinners!

Jesus started to write on the ground. Some would say that he was writing the sins of the others in the crowd, but that seems out of character for Jesus. He was, perhaps, doodling; perhaps he was bored. What concerned Jesus was not this woman's sin, but their attitude toward her. He was not interested in their questions, but in the sinister motives which had led to this whole scene. "Let the man among you who has no sin be the first to cast a stone at her." Jesus was not calling for a remembrance of past offences; he was calling attention to the very sin they were at that moment involved in: judging the woman, and judging him. "Then the audience drifted away one by one." Perhaps they were realizing the immorality of their condemnation of her; perhaps they were embarrassed, as violence and revenge are when met with gentleness and forgiveness. The woman is left standing alone before Jesus.

What is God like? "Remember not the events of the past." Jesus has his chance to question her privately, to ask why, to lay a little guilt on her. But no, he is only compassion. He does not speak of her past; instead he gently teaches her that she is not alone in her weakness, and that no one has the right to condemn her. He says, "Nor do I condemn you,— and then encourages her to go on, to begin again. No lecture, no penance, just forgiveness.

Jesus teaches us a lot too. He reminds us that you don't achieve conversion by stones and condemnation, but by loving and accepting love.

Isaiah writes, "Remember not the events of the past." There are many places in Scripture when we are enjoined to remember as well. We are asked to remember our Creator, to remember his love for us and his covenant. We remember Jesus: his words and deeds. We celebrate the Eucharist that we might recall his teachings and have his memory permeate our lives. All of these rememberings though are joyful celebrations, not depressing recollections.

Lent should be not a time for morbid dwelling on our past sins, but a time of training to strengthen us for the race. We too experience conversion not through self-imposed stonings, but by accepting God's forgiveness and love.

"Remember not the events" that tie you down to a limited vision of God's love; "remember not the events" which proved your own weakness or that of others. Remember God's love and forgiveness, and keep your eye on the finish line.

Carole M. Eipers

Passion (Palm) Sunday

Cycle C

Is 50:4–7
Phil 2:6–11
Lk 22:14—23:56

How can anyone celebrate when suffering is imminent? Jesus did. He did it throughout his life and he did it on Palm Sunday. Palm Sunday is not a feast for the cynics nor the skeptics, for to them it would be absurd to accept momentary adulation in the face of death. Palm Sunday can be celebrated only by those who, like Jesus, have chosen to serve the Father. Only they can see that the road we travel on Palm Sunday leads not just to Calvary, but to Easter.

Luke's account of Palm Sunday is read for the procession. This reading reminds us how much more simple life was in the time of Jesus. Who today could borrow a donkey or a car or anything else by saying, "The Master has need of it?" Can you imagine being approached to lend something by someone who simply says, "The Master has need of it?" Thank God the donkey owner was not a cynic. He obviously knew who the Master was and trusted him. His belongings were at the disposal of Jesus; he was a servant. He was probably denounced in his neighborhood as being idealistic and impractical, like the servant in the reading from Isaiah.

The "Servant Song" is a real stumbling block for skeptics. Why use your tongue and ears for a job that will bring suffering? But the servant sees beyond the suffering to ultimate triumph. The skeptic's vision is limited by lack of trust; the servant's whole life is based on trust. The skeptic can appear wise at the moment: questioning, cautioning, focusing on the inevitable consequences of speaking truth and love. His arguments are plausible. If we listen to the skeptic long enough we can avoid our Palm Sundays, and perhaps some Calvarys too, but then we deny ourselves the Easters as well.

We can decide to be temporarily "wise," to choose the way of the skeptics and cynics and watch our predictions of betrayals and crucifixions come true. Or, we can empty ourselves, as Paul tells us Jesus did, and let God's wisdom direct us. Then we will go to our Jerusalems and enjoy our momentary triumphs, and yes, we will go to our Calvarys as well, but we will travel beyond those sufferings, even beyond death, to Easter. Jesus chose to cast his lot with the servants. He faced the cynicism of his opponents and the skepticism of his own followers. He knew that in the short run, they made sense, but he had come to show us wisdom for the long run. Jesus made his triumphal entry into Jerusalem, not as the inane exercise of a fool, but as the meaningful journey of one who had fully accepted the conditions of human life as the road to ultimate victory.

The liturgy of Palm Sunday includes the Passion according to Luke. While the hosannas still ring in our ears, we are reminded that the shouts of praise soon turned to, "Crucify Him!" "Ah ha!" says the cynic, "I knew it would come to this!" Indeed, so did Jesus. He knew as he celebrated his last meal with his friends that Judas would betray him, that Peter would deny him, that the others would desert him. How can one celebrate when suffering is imminent? It takes trust; it takes a faith which sees this celebration as merely a foreshadowing of the eternal celebration. Skeptics and cynics don't celebrate much at all, but they would certainly never share a meal with fickle friends. One canon of the Mass says that it was "on the night he was betrayed" that Jesus took bread, blessed it and gave it to his disciples. In the shadow of betrayal, Jesus gives himself to his disciples; in the shadow of our future betrayals he gives us the Eucharist. A cynical Christian seems to be a contradiction in terms.

Palm Sunday makes sense to Jesus, and if we are servants it makes sense to us too. We too are surrounded by the cynics and skeptics of our time who caution us to be careful, to not trust, to leave hope to the fools. We too are asked to give ourselves for others, whether it be in moments of triumph, or on the nights we are betrayed. Jesus shows us what it means to trust the Father, and what it means to trust each other. If we buy into the skepticism and cynicism which breed doubt and seek self interest above the good of others, then we have not only compromised the Kingdom, we have defected.

Palm Sunday is a feast for those who know how and why to celebrate in the face of suffering. Palm Sunday is for those who will lend their donkeys, or their tongues and ears, if the Master needs them. If we can't enjoy our moments of triumph because there is the possibility—even the certainty—of betrayal and death, then we have missed the message of Jesus' triumphal entry.

Carole M. Eipers

Easter Sunday

Cycle C

Acts 10:34, 37–43
Col 3:1–4
Jn 20:1–9

A few days before Easter last year, I was shopping at an extremely crowded grocery store. The lines extended all the way to the other side of the store. There was a grandmother in front of me, tending her toddler grandson, who was doing his best to amuse himself during the interminable wait. The grandmother became increasingly irritated with the child's harmless antics, and began threats of "telling Mother." The boy began to cry and reached his arms out to hug his grandma. Grandma ignored his plea to be held and declared, "You are bad. Grandma doesn't know you when you're bad."

Have you ever been re-introduced to an acquaintance who claims, "No, we've never met"?

It can be a devastating experience to be unrecognized; we cannot be loved if we are not known. Today's Gospel tells us that Jesus' resurrection was first discovered by a reformed prostitute and an impetuous man who had denied him. That is good news! Jesus didn't abandon those who had abandoned him. Even though the apostles had not shared Jesus' crucifixion, he still shared his resurrection with them. Jesus knew them. He knew them as the Israelites "knew" God, with the heart. The scriptural meaning of "know" is far richer than our concept of an intellectual exercise. To know someone meant to have experienced that person, to have recognized and accepted him. Mutual knowledge was equated with love.

Jesus' resurrection is good news, but the even better news is that he still knows us—even when we are bad. In returning to his apostles, he has shown us that even betrayal and denial are forgiven. If we reach for Jesus we will never be told, "I don't know you."

But, is our relationship one of mutual knowledge? Of love? The first two readings help us to answer whether or not we know Jesus.

In the first reading from Acts, Peter speaks of what it means to know Jesus: to be his witnesses. To know Jesus is to have experienced him; to be his witness is to share those experiences with others. We, like the apostles, have eaten and drunk with him after his resurrection, but the eating and drinking with Jesus was not an end in itself for them, nor should it be for us. Jesus ate and drank with his apostles that they might believe, and that belief would lead to their sharing the Good News of his life, death, and rising.

Peter proves that he knows Jesus by his preaching, but also by the fact that his audience is Gentile. Peter, in knowing Jesus, recognizes the Gentiles as co-heirs of the Kingdom. To know Jesus is to be his witness, not only by our preaching, but by our lives. Practically speaking, that means we cannot be selective in sharing the Good News. To know Jesus is to know each other—with our hearts.

The reading from Colossians takes the question of whether we really know Jesus yet deeper. Paul says that if we know Jesus (recognize him, accept his teachings) we will, "look for the things that are in heaven." His words are a restatement of Jesus' "seek first the Kingdom of God." To know Jesus is to work for his Kingdom, to hold our relationship with him as our highest value. It means dying to our former selfish ways. To know anyone with our hearts means dying a little. It means putting aside self-seeking; it means caring enough to find out how someone else thinks and feels. And it means recognizing others—even when they are bad.

Easter means more to me because I saw that grandmother and boy in the grocery store. That scene of rejection, complete with our carts brimming with food for Easter celebrations, reminded me that the Father knows me, and that Jesus knows me. It reminded me that when I reach out the Father is always there. It reminded me, too, that sometimes God is reaching and I'm the one who says, "I don't know you."

The best news about Easter is that Jesus still knew his apostles. He didn't rise in glory and look for a more faithful band of followers. Easter celebrates life conquering death, and forgiveness conquering betrayal.

Jesus always knows us. If the Kingdom is to come we have got to know him—with our hearts.

Carole M. Eipers

2nd Sunday of Easter

Cycle C

Acts 5:12–16
Rv 1:9–11, 12–13, 17–19
Jn 20:19–31

Today's first reading presents a positive picture of the early Christian community: they met regularly, there were apparently miracles and wonders which enhanced their beliefs, many were healed by their faith, and, to top it off, non-believers spoke highly of them. It strikes me as rather curious, then, that the writer of Acts records the fact that "nobody dared to join them."

With all of the good features of this Christian community, why would no one join them? Was it the memory of what had happened to the man who had first gathered this group? Was it the threat of persecution? Was it the fear of rejection by their families and community? Were they hesitant to abandon comfortable traditions and beliefs?

Upon reflection on their situation, I can not judge those who did not dare to join the Christians. I find instances in my own life of times when I spoke highly of groups which I, nonetheless, did not dare to join.

I have spoken often of those who are involved in the Peace Movement, yet their frequent call to accept the call to personal freedom has kept me distant; I have spoken positively of those who work for Pro-Life, yet I do not formally join them for they face persecution by unbelievers and by fellow Christians as well; I have spoken highly of those who press for full equality for women in the Church, yet I do not stand with them, perhaps because I am also hesitant to abandon comfortable traditions; I have praised ecumenical leaders, yet often fail to join them because I fear rejection by my own ecclesial community; I have praise for Charismatics, and have asked such communities to pray for healings, yet I do not pray with them, perhaps out of fear of God himself and what his Spirit might ask of me.

So, I too stand at a distance from Christian groups as they meet on contemporary counterparts of Solomon's Portico. It is so much easier to admire goodness from afar and to speak highly of it than it is to join in, to be a part of the struggle, and to be a responsible risk-taker in the thick of activity and often in the midst of controversy.

I also identify with those in today's first reading who wanted Peter's shadow to fall on them. They wanted to be close enough to benefit from the goodness and faith of the community, to be healed by it, but not to commit themselves to the community. I too stand in the shadows which bring healing: not only the shadows of those who have gone before me and whose faith I benefit from, but in the shadows of those contemporary miracle-workers who work for a better Church and a better society. I want to benefit from their efforts, to be made more whole by the changes they effect, but will not fully commit myself to their cause. "Work miracles of healing for me with your shadow," I seem to declare, "but do not really touch me, nor suggest that I must change in order to be healed."

Does Jesus accept my doubts and understand my noncommittal attitude as he accepted Thomas' reluctance to believe the word of the disciples? I too doubt what I have not seen and am sometimes loathe to relinquish the tried and true even when I know it is not the best. It is much easier to join a group which treads familiar pathways and gets predictable results than to cast our lot with the trailblazers whose outcome is uncertain.

"Don't be afraid" the reading from Revelation says, reiterating Jesus' familiar words. Those words have echoes, not only to the ears of those who stood on Solomon's Portico, but to our own ears and hearts as well. "Don't be afraid" to become a miracle-worker, a healer. Don't be afraid to step out of the shadow of the Saints and into the sunlight of personal sainthood.

A tempting invitation, but, nonetheless, one that demands a risk of faith. I hope that those Christians with whom I have yet failed to cast my lot will heed what Revelation says: "Write down the things you see, both the things that are now and the things that will happen afterward." Perhaps if others—like me—will read of their struggle, their faith and their vision, we will finally have the courage to join them and so to know the joy of having cast our lot with Jesus himself.

Carole M. Eipers

3rd Sunday of Easter

Cycle C

Acts 5:27–32, 40–41
Rv 5:11–14
Jn 21:1–19

Fr. Eugene LaVerdiere, a well-travelled scripture scholar, tells the story of a dinner invitation on one of his journeys to the Far East. In an afternoon break during one of his sessions, he met one participant who invited Father to dinner that night. Anxious to respond to this hospitality, Fr. Gene accepted. When the supper hour approached, Father asked his workshop host to join him for dinner. The host stopped Father and asked him if the person made the invitation three times. "No," was the reply. Then his host told him that he really wasn't invited to supper. The invitation was only a friendly formality. To show up for dinner would be an embarrassment because the household would not be expecting him without a three-fold invitation.

I am reminded of this story whenever I hear today's gospel story. The three-fold question of Jesus to Peter emphasizes the seriousness of Jesus' inquiry. To love Jesus is not just a single response—it takes a lifetime of service. Sometimes we can very casually answer "Yes" when those close to us ask us if we love them. But the real proof of it is demonstrated when we stick by them when the going gets tough.

Tevye, in *Fiddler on the Roof,* asks his wife if she loves him. She doesn't say "yes" or "no"; she just enumerates how she has fed him, raised his children, and shared his bed all those years. Didn't that say "yes" to the question?

Peter, too, is told that his love will cost him. Feeding the sheep—ministering to people—takes time and energy. In Peter's case, it meant giving up his very life.

The "Do you love me?" question is answered differently on one's wedding day than when it is asked again years later after the truth of living together brings out the good and bad in both partners. A "yes" now embraces much more of life.

The apostles in today's reading from Acts also realize that saying "yes" to love involves taking risks. When they began to realize what kind of commitment Jesus had made to them by giving his life for them, they began to return this commitment in their own lives. In spite of being threatened by the dangers posed by the religious leaders of the day, the apostles were willing to remain faithful to their lifestyle.

Some people today continue to risk imprisonment for harboring refugees fleeing for their lives. This is an authentic "yes" to Christ's question.

As the reading from Revelation points out, the many who risk a firm "yes" to love rejoice in the peace and freedom that comes from such fidelity.

John R. Schmitz

4th Sunday of Easter

Cycle C

Acts 13:14, 43–52
Rv 7:9, 14–17
Jn 10:27–30

Recently I read the local advice columnist as I was browsing through the paper. The person asking for advice described a situation where she felt she should be of help to another family but the decision was causing her great distress. The advice columnist told her not to come to the aid of the family because "anything which causes conflict within should be avoided. Peace of mind is our goal. Forget about helping the family until you can do it peacefully." It struck me that the advice columnist was wrong just as the Jews are wrong in today's first reading from Acts. In this story, the Jews throw out Paul and Barnabas because they issue a challenge the Jews cannot stand to hear. What all this means to us is an investigation of the question: "How do we handle conflict?"

One way to approach today's reading from Acts is from a Jungian perspective. It is a story of the Self. Within all of us is a challenging voice calling us to be better people. Within us is a dimension symbolized by the Jews in today's story: we want to throw the challenging voice out. And within us is a receptive, listening place—symbolized by the Gentiles.

Ask your congregation to get in touch with the voice within which challenges. Is there a voice within calling you to be more? A voice asking you to be selfless, to give, to forgive, to be actively compassionate? Is it a difficult voice to hear? Does it seem to be demanding too much? Don't let this be an idealistic voice of easy piety. Get in touch with the voice that demands you immerse yourself in a life-affirming reality. It could be similar to the voice which drove Dorothy Day to work with the most destitute of the poor, where she was confronted with a people who "do not just ask you to go the extra mile and then request your coat. These people, after you go another mile and give away your coat, will demand you go five extra miles, at the conclusion of which they will knock you over the head and take your hat and shoes." The challenging voice might lead us to a place we are unprepared for.

Now that you know your challenging voice, what are your feelings? Is there anything in you reacting like the Jews in today's reading so that you want to dismiss this voice? Many of us have this dimension within and often it takes the form of rationalizations. "It is not practical to respond to my challenging voice." Or, if the voice comes from the example of others, how often do we put down another aspect of the prophet issuing the challenge? Have you ever been in conversations where a person is praised for a generous deed and people respond with, "Yes, she works two nights a week at the shelter. But then who is at home taking care of her kids? I know that little Brian is constantly in trouble in the neighborhood." "Yes, he does bring communion to the sick. But he thinks he is a pillar of the church." Even our sophisticated psychology can lead us in this direction: "What do you think he is gaining by taking care of his elderly parents?" "What need is she fulfilling in herself by taking back her alcoholic husband again and again?"

Are you allowing yourself to listen to the challenging voice? Or would you like to "expel it from your territory"? Our advice columnist would suggest the latter, since it might safeguard your "peace of mind." But is there another place within that listens? You might not resolve the conflict, but is there a place in you that listens as the Gentiles did? A wonderful example of this comes from the movie "Choices of the Heart," about Jean Donovan, the American churchwoman killed in El Salvador. In this movie her fiancé asks her to not go back to El Salvador. She has done enough. He loves her but will leave her if she goes back. It would be easy to silence the voice which asks her for more time in Central America. One can see the conflict all over her face. But she says "I must go back. My life is worth more in Salvador. I must do it for the kids."

We can't all respond to our challenging voices the way Jean Donovan did—although some might. What we can do is live with the conflict the voice brings.

This morning let's lend an ear to the challenging voices within us. Let's live with the conflict they create knowing that perhaps living and learning from the tension will eventually make us a people who, like the disciples, "know only how to be filled with joy and the Holy Spirit."

Douglas Fisher

5th Sunday of Easter

Cycle C

Acts 14:21–27
Rv 21:1–5
Jn 13:31–33, 34–35

"Witnessing" about one's faith in the stand-up-and-tell-how-you-met-Jesus style is not as common a practice among Roman Catholics as among some other Christian denominations. Yet, "witnessing" is part of our faith life. Someone in our life "witnessed" to the presence of Jesus in their lives.

To "witness" means to "testify to" something. Many of our parents "testified" to us through their example, and through church related participation, or home devotions. Through these things, they spoke to us of Jesus. The faith community also witnessed by their coming together to worship. In the liturgy, the Mass, the priest, deacon, servers, readers, ushers, and other ministers told us something about Jesus. All of these "witnessed" in a true sense of the word.

Paul and Barnabas had the task (and privilege) of proclaiming the good news, announcing out loud to groups of people who had never heard of Jesus the new truth and reality present in the world. They must have been strong in their conviction, and gifted and effective in their "articulation" of the message, because communities of faith formed around them. What an exciting thing: people hear your witness, and gather round you to hear more! That was only the beginning.

After people started believing in Jesus, they needed more teaching and a way to celebrate this new faith. Thus, new leadership and liturgy emerged. Paul and Barnabas prayed and fasted, and laid their hands on those called to lead. The Church joined in this prayer. Church "structure" began to emerge. Paul and Barnabas moved on, occasionally returning to local communities to encourage and reassure the congregations and their leaders. In the course of history, the role the apostles played continued in the ministry of "bishops." Other ministries likewise developed.

"Witnessing," though, is the primary way in which we come to know Jesus. It is a task for us all. When I was young, my mother helped a lady become Catholic. My mother felt privileged and humbled, and the lady to this day speaks of my mother's witness and help. By her life, somehow, my mother had "witnessed" about God, and attracted this lady.

It is a great experience to bring another to faith! Have you ever had the experience? Often, we leave it up to others, but the Church would never grow if someone did not witness.

Of all kinds of "witnessing," the greatest and most effective is love! Isn't that Jesus' commandment today in the Gospel? To love is the greatest way to convince others of our faith. To experience being loved, *is* to experience "good news." Any act of love, then, is an act of "witness"!

I believe that love is the greatest experience people can have. Oftentimes in our lives, there are moments of tragedy, hurt, loneliness, frustration, etc. The only thing others can offer is their presence, their love and their compassion! Mysteriously enough though, this is often the greatest gift, the only thing a person who is hurting *can* receive. Explanations, rationalizations, and reasons can't help, but love does.

Jesus told us: "This is how all will know you are my disciples: your love for one another." When someone is in deep pain, or has lost a loved one, or has sinned grievously, we *can* love them! We *can't* answer questions maybe, or remove the pain, or restore lost persons. But, we *can* love them, care for them, be with them. This works powerfully. It is the greatest witness to Jesus.

The day will come when God will "wipe away every tear from their eyes, and there shall be no more death or mourning, crying out in pain, for the former world has passed away." We believe this. It is our hope and goal. In the meantime, we "must undergo many trials if we are to enter the reign of God." Ultimately, what we *can do* in every situation is love! As popular music tells us: "Love will keep us together" and "love will see us through." Let our lives be a witness to this truth in our daily lives.

Jeffrey Archambeault

163

6th Sunday of Easter

Cycle C

Acts 15:1–2, 22–29
Rv 21:10–14, 22–23
Jn 14:23–29

Although today's first reading from the Acts of the Apostles is about conversion, it brought to my mind some current efforts at ecumenism.

One parish began what they proudly termed their "Ecumenical Committee." When asked to join, I was somewhat taken aback upon discovering that this "Ecumenical" group's membership consisted of all Roman Catholics. I was further amazed to discover that the purpose of their meetings was to expound the Roman Catholic doctrines and get "the Church's" position on ecumenism straight before they began meeting with "non-Catholics." As far as I know, this "Ecumenical Committee" is still meeting, still busy circling the wagons around Roman Catholic doctrine. I wonder if they ever will get around to inviting people of other ecclesial communities; I wonder if people of other ecclesial communities will ever want to join them.

Paul and Barnabas really got into it over the law of circumcision. It was no simple matter either, for circumcision had been a practice related to the covenant for generations. Like the Ecumenical Committee I met, the early Church had to make some rules about new members. Paul and Barnabas recognized that the Spirit resides in the Christian community, and so, they traveled to Jerusalem in search of the shared wisdom of Jesus' followers.

I would love to have been there for that discussion! Circumcision was an emotional issue, a custom intertwined with the very identity of the Jewish people. There had to be a delicate balance between respecting a cherished tradition which had, nonetheless, become more cultural than spiritual, and respecting the teachings of Jesus who had accepted—and called—both Jew and Gentile into relationship with the Father.

Circumcision was deemed unnecessary for Gentile converts. I wonder if some of the Jews left the Church over this decision. Perhaps they felt it watered down their beliefs; perhaps they felt that not requiring circumcision of the Gentiles lessened the significance of circumcision for themselves. It must have been a kind of "post-Vatican II" time for the Church: who will leave, who will stay, who can accept the change, did we do the right thing?

I guess that Ecumenical Committee I know is struggling the way the Church in Jerusalem did with the circumcision question. The bottom line is, "What should we require of non-Catholics who join us?"

It is a legitimate question, I suppose, but hardly a perfect starting point for unity. And, as much as we all desire unity, it is still a scary concept. We're afraid of losing something; we're afraid that we—and perhaps our Church as well—will be lessened if everyone is included. We want new members to be like us, whether that means being circumcised or having a belief in papal infallibility or a common understanding of the Eucharist.

Jesus invited everyone to join him. Today's Gospel sets out the requirements: love Jesus and obey his teaching. Then Jesus and the Father will live with us, and they will send the Spirit to us, not for our exclusive possession, but to possess us, and to use us for the common good. Jesus' message, like his own life, was one of relationships: relationship with the Father and with other people. Those relationships are far more difficult to live out than going through a simple rite of circumcision or giving verbal assent to a specific doctrine.

The writer of today's reading from Revelation has a dream in which the Spirit "takes control" and transports him to a "new Jerusalem" where there is no temple, for God himself is the temple. My dream for ecumenism is that the Spirit will take control and will enable us to think more creatively about the unity for which Jesus prayed.

My own experience has taught me that we need not be afraid of joining with other Christians. It has shown me that the blessings of ecumenism come, not so much from our common ground, but from the uniqueness of our traditions and the diversity of our views.

The only prerequisite for membership on an Ecumenical Committee should be openness to the Spirit of Jesus. And we should make certain that we have met that requirement before we invite anyone else to join.

Carole M. Eipers

7th Sunday of Easter

Cycle C

Acts 7:55–60
Rv 22:12–14, 16–17, 20
Jn 17:20–26

Today's readings tell us that following Jesus is a costly venture. The death of the first martyr, Stephen, is modeled after the death of Jesus. Discipleship is always, in a hidden or open way, a bearing of the cross. And yet, this is the way to life and to victory. The reading from Revelation promises a share in Christ's victory over evil to all who remain faithful to him. Lest we lose courage in the face of the demands of discipleship, Jesus' farewell discourse to his disciples recalls our ground for hope. He lives in us and we in him. These three themes help us understand our own efforts to follow Jesus.

Jesus never told us to seek out suffering for its own sake. What he did say is that we will meet suffering in our efforts to follow him, and we must not allow it to turn us away from the call to discipleship. The Lutheran pastor, Dietrich Bonhoeffer, who was hanged in a Nazi concentration camp during World War II, wrote a book called *The Cost of Discipleship*. In it he said that discipleship is demanding because it may cost a person his or her life. Yet it is a grace, because it gives the only true life. Bonhoeffer's discipleship cost him his life, but it also enabled him to live with peace and forgiveness. In the concentration camps, his courage, unselfishness, and goodness inspired all who came in contact with him, even his prison guards.

For most of us the cross to be borne is not as heavy as Bonhoeffer's. Discipleship for us may mean simply bearing the cross of everyday life. It comes in daily obligations, challenges and misunderstandings. Scott Peck begins his best-selling book, *The Road Less Traveled*, with a simple, thematic sentence: "Life is difficult." He continues by pointing out that it is our effort to avoid life's difficulties and problems, in a word to escape the cross, which accounts for most of our neuroses and deeper sufferings. Being a student, a parent, a friend, or a spouse inevitably involves suffering. The painful struggle arises from that central command of Jesus that we love as he loved. C.S. Lewis illustrates this fact very well in his book, *The Four Loves*. "Love anything," he says, "and your heart will certainly be wrung and possibly be broken." But if we refuse to love, wrapping up our heart in the coffin of our selfishness, it will become impenetrable and irredeemable.

To risk loving as Jesus does, we must believe in his victory over evil. It is difficult to remain steadfast in discipleship to the end. The Book of Revelation gives us the image of Jesus as victorious to sustain our faith. The first Christians were tempted, as we are, to give in to the prevailing values, the gods of the moment. We face this same challenge in the temptation to substitute fear, revenge, and war for Jesus' message of trust, reconciliation, and forgiveness. We meet it again in the ease with which we slip into a life of consumerism, ignoring the needs of others as we acquire more possessions. Like the early Christians, we need to be reminded of the victory of Jesus who is Alpha and Omega, the Beginning and the End.

When we struggle to be disciples of Jesus and find ourselves failing to live up to our resolve, we can draw strength from the words of Jesus in his farewell discourse. In it, he prays for his disciples, knowing the difficulties we will meet in our attempts to follow him. Not only that, he tells us that our discipleship is not just an external imitation of him. Rather, we live it out of a union with him and his Father. We share the intimacy with God which he knows: "That they may be one, as we are one—I living in them, you living in me." Discipleship is not only the way to a future victory over evil; it is a life lived out of the wellsprings of God's grace, an existence, therefore, filled with a deeper life and joy than we could otherwise know.

Kathleen R. Fischer
Thomas N. Hart

Pentecost Sunday

Cycle C

Acts 2:1–11
1 Cor 12:3–7, 12–13
Jn 20:19–23

The Holy Spirit is the one who surrounds us while we are busy looking for God. The Spirit comes, as the account of Pentecost tells us, like fire and wind.

Fire is a good symbol for the Spirit. We understand warmth and light and energy. We know a well-kindled fire can spread. We have known moments of "being on fire" with faith; the Spirit's spark has on occasion illumined our minds so that we recognized our common humanity and acted compassionately.

Wind is a good symbol for the action of the Spirit. If you have ever sailed, you know the uncontrollable nature of the wind, its apparent sudden shifts which have reasons and causes beyond our comprehension. The man who taught me to sail when I was a child would say, "You gotta go this-a-way to go that-a-way." He had mastered the art of working with the wind, and what seemed to me to be pointless meandering was, in fact, the only way to reach our destination. The Spirit, like the wind, may indeed take us off our previously planned course, but the journey is the important thing.

The problem of Pentecost is not that we don't understand the gift of the Spirit, we're just not certain that we want wind and fire in our lives. There is no doubting from the symbols used that this gift is not for our manipulation. The Spirit is not to possess, he possesses. Fire and wind can be frightening, but our belief is that we are not at the mercy of some hapless elements, but being moved by a loving God. The trouble is, we'd all rather be drivers than riders. We hesitate to turn over the controls, even to God. What will happen if we do?

Saint Paul tells us what will happen in the second reading: "To each person the manifestation of the Spirit is given for the common good." If we accept the gift of the Spirit, we will serve others. The common good will take precedence over personal goals and glory, but, even more radically, the Spirit's vision of the common good will guide us so that our sometimes culturally-tainted visions must be yielded.

That is why we are busy looking for God. We are surrounded by the Spirit. He is as common an experience as fire and wind, but he is counter-cultural. And, even worse, he expects us to be counter-cultural as well!

Jesus said that all sins would be forgiven except sins against the Spirit. Our society tells us that the greatest "sin" is to be counter-cultural. It seems we trust our culture to direct our lives rather than God.

I recently read about a woman's struggle to hide her virginity from her new boyfriend. The fact that her love, morality, and self-respect had kept her from pre-marital sex was an embarrassment to her. Honest men lie about cheating on income tax or in business so that others will praise their cunning. Those who are conscientious objectors to graft, abortion, or the myriad moral pitfalls which are everywhere must pretend they are not. Those who oppose nuclear war or any form of violence disguised as self-defense are named "Un-American."

In the Gospel, Jesus breathes on the disciples and says, "Receive the Holy Spirit." Breath is a gentler wind; you have to be very close to someone to feel her breath. The Spirit comes to us in breath. He resuscitates us when our society has deadened us to our own conscience and to the needs of others. He breathes into us the life and power of Jesus; he gifts us for the common good. Sometimes he comes in the breath of others who speak to us words of encouragement, challenge, and love.

The Spirit is the fire of outrage in the eyes of those who fight injustice; the wind which dishevels our complacency in the face of other's suffering; the reserve breath we find to speak love when hurt has left us breathless.

He is a common Spirit, surrounding us, warming us, moving us: always for the common good.

We are free to accept this gift whom Jesus sent on the first Pentecost, to hoist our sails, and to learn to trust and to risk ourselves for others.

Or, we can reject this difficult challenge, ignore fire, wind, and breath, and go off, motors running to search for other gods.

Carole M. Eipers

Trinity Sunday

Cycle C

Prv 8:22–31
Rom 5:1–5
Jn 16:12–15

I received a beautiful card from a friend of mine the other day which said, "I found God within me . . . and I loved HER." Perhaps reading that quotation made you smile as it made me smile. In our awakening to identity, in our struggle for equality, we change our language. Some people dismiss these efforts as "merely playing with semantics," but for many people language not only reflects reality, but can act as an agent to change reality as well.

The him and/or her-ness of scriptural language never really bothered me. I was conditioned to feel included even when addressed as "brother." My attitude changed somewhat, though, when I experienced an Evening of Renewal with the Fountain Square Fools. The scriptural story they re-enacted was the one about the prodigal son. However, they re-told it as the tale of the prodigal daughter. I found myself touched—emotionally and spiritually—by this daughter as I had never quite been touched by the son. I realized that part of our being reached by any story, or movie or Bible passage, is our identification with the characters. I could identify with the prodigal son in many ways, but the prodigal daughter was really me. Sometimes the sexual identity of the character does make a difference. It was the word "daughter" that struck me; it was the uniqueness of the father-daughter relationship which touched me. The scenes between the young girl and her father recalled my own father's love for me, and caused me to understand the Father God's love for me in a new way. The daughter's failure to respond to her father's generous love moved me to regret my own failures more deeply.

As we celebrate Trinity Sunday, we could just as easily refer to God as "Mother, Daughter and Holy Spirit" I suppose. Yet, this poses some real historical difficulties. Jesus was, in fact, a man, who referred to himself as "Son"; He called God his "Father." I do not see "Son" and "Father" as a statement of sex, but rather a description of roles.

We go to great lengths sometimes to try to make God like us: in God's "thoughts," in God's "Will," in God's "sexuality." Perhaps we need to concentrate more on making ourselves like God. Whatever "sex" God is, if God is either, only 50 percent of us have a chance of resembling God in that. But, we are made in the image of God. We are meant to be like the Father, the Son, and the Holy Spirit, not in their sex, but in their roles, in their relationships with each other and with people.

Am I like God the Father?
Do I create and enrich creation?
Do I work, as he did, with Wisdom
and take delight in wise choices made?
I am made in the image of
the God who created me.

Do I perceive his presence
in all the creatures of his hand
and care for them as their Creator would?
Do I echo his blessing on the earth
and pronounce all his creation good?

Am I like God the Son?
Am I a channel through which
others might come to believe?
Are others at peace with God
through my presence in their lives?
Do I suffer afflictions willingly
that I, too, might rise again?
Is my spirit one of hope
which I joyfully share with others?
Do I image God the Son
for those who seek him in our world?

Am I like God the Spirit?
Do I hold my words of sadness or joy
until my listeners are ready to hear?
Do I speak only truth—
the truth received from God's own Son—
even when that truth
is painful for me to live?
Do I encourage openness
in myself and those around me?
Do I image the Spirit faithfully
in spite of personal cost?

It would be so much easier if God were simply male or female, and to be God's image we had only to match God's sex. From the life of Jesus, we know that to image God means far more. Let's celebrate Trinity Sunday by trying to image God in our attitudes and actions rather than trying to have God match our sex. I'm sure She will be delighted.

Carole M. Eipers

Corpus Christi

Cycle C

Gn 14:18–20
1 Cor 11:23–26
Lk 9:11–17

In Virginia, we find Ken and Ray who are called "The Potato Pastors." Several years ago, they discovered that millions of pounds of potato rejects were left to rot in the fields annually. They decided to collect these for soup kitchens in their area. Before long, the news was out; farmers from all the surrounding communities began donating their unsalable potatoes and other vegetables to what became known as the "Potato Project."

In June of 1983, the first load of potatoes was distributed. By the end of the year, 1.6 million pounds of potatoes (otherwise left to rot) filled hundreds of empty stomachs. As of today 14,597,551 pounds of potatoes have been distributed.

"Do this in memory of me."

His name is Sydney; he's nearly seventy. Every Monday evening for over thirty-five years, he has traveled to a large veteran's hospital in the Bronx. Once there, he sits at an old piano and helps each patient sing a solo that is taped and played back. According to the medical personnel and psychiatrists of the hospital, this personal touch has been very beneficial for the patients. Yet Sydney, a composer and pianist, has never received any pay for his services.

"Do this in memory of me."

According to the newspaper, these people were hungry. They were a group of street people who gathered regularly in a soup kitchen in a California city to get something to eat. They heard of the starving people in Ethiopia. Over a period of time, these poor pooled their pennies, nickels, and dimes. In the end, they donated over $150 to those who were really hungry.

"Do this in memory of me."

One of the parishioners of St. Mary's Church of Hales Corners, Wisconsin, returned from a visit to Washington, D.C. with a project she had heard about in a parish there; it was called "Circle of Love." She gathered people around her and organized it for St. Mary's. Parishioners were invited to send in requests for the neighbors they knew were in need of food, clothing, and gifts for Christmas. No one knew who these people were except for their sponsors. Through the initiative of this one woman, over 400 people celebrated a happier Christmas in 1984.

"Do this in memory of me."

The television program "60 Minutes" devoted a twenty-minute segment to a married couple in Oregon who had 33 children! They didn't live in a shoe but in a house that was added on to with the help of neighbors.

Six of the children were the couple's own; the rest were adopted, and most of them had special needs. The children were taught how to help themselves and one another. On the salary of a postal worker and with the help of neighbors, this couple gave a home to many who never had one.

"Do this in memory of me."

John R. Schmitz